Anti-Apartheid and the Emergence of a Global Civil Society

Håkan Thörn
Professor of Sociology, Göteborg University, Sweden

palgrave
macmillan

First published in hardback 2006
First published in paperback 2009 by
PALGRAVE MACMILLAN

Palgrave Macmillan in the UK is an imprint of Macmillan Publishers Limited, registered in England, company number 785998, of Houndmills, Basingstoke, Hampshire RG21 6XS.

Palgrave Macmillan in the US is a division of St Martin's Press LLC, 175 Fifth Avenue, New York, N.Y. 10010

Palgrave Macmillan is the global academic imprint of the above companies and has companies and representatives throughout the world.

Palgrave® and Macmillan® are registered trademarks in the United States, the United Kingdom, Europe and other countries.

ISBN–13: 978–1–4039–3937–1 hardback
ISBN–10: 1–4039–3937–3   hardback
ISBN–13: 978–0–230–23496–3 paperback
ISBN–10: 0–230–23496–8   paperback

This book is printed on paper suitable for recycling and made from fully managed and sustained forest sources. Logging, pulping and manufacturing processes are expected to conform to the environmental regulations of the country of origin.

A catalogue record for this book is available from the British Library.

A catalog record for this book is available from the Library of Congress.

10 9 8 7 6 5 4 3 2 1
18 17 16 15 14 13 12 11 10 09

Printed and bound in Great Britain by
CPI Antony Rowe, Chippenham and Eastbourne

St Antony's Series

General Editor: **Jan Zielonka** (2004–), Fellow of St Antony's College, Oxford

Recent titles include:

Motti Golani
THE END OF THE BRITISH MANDATE FOR PALESTINE, 1948
The Diary of Sir Henry Gurney

Demetra Tzanaki
WOMEN AND NATIONALISM IN THE MAKING OF MODERN GREECE
The Founding of the Kingdom of the Greco-Turkish War

Simone Bunse
SMALL STATES AND EU GOVERNANCE
Leadership through the Council Presidency

Judith Marquand
DEVELOPMENT AID IN RUSSIA
Lessons from Siberia

Li-Chen Sim
THE RISE AND FALL OF PRIVATIZATION IN THE RUSSIAN OIL INDUSTRY

Stefania Bernini
FAMILY LIFE AND INDIVIDUAL WELFARE IN POSTWAR EUROPE
Britain and Italy Compared

Tomila V. Lankina, Anneke Hudalla and Helmut Wollman
LOCAL GOVERNANCE IN CENTRAL AND EASTERN EUROPE
Comparing Performance in the Czech Republic, Hungary, Poland and Russia

Cathy Gormley-Heenan
POLITICAL LEADERSHIP AND THE NORTHERN IRELAND PEACE PROCESS
Role, Capacity and Effect

Lori Plotkin Boghardt
KUWAIT AMID WAR, PEACE AND REVOLUTION

Paul Chaisty
LEGISLATIVE POLITICS AND ECONOMIC POWER IN RUSSIA

Valpy FitzGerald, Frances Stewart and Rajesh Venugopal (*editors*)
GLOBALIZATION, VIOLENT CONFLICT AND SELF-DETERMINATION

Miwao Matsumoto
TECHNOLOGY GATEKEEPERS FOR WAR AND PEACE
The British Ship Revolution and Japanese Industrialization

Håkan Thörn
ANTI-APART~~~ ~~~OCIETY

St Antony's Series
Series Standing Order ISBN 978–0–333–71109–5 (hardback) 978–0–333–80341–7
(paperback)
(outside North America only)

You can receive future titles in this series as they are published by placing a standing order. Please contact your bookseller or, in case of difficulty, write to us at the address below with your name and address, the title of the series and one of the ISBNs quoted above.

Customer Services Department, Macmillan Distribution Ltd, Houndmills, Basingstoke, Hampshire RG21 6XS, England

Contents

Acknowledgements

This book, and the research project on which it is based, would not have been possible without the assistance of a number of generous people. I would like to thank my wife, Catharina Thörn, for continuing support, intellectual discussion and comments on the final manuscript. The support of William Beinart has also been crucial for the project and the book. My stay at St Antony's College, Oxford in 2003, which made it possible to engage in a number of stimulating seminars and discussions with William and others, provided an important starting point for the writing process. Thanks also to Robert J. C. Young for stimulating discussions on new social movements and postcolonialism. At an early stage discussions and seminars with a small group of people in London and Sussex, including Saul Dubow, Shula Marks, James Sanders, David Rhodes and Rob Skinner, were also important.

The work with this project has been an extremely interesting and challenging intellectual journey also thanks to the many previous anti-apartheid activists, who shared their experiences, recollections and reflections on life-long commitments. Christabel Gurney, Enuga S. Reddy and Anne-Marie Kihlberg have been particularly helpful, as they have been eager to assist both with contacts and by giving informative and detailed responses to questions that I have put via e-mail. In the final phase Christabel also read, and provided valuable comments on, the manuscript. So did Genevieve Klein, Martin Peterson, Ann Schlyter and Per Wästberg. Comments on individual chapters were provided by Enuga S. Reddy, Jan Ekecrantz, Bertil Högberg, Sören Lindh, Margaret Ling, Michele Micheletti and Mai Palmberg. Thanks to all of you for taking time! Thanks also to Lucy McCann at the Bodleian Library, Oxford, for important assistance. Lucy's work with the AAM Archive has made it an indispensable source for anyone who wishes to do research on the British as well as the transnational anti-apartheid movement.

While carrying out the project, I have been based the Department of Sociology, Göteborg University. Funding was provided by the Swedish Council for Research in the Humanities and Social Sciences (HSFR), the Bank of Sweden Tercentenary Foundation, The Jubilee Foundation at Göteborg University and Magnus Bergvall's foundation. Thanks also to the Centre for Cultural Studies at Göteborg University for many stimulating seminars.

Finally, I would like to thank my children Andreas, Klara, Teresia and Teodor for constantly reminding me of, and involving me in, some basic things that makes life meaningful; things that also support research and other intellectual activities.

List of Abbreviations

AAM	Anti-Apartheid Movement (Britain)
AAAM	Australian Anti-Apartheid Movement
AB	Aftonbladet (Sweden)
ACOA	American Committee of Africa
ACTSA	Action for Southern Africa
AFL-CIO	The American Federation of Labor and Congress of Industrial Organizations
AGIS	Africa Groups in Sweden
ANC	African National Congress
AP	Associated Press
APLA	Azanian People's Liberation Army
AZAPO	Azanian People's Organization
BBC	British Broadcasting Corporation
BCC	British Council of Churches
BCM	Black Consciousness Movement
BM	Boycott Movement
BoSS	Bureau of State Security (South Africa)
BPC	Black People's Convention
CAO	Committee of African Organizations (Britain)
CND	Campaign for Nuclear Disarmament
CCETSA	Canon Collins Educational Trust for Southern Africa
CCHA	Consultative Committee of Humanitarian Assistance (Sweden/SIDA)
CFS	Committee for Fairness in Sport
CI	Christian Institute (South Africa)
CIA	Central Intelligence Agency (USA)
CLAAG	City of London Anti-Apartheid Group
CONCP	Confêrencia das Organizacoes Nacionalistas das Colónias Portuguêsas
COREMO	Comité Revolucionário de Mocambique
COSATU	Congress of South African Trade Unions
CPC	Coloured People's Congress
CSM	Church of Sweden Mission
DN	Dagens Nyheter (Sweden)
FLN	Front de Libération Nationale (Algeria)
FNL	Front National de Libération du Viêt-nam du Sud

FNLA	Frente Nacional para a Libertacao de Angola
FPU	Folkpartiets ungdomsförbund (Liberal Party Youth League in Sweden)
FRELIMO	Frente de Libertacao de Mocambique
GATT	General Agreement on Tariffs and Trade
ICFTU	International Confederation of Free Trade Unions
IDAF	International Defence and Aid Fund
IGO	Inter-Governmental Organization
ILO	International Labour Organization
IFP	Inkatha Freedom Party
IMF	International Monetary Fund
INGO	International Non-Governmental Organization
ISAK	Isolera Sydafrika-Kommittén (Sweden) (Isolate South Africa Committee)
IUEF	International University Exchange Fund
JSAK	Jönköpings Sydafrika Kommitté (Sweden)
LO	Landsorganisationen i Sverige (Swedish Trade Union Confederation)
LP	Labour Party (Britain)
MCC	The British Cricket Council
MCF	Movement for Colonial Freedom
MK	Umkhonto we Sizwe (Spear of the Nation), the armed wing of the ANC and the SACP
MP	Member of Parliament
MPLA	Movimento Popular para a Libertacao de Angola
NAI	Nordic Africa Institute
NATO	North Atlantic Treaty Organization
NF	National Forum (South Africa)
NGO	Non-Governmental Organization
NP	Nationalist Party (South Africa)
NSM	New Social Movements
NTA	National Tennis Association (Sweden)
NUSAS	National Union of South Africa Students
OAU	Organization of African Unity
PAC	Pan-Africanist Congress of Azania
PAIGC	Partido Africano para a Indepêndencia da Guiné e Cabo Verde
POS	Political Opportunity Structures
RCG	Revolutionary Communist Group
RENAMO	Resistencia Nacional Mozambicana
RMT	Resource Mobilization Theory

SABC	South African Broadcasting Corporation
SACP	South African Communist Party
SACOD	South African Congress of Democrats
SACTU	South African Congress of Trade Unions
SADF	South African Defence Force
SAIC	South African Indian Congress
SAN-ROC	South African Non-Racial Olympic Committee
SAP	South African Police
SASO	South African Student's Organization
SDP	Social Democratic Party (Sweden)
SDS	Students for a Democratic Society (USA)
SEK	Swedish Kronor
SIDA	Swedish International Development Agency
SMOs	Social Movement Organizations
SSU	Sveriges Socialdemokratiska ungdomsförbund (Youth League of the Swedish Social Democrats)
STST	Stop the Seventies Tour (Britain)
SvD	Svenska Dagbladet (Sweden)
SWAPO	South West African People's Union
TCO	Central Organization of Salaried Employees/Tjänstemännens Centralorganisation (Sweden)
TGWU	Transport and General Worker's Union (Britan)
TRC	Truth and Reconciliation Commission
TUC	Trade Union Congress (Britain)
UDC	Union of Democratic Control
UDF	United Democratic Front (South Africa)
UM	Unity Movement
UN	United Nations
UNITA	Uniao Nacional para a Independencia total de Angola
UPI	United Press International
WAY	World Assembly of Youth
WCC	World Council of Churches
WFTU	World Federation of Trade Unions
ZANU	Zimbabwe African National Union
ZAPU	Zimbabwe African People's Union

Prologue: Apartheid as a Dark Side of Modernity

> The previous day it was Christmas. We saw these people with white scarves, the *witdoeke*, and other people who were blowing whistles. When I came home, I saw there were many white men, they kicked my door, they kicked it and they went in. I am sure I nearly died that day. They missed me when they shot – they missed me on my forehead ... After they killed my husband Jackson, they threw him in the garden. These people with white scarves came into the house ... I heard bullets going into the toilet, somebody hit my door, one of the children said 'Mama, let's leave, let's go out, my father is coming, he's calling us'. Apparently that was the last time he spoke. The white-scarf people axed him, houses were on fire, there was just fire all over.[1]

This is just one of many accounts of the violence of apartheid that was narrated before the Truth and Reconciliation Commission (TRC), set up in order to reconcile South African society, torn by decades of racist violence, through seeking the truth about what had happened to the many people that died or were injured from violence occurring during the apartheid era.[2] The hearings were broadcast on television in South Africa, but they were not 'news'. There were people in post-apartheid South Africa who, just like in post-war Germany, claimed that they did not know. However, the TRC hearings showed that this ignorance was only possible for those who, confined in their isolated white suburban communities, *actively* turned a blind eye.[3] For most people in South Africa however, the TRC accounts were much too familiar, like the horror of a bad dream. To black people in South Africa, the violence of apartheid was an everyday experience.

The violence of the apartheid State was also widely known to people in many countries around the world, especially so after the massacre in Sharpeville in 1960, widely reported by the international media, and often referred to as a turning point in modern South African history as well as a starting point for international anti-apartheid mobilization. 'Sharpeville' does however also represent a dominant way of framing apartheid in the international media. In the reports from Sharpeville, apartheid repression appeared as outbursts of violence, irrational, disorganized. The same goes for the reports of the shootings in Soweto

16 years later, when apartheid once again gained huge international media attention after many years of relative silence.

But apartheid repression was not mainly about irrational outbursts of violence. It was an everyday terror, highly organized and systematic. Apartheid discourse contained elements of pre-modern thought, including a construction of a Boer identity that was based on an interpretation of the Bible. However, its ideas of race and segregation were based in modern scientific discourse, and its actual practices of organizing society was highly modern, its segregationist politics representing a form of modern social engineering.[4] Apartheid articulated a dark side of modernity – in the same sense as German National Socialism did, as showed by sociologist Zygmunt Bauman in his *Modernity and the Holocaust*.

If apartheid violence largely appeared as disorganized outbursts of violence at those moments when international media attention was at its peak, South African anti-apartheid resistance was often depicted in the same way. In many cases the media were presenting the shootings as responses to rioting black Africans armed with stones and sticks. However, a highly organized repressive system like apartheid demanded organized resistance. From the late 1950s to the 1990s the anti-apartheid movement performed increasingly well-organized transnational collective action, based on a collective identity, an imagined community of solidarity activists, uniting people across large distances.

And just as the organization and articulation of apartheid needs close examination and analysis in order for us to understand how it was made possible, so does the organization and articulation of anti-apartheid. This book is meant as a contribution to the analysis of the transnational anti-apartheid movement, whose history has only begun to be written. Analysing a part of twentieth-century post-war history mainly from a sociological perspective it also highlights dimensions of globalization in an era in which we still live; the power of the media; and the power of collective action.

Introduction: Anti-Apartheid, the Media and 'New Social Movements' – Beyond Eurocentrism

The long journey

> Even through the thickness of the prison walls ... we heard your voices demanding our freedom.
>
> (Nelson Mandela, Wembley stadium, London, 16 April 1990).[1]

Soon after he was released from prison on the 11 February 1990, Nelson Mandela travelled abroad. He visited Zambia, Zimbabwe, Tanzania and then Sweden, where he saw Oliver Tambo, African National Congress (ANC) president in exile, who at the time was hospitalized in Stockholm. Here, he also appeared in front of thousands of cheering people in the Globe Arena. In April, he went to London, where he attended the second 'Mandela concert' at Wembley Stadium, organized by the British AAM (Anti-Apartheid Movement) and broadcast by BBC on television globally.

This was the beginning of the end of the long journey, or as Mandela puts it, 'the long walk', to freedom from the brutal apartheid system in South Africa.[2] As a prisoner for 27 years, Mandela's movements had in a literal sense been limited to walking within an extremely limited space for most of the period of which the anti-apartheid struggle lasted. However, for many of his fellow anti-apartheid activists, journeys across borders were an important and necessary part of the anti-apartheid struggle (as for Mandela himself before and after he was imprisoned). In order to defend its system, the apartheid regime did not just imprison many of its opponents, it also fenced the country in, attempting at strict control over movements across, as well as within, its borders, be it of people or information. However, in an era of increasing cultural, political and economic globalization, this became increasingly difficult.

Across borders

Through the years millions of people participated in the movement to abolish apartheid in South Africa. A large number of them were living in South Africa and were experiencing the violence of the apartheid system as part of every day life.

But the struggle against apartheid in South Africa also benefited from the support of large numbers of people around the world who were not sharing this direct experience of the apartheid system. People living in various countries like Japan, Holland, India, Sweden, Guyana, Britain, Ghana, Jamaica, Cuba, New Zealand and the United States made contributions through taking part in collective action. Most of them had not even been to South Africa. Their support was an act that in the context of the movement was defined through the concept of 'solidarity'.

There are a number of different opinions and theories about the causes of the end of apartheid in South Africa – and about the role that the anti-apartheid struggle played in the process that led to the transformation. In these discussions, a distinction between 'internal' and 'external' factors has been central. On the 'internal side', attention has been paid to the intensified internal struggle during the 1980s, led by the United Democratic Front (UDF), and in which youth movements and trade unions played a significant role.[3] It is argued that this struggle in the end made South Africa 'ungovernable' from the point of view of the apartheid regime. Yet others point to the economic decline in South Africa during the 1980s, and South African big business' changing attitudes towards the apartheid regime, leading to negotiations with the ANC.[4] On the 'external side', one argument emphasizes strongly that it was the shift of international power balance that followed the end of the Cold War that ultimately brought apartheid down. This meant that the 'communist threat' that had helped the South African government to sustain its position internationally was no longer there and that the Western powers and the Soviet Union started to negotiate about finding solutions to conflicts in Southern Africa.[5] Others emphasize the pressure of the international solidarity movement, resulting in boycotts and sanctions against South Africa.[6]

During my research on the anti-apartheid movement, I have come across a number of accounts about how the struggle 'inside' South Africa was constantly influenced by the 'outside', just as the struggle 'outside' was influenced by, and dependent on, the struggle 'inside'. This displays the difficulty to establish a clear, unambiguous 'inside' and 'outside' of South Africa in the struggle against apartheid, just as it is difficult to establish *any* fixed or clear-cut borders in an increasingly globalized world, where people and information increasingly are moving across borders, be it geopolitical, cultural or 'racial'.

Such an account is for example provided by Michael Lapsley, to many known as 'Father Michael', one of many anti-apartheid activists that embodied the movements across borders that characterized the anti-apartheid struggle. Lapsley, born and raised in New Zealand, and trained as an Anglican priest in Australia, was sent by his church community to South Africa in 1973 to study at the University of Natal. Here, he also worked as a chaplain to students at campuses, most of them black, and got involved in anti-apartheid activities. Because of this, he was expelled in 1976, and went to live in Lesotho, where he also became a member of the ANC. In the early 1980s he spent nine months in London, working in the ANC office, speaking at meetings organized by the British AAM. He then went to Zimbabwe, where he continued to work against apartheid.[7]

Lapsley gives the following examples of the important role of both media and travel, as the anti-apartheid movement outside South Africa also became present within its borders:

> To give you an example of a specific moment, there was a particular day, where three o' clock in the morning in South Africa, white South Africa got up to watch a rugby match in New Zealand. And the rugby match was stopped by this massive anti-apartheid movement. And it was electrifying, because we were told in South Africa, people were being told, look there is a few longhaired layabouts, and suddenly it's not a group of longhaired layabouts, but it's actually a broad cross section of society in New Zealand. I think there was enormous appreciation in the majority community that there was an international movement there. And also the (anti-apartheid) leadership and many people in prison talked about that.
>
> Obviously, there were always people who travelled, church people loved travelling. I think that the international church network was often a vehicle for communication, because often political people couldn't necessarily travel, they didn't have passports, they were detained, whatever. The churches were having conferences everywhere, so that the South African connection of the faith community coming back

into the country I think was very significant, a very significant gateway of communication. And there were people from church networks visiting South Africa as well, those communications remained throughout, they never really stopped. So there was that vehicle of communication in both directions.[8]

As I see it, these quotes show that an adequate analysis of the anti-apartheid movement has to pay attention to the construction of networks, organizations, identities, action forms and information flows that transcended borders. In this sense the anti-apartheid movement could be seen as a part of a complex and multi-layered process that could be defined as a globalization of politics.

The globalization of politics

I would like to argue that the global struggle against apartheid must be seen in the context of the emergence of the 'new social movements', that have addressed *global issues* in new ways, for example, solidarity, anti-colonialism, ecology, peace and gender inequality, *as well as* the increased internationalization of 'old movements' (predominantly labour and church movements).[9]

During the last decade, these phenomena have begun to be discussed and analysed in terms of a global or international civil society. There has also been an increasing interest in these issues after the 'global justice movement' (sometimes called the 'anti-globalization movement') became visible in the the World Social Forums in the South and in the streets in cities in the North (Seattle, Genua), as well as in a globalized media space.[10] In these more recent discussions, the Internet is often highlighted as something that has made the construction of an effective global civil society possible. However, I would like to argue that more important, the present 'global civil society' has historical links to the post-war, transnational political culture that the anti-apartheid movement was part of.

This political culture can be understood as part of an increasing *globalization of politics*, taking place predominantly after the Second World War. In this historical context a new, global political space emerges, constituted by three interrelated phenomena: (a) the new media which creates new possibilities for global communication, the creation of (b) *transnational networks of individuals, groups and organizations*, made possible not only through the new media, but also by face-to-face interaction facilitated by the new possibilities of travel. Not the least important, these networks must also be seen in the context of de-colonization and post-colonial migration and (c) the rise and consolidation of new 'global' organizations and institutions.

This book emphasizes the importance of a historical perspective on political cultures, social movements, and political globalization. It looks at anti-apartheid as part of the history of present global politics. It analyses the crucial action forms and identification processes of the anti-apartheid movement as a transnational phenomenon, relating it to relevant political and historical contexts. I argue that the anti-apartheid movement could be seen as part of the construction of an emerging global civil society during the post-war era. Consequently, the transnational anti-apartheid struggle proves a relevant case for recent theorizing and research on transnational movements and global civil society.

Anti-apartheid and human rights

Given the number of people that participated in the transnational anti-apartheid movement, as well as its geographical dispersion and its achievements, there is no doubt that it was one of the most influential social movements during the post-war era. In addition to the South African movement organizations, the transnational anti-apartheid network connected thousands of groups and organizations, including solidarity organizations, unions, churches, women's, youth and student organizations in more than 100 countries.[11] For example, only in Britain more than 184 local groups were affiliated to the British AAM in 1990; and its list of international contacts included anti-apartheid solidarity organizations in 37 countries.[12] Existing as a transnational movement for more than four decades, anti-apartheid's impact was not limited to the South African context, as it created transnational networks, organizations and collective action forms that made – and still makes – an impact on national as well as transnational political cultures.

The significance of this movement has often been recognized in the context of social movement studies and international relations.[13] However, little research has been done on anti-apartheid, especially from the perspective of social movement theory. Further, while one of the most crucial aspects of this movement was its construction of transnational networks and forms of action, most research has focused on its national aspects, looking at the Australian, American, British or South African anti-apartheid movement.[14]

In the context of international relations, Audie Klotz argues that the history of the anti-apartheid struggle refutes the realist notion of international politics as *purely* dominated by the self-interest of states. In an attempt to move beyond the debate on realism versus idealism, she argues for considering norms as a force of change in international politics.[15] Although the focus of her analysis is not on the level of civil society, it nevertheless implies a strong role for the anti-apartheid movement. Through advocating *the global norm of racial equality*, initially emerging in the context of the anti-slavery movement, and through connecting this norm to demands for sanctions, the transnational anti-apartheid movement could become a powerful actor in world politics, influencing the interests and actions of states, corporations and intergovernmental institutions. Klotz also argues that the transnational anti-apartheid movement was related to, and supported by, the emergence and strengthening of issues like human rights and democratization in a global political context during the last decades.

This analysis might also explain the increasing interest in social movements among international relations theorists, as well as the fact that social movement theorists are turning to international relations in order to borrow theoretical concepts when formulating theories of transnational social movements.[16] An important example in this respect is Margaret E. Keck's and Kathryn Sikkink's *Activists Beyond Borders: Advocacy Networks in International Politics*. Advocacy networks are distinguished from other types of transnational networks through 'the centrality of principled ideas or values in motivating their formation'.[17] In the book, the authors identify the anti-apartheid struggle as one of the most successful transnational campaigns in history. However, it is not included as a case in their study.

Although emphasizing historical predecessors in the nineteenth and early twentieth century, such as the anti-slavery campaign and the international suffrage movement, Keck and Sikkink argue that a major change regarding the global diffusion of human rights discourse and practice took place between late 1960s and early 1990s. Before this human rights had, with a few exceptions, been an empty declaration rather than a forceful political discourse. It was only through the emergence of transnational networks, launching successful campaigns during this period, that human rights became powerful as a discourse.

I would argue that this process started a bit earlier, in the early 1960s. Important in this respect was not just the forming of Amnesty International, but also the emergence of the transnational anti-apartheid movement. In 1956 Canon John Collins formed the Treason Trial Defence Fund out of Christian Action, which in turn had roots back to the British Anti-Slavery Society. Later it changed its name to the British Defence and Aid Fund, and in 1965 the International Defence and Aid Fund (IDAF) was set up with the purpose of providing legal support to individuals prosecuted for violating the apartheid laws and to support the families of 'apartheid prisoners'.[18] It became one of the most important international anti-apartheid organizations. However, the broader international campaign against apartheid took off after the All Africa People's Conference in Accra made a call for an international boycott of South African goods in December 1958. Four months later the ANC, who had been discussing a boycott since the early 1950s, launched a boycott in South Africa.[19] In Britain the anti-colonial Committee of African Organizations (CAO) responded to the call at a meeting in Holborn Hall in London. Invited to the meeting as Speakers were Julius Nyerere, president of the Tanganyika Africa National Union, and Father Trevor Huddleston.[20] A boycott committee was formed, and soon it evolved into the independent Boycott Movement, which in 1960 changed its name to the AAM, consisting of South African exiles and a few of their British supporters.[21] In March 1960, the campaign was fuelled by the Sharpeville shootings, which was reported globally by the media and caused a moral outrage all over the world. In various countries anti-apartheid protests occurred, demanding that governments and the United Nations (UN) put pressure on the South African government to end apartheid.

Partly as a result of this emerging global mobilization, the UN General Assembly a year later passed a resolution, explicitly referring to the demands of the 'world public opinion'. It declared that the 'racial policies being pursued by the Government of the Union of South Africa are a flagrant violation of the Charter of the United Nations and the Universal Declaration of Human Rights'.[22] The British AAM, which in 1965 decided to pay special attention to co-ordination of the transnational anti-apartheid network,[23] continued to refer to apartheid as a human rights issue in its internationally distributed *AA News* in the 1960s. In the Human Rights Year of 1968, AAM sent a circular letter to all organizations in the international anti-apartheid network, urging them to campaign about the apartheid issue as a violation of human rights.[24]

This might prove a case to conceptualize the transnational anti-apartheid struggle in Keck's and Sikkink's terms as a human rights advocacy network. However, in this book, I will argue that such a conceptualization is not sufficient, as the anti-apartheid struggle clearly took the shape of a *social movement*.

Anti-apartheid and new social movements

In the cases where the anti-apartheid struggle has been analysed in terms of a social movement, it has often been related to the discourse on 'new social movements' (NSM). In an article on the British AAM,

Stuart Hall argues that it could be seen as one of the new social movements, since it 'cut across issues of class and party, and organizational allegiance'.[25] In a similar mode Christine Jennett has analysed the Australian anti-apartheid movement as a new social movement, emphasizing its cultural orientation.[26]

I agree that the anti-apartheid movement displayed many of the central features of new social movements as these have been defined in the context of NSM theory.[27] The struggle against apartheid was as a part of the emergence of a new transnational political culture during the post-war era, that also included other solidarity movements, as well as student's, green, peace and women's movements, often conceptualized as 'the new social movements'. The anti-apartheid movement was able to unite an extremely broad 'rainbow coalition' of organizations and groups, with a socially diverse support base and ideological orientation. Further, the anti-apartheid movement had a strong cultural orientation, it was highly media oriented and the production and dissemination of information was one of its central activities. Finally, although its actions often had the purpose of putting pressure on governments and political parties, it engaged in extra-parliamentary political action, such as civil disobedience and boycotts, the latter its most important form of collective action.

However it is not possible to use NSM theory to analyse the transnational anti-apartheid movement without making a few modifications. *First*, 'old social movements', predominantly labour and church movements, and their increased internationalization during the post-war era, were an integral part of anti-apartheid, as a 'movement of movements'. *Second*, and more important, the case of anti-apartheid as a transnational social movement reveals some highly problematic Eurocentric assumptions made in the context of NSM theory. I would like to argue that this implicit Eurocentrism to a large extent is related to a lack of a theoretically developed global perspective on contemporary collective action in the theoretical literature on new social movements. Although the global dimensions of contemporary collective action has often been pointed out, Western nation states have been the point of departure for theorizing on new social movements. Theorists of new social movements have pointed to the *new* social conditions of 'post-industrial', 'complex' or 'informational' societies as a precondition for the emergence of these movements. Consequently, where no such new conditions are clearly present, no new movements can possibly emerge.

In spite of this, the concept of new social movements has in a few cases been applied in analyses of collective action in the South, however often without theoretical debate.[28] One important exception is Ernesto Laclau, who has argued that:

> is it not the case that this plurality of the social and this proliferation of political spaces which lie behind the new social movements, are basically typical of advanced industrial societies, whilst the social reality of the Third World, given its lower level of differentiation, can still be apprehended in terms of the more classical categories of sociological and class analysis? The reply is that, besides the fact that this 'lower level of differentiation' is a myth, Third World societies have never been comprehensible in terms of a strict class analysis. We hardly need to refer to the Eurocentrism in which the 'universalization' of that analysis was based.[29]

The Eurocentric and evolutionist thinking often implied in NSM theory is clearly expressed by Christine Jennett as she is applying Alain Touraine's theory of social movements in her analysis of the Australian Anti-Apartheid Movement (AAAM). The organization AAAM, consisting of predominantly middle-class Australian solidarity activists, is by Jennett defined as a new social movement, characterized by its orientation toward participatory grassroots democracy. The exile liberation movements, including organizations such as the ANC, the Pan-Africanist Congress of Azania (PAC) and South West African People's Union (SWAPO), are by the same author defined as 'historical movements', characterized by hierarchical forms of organization and nationalist ideology.[30]

In a sense NSM theory has often implicitly been reproducing the Eurocentric evolutionist thinking of classical modernization theory, in which each country in its development has to pass through similar stages, and where the 'underdeveloped' countries of the South are always lagging behind the developed countries of the North. This mode of thinking is also based on what has been called 'methodological nationalism' in the sense that the nation state is always the basic unity of the analysis, and development/underdevelopment thus always is related to 'internal factors'.[31] This paradigm ignored the existence of global power relations and economic and political interdependence. In the case of theories of post-industrial society, it was often 'forgotten' that the transformation to post-industrial economies in the North presupposed moving industrial production to so called 'low-wage' countries in the South. Although few advocates of classical modernization theory are to be heard today, many of its assumptions are still implicitly present in current social theory. This is the case even in recent globalization discourse, as social conditions and trends specific to countries in the North are often being universalized.[32]

As I see it, this is not to say that NSM theory has not contributed with valuable insights regarding contemporary collective action. However, it has to be de-linked from its Eurocentric implications. Social movement studies could thus benefit from integrating perspectives from postcolonial theory. Postcolonial studies have not only emphasized the presence of a colonial legacy in the context of the latest phase of the globalization process, but also the presence and influence of the de-colonization process and the politics of anti-colonialism on present-day politics.[33]

Applying this perspective to the transnational anti-apartheid movement, and relating it to the debate on 'new social movements', it is evident that this movement, displaying all the characteristics associated with new social movements, emerged out of transnational interactions located in the context of de-colonization. It was initiated under strong influence not just of South African anti-apartheid organizations and exiles, but also of the broader anti-colonial struggle. The de-colonization process clearly marked established politics as well as the emerging alternative political culture in Britain at the time when the two internationally important solidarity organizations, IDAF and AAM, were initiated. These organizations were part of what in Britain in the late 1950s and early 1960s was called 'new politics', as I see it an early conceptualization of certain forms of collective action, foreshadowing the latter 'new social movements'.

In 1952, the same year that Canon John Collins initiated the activities that would subsequently lead to the formation of IDAF, the British peace movement initiated a mobilization process influenced by the Indian anti-colonial movement. It was called 'Operation Gandhi', and organized 'sit-ins' in central London.[34] The founder of IDAF, Canon John Collins, was also the chairman of the Campaign for Nuclear Disarmament (CND), the dominant peace movement organization in Britain at the time. A public personality involved in the more militant civil disobedience actions that the peace movement at this time continued to stage (and which amongst other things led to the trial against Bertrand Russell, that gained media attention around the whole world) was Reverend Michael Scott. Scott had been participating in militant Indian civil disobedience actions as well as black political activism in South Africa. Banned in South Africa in 1950, Scott initiated the Africa Bureau in London in 1952, supporting African de-colonization. Just like the Movement for Colonial Freedom, The Africa Bureau was an important part of an emerging anti-colonial political culture in Britain in late 1950s.

When the Boycott Movement, initiated by the Committee of African Organizations, in 1960 changed its name to AAM, and started to reach outside of the exile circles, it attracted individuals who participated in this political culture.[35]

To conclude the discussion on the implications of the case of the anti-apartheid movement in relation to the theoretical debate on new social movements: I argue that when using this concept, it must be recognized that new social movements in the West partly emerged out of the *global context* of de-colonization, and that the collective experiences and action forms of the anti-colonial struggles in the South were extremely important sources of influence.

I think that the reason for this influence being largely neglected in the context of NSM theory, is partly due to the methodological nationalism which for a long time has dominated not just social movement studies but the social sciences in general. However, as has already been mentioned, recently a new interdisciplinary field of research has emerged, dealing with transnational collective action and the changing role of the nation state in the context of the increasing importance of processes of globalization. As Keck and Sikkink have showed, this approach is not only valid in relation to the recent wave of transnational collective action, but also to historical cases.

Defining anti-apartheid as social movement

I define a *social movement* as a form of collective action that ultimately aims at transforming a social order. A social movement is a process involving as central elements the articulation of social conflicts and collective identities. It is constituted by different forms of practices: production and dissemination of information, knowledge and symbolic practices, mobilization of various forms of resources, including the construction of organizations and networks, and the performing of public actions of different kinds (demonstrations as well as direct actions).[36] This means that a social movement should not be confused with an 'organization', or an NGO (although it can include NGOs), and that it does not consist of the sum of a number of individuals – that is, it does not presuppose 'membership' – but should rather be seen as a space of action. For example, by participating in a boycott against South African goods you performed an action that was a part of constituting anti-apartheid as a social movement.

While this analytical understanding of a social movement departs from the so-called 'identity paradigm', I will also make use of the Resource Mobilization Theory (RMT), particularly its emphasis on the importance of previously established networks for the emergence of a social movement, and the notions of 'action repertoire' (designating the available, historically accumulated, stock of action forms) and 'social movement organizations' (SMOs).[37] Resource Mobilization Theory has also been reformulated as the Political Process Perspective, an approach that emphasizes the role of political opportunity structures (POS), often being used for cross-national comparisons. Although the POS approach recently has been modified in order to be adapted to the emergence of transnational social movements that address supra-national institutions, it still tends to treat the nation state as a 'pre-given', largely unproblematized, context for social movement action.[38]

Rather than presuming that explanations for both national and transnational collective action are primarily to be sought in the context of the internal dynamics of a nation state, I will shift emphasis, suggesting that any analysis of the emergence of social movements, national and transnational, in the twentieth (and the twenty-first) century, must consider their relations to transnational processes. Further, as a consequence of its emphasis on political structures, the POS mode of analysis has in some cases tended to downplay the role of culture and history. In this book, I will use a number of concepts that emphasize global processes, history and culture.

On the most general level of analysis, I will use the concept of *structural context*, including the economic, political and cultural structuring of social action. In its widest sense the appropriate structural context for the transnational anti-apartheid movement is the process of intensified globalization during the post-war era.[39] Further, situated in *the context of postcoloniality*, the issue of anti-apartheid was articulated as an issue of de-colonization, particularly by newly independent states and anti-colonial movements, and the patterns of conflicts and positions taken in the context of international communities were to a large extent conditioned by the political history of colonialism. Finally, situated in *the context of the Cold War*, the anti-apartheid struggle, like any significant political field during the post-war era, national as well as transnational, was divided along the conflict lines that constituted the bipolar political world order. The Cold War was a crucial factor in the circumstances that made it possible for the South African apartheid government to sustain its position internationally. It was also the Cold War that made it possible to define ANC as part of a bloc that threatened world peace and security.[40]

Further, in order to emphasize the importance of the cultural dimension of collective action, I will use the concept of *political culture* to signify a more specific and highly relevant context for the analysis of how national and transnational collective action at any given time is structured not just by the presence of formal political institutions, but through historically instituted discursive formations and processes of identity construction on different levels.[41] 'Political culture' refers to processes of communication and articulation of political experiences, identities, action strategies and projects – and to the institutions in which these processes are embedded.[42] On a transnational level, the political cultures established by the anti-colonial movements and previously existing solidarity movements played a crucial role in shaping the character of the transnational anti-apartheid movement (Chapter 1). In Britain and Sweden, specific national political cultures influenced the anti-apartheid movements in the two countries (Chapter 3).

Further, I will use *social movement culture* as a more specific context, in which historical movement traditions (in terms of collective identifications, action repertoires, and organizational forms) are being reproduced, modified and/or transformed. Finally, *key organizations* and *key activists* denote an even more specific and methodologically relevant focus for an analysis of a social movement. A social movement can include a number of SMOs, and certain SMOs can be part of several social movements. For example, the anti-apartheid movement included SMOs that were also part of other movements (such as labour organizations or women's organizations). Key organizations are however those SMOs that solely focus on the main conflict/issue that defines the 'common ground' of a movement, and therefore play a key role in constructing its collective identity. In the case of anti-apartheid, key organizations in South Africa at different times were the ANC, the PAC (1950s and early 1960s), the Azanian People's Organization (AZAPO, related to the Black Consciousness Movement emerging in the late 1970s), the Inkatha Freedom Party (formed in 1975 out of Mangosuthu Buthelezi's Inkatha Movement) and the UDF (formed in 1983).[43] In countries outside of South Africa, key SMOs were the organizations that specifically focused on solidarity with the former. In the context of the transnational anti-apartheid movement, the key movement organizations were mainly the ANC, the PAC and the two British key solidarity organizations, AAM and IDAF.

Key activists should be understood as those who perform the crucial role of being spiders in movement networks, combining the possession of information and knowledge particularly relevant in a movement context (a kind of 'movement capital' in Bourdieu's terms) with strategically relevant spatial moves and movements as networks are spun across borders. Thus key activists have the function of being 'nodes' in the information networks of the movement, in retrospect often being able to provide a general view of certain processes as well as contexts of the movement. The function of key organizations and key activists in an empirical study of social movements is thus that they facilitate the analysis of the crucial dynamics of the processes of identification, as well as to the informational, cognitive and spatial networks of a social movement.

The approach that I am suggesting implies mainly focusing the analysis on the complex process of interaction through which a social movement is constructed. This is a process that not only involves consensus building but also tensions and conflicts. Although social movements may appear as homogenous phenomena in public space, they must be understood as constituted by heterogeneous and sometimes contradictory constellations of actions. I would even like to argue that tensions and conflicts are fundamental elements in the dynamic of social movement processes. An adequate analysis of a social movement, including its relations to the social and historical context in which it acts, must therefore not only focus on conflicts between a movement and its adversaries, but on the *internal* conflicts through which the strategies and identities of the movement are articulated. Such an approach is highly relevant in the case of anti-apartheid, that to a large extent was a 'movement of movements', consisting of an extremely broad alliance between liberation movements and solidarity movements, the latter composed of different 'blocs' – churches, unions, political parties, student movements and solidarity organizations.

Social movements are frequently referred to in current discussions on democracy and civil society. Since this book relates to this theme it must underlined that the concept of 'social movement', in the way it is used here, does not *per se* refer to democratic processes. However, in the history of modernity there have seldom been processes of democratization without the involvement of broad social movements. The transformation of South African society in the 1980s and 1990s is, of course, one of the latest examples of this.

This theme connects to the discussion on the relation between social movements and social change. The fact that social movements are defined by an orientation toward social change does of course not mean that they always achieve the changes that are struggled for. Sometimes they do, but not exactly the way it was imagined in movement discourses. Sometimes unimagined changes might come about in the form of unintended consequences of collective action. Although there are disputes as to what extent the anti-apartheid movement contributed to the end of apartheid system, it might still be argued that it by large was a success story. Still, present day South African society might not look the way it was imagined in the utopias of the anti-apartheid movement. However, more important, simply to asses to what extent a movement achieved the goals that were formulated in its programmes might not be the most fruitful way of reaching an understanding of the impact of its collective actions. To be able to reach a more complex analysis of the relations between social movements and social change it might be useful to introduce the notion of 'learning process' as an important aspect of social movement praxis.[44] In the practices of social movements, collective experiences are made, that to its individual participants constitute learning processes, which might be carried into other contexts.

To what extent learning processes of social movements actually contribute to significant social change is of course open to careful empirical investigation in any given case. In any case this is not an easy task to assess, since it really cannot be measured. To find out about the number of participants is of course not unimportant to be able to assess the impact of a movement. But the main task for the approach that I am using is to find out about the *quality of action*. What were the important forms of action and interaction and what did they mean in the different contexts in which they were performed?

Social movements and the mediatization of politics

In March 1960, the international campaign against apartheid that was initiated the year before was fuelled by the Sharpeville shootings, which was reported globally by the media and caused a moral outrage all over the world. In various countries, anti-apartheid protests occurred. However, media attention related to dramatic events in South Africa was short-lived. During long periods anti-apartheid activists experienced difficulties to get a voice in public space. In response to this, an active approach to media was developed. This involved the two interrelated strategies of trying to influence established media, and to develop alternative media.

The rise of the transnational anti-apartheid movement was parallel in time, and was indeed part of, the mediatization of politics, which followed the changes in the media structure in societies all over the world, beginning in the 1960s. The changes included the expansion of the tabloid press and the increasing importance of television.[45] These changes brought about (a) *new national media spaces*, where political identities are constructed in new ways and where local problems can become national issues; (b) *a visualized transnational media space*, which can be seen as a part of the process of globalization.[46] This is not only a space for the immediate transmission of news across the globe, but also a site of political struggle, where different political actors, through symbolic actions, are trying to influence opinions (such as in the case of, for example, Greenpeace). In relation to this John Keane, in his influential book *Media and Democracy*, argued that we have seen a 'slow and delicate growth of an international civil society'.[47]

The media orientation that is characteristic of new social movements must be seen in relation to the broader context of the construction of a new movement culture, beginning in the late 1950s. Although often involving antagonistic relationships the different movements had in common that their identities were defined in anti-establishment terms, and together the various groups, organizations and networks made up an 'alternative culture'. This was a context for articulating new issues and identities, related to regular activities taking place in 'invisible networks' as well as within the framework of 'visible' movement organizations and institutions: journals, small publishing houses, co-operatives and festivals including performances, theatres and rituals related to political issues. It has been argued that this alternative political culture can be seen as a reaction to the decline in the public sphere that Jürgen Habermas was referring to in 1962 and that the movements represented an attempt to revitalize and redefine civil society and politics itself.[48]

Just as in the case of the new media structures, the rise of new social movements is not only a part of the changing character of national political cultures, but also *contributes to the emergence of a new transnational political space*. In 1968 the protesters outside the Democratic Presidential Convention chanted 'the whole world is watching', and since the 1960s new social movement groups and organizations are increasingly staging media oriented public manifestations addressing a global audience.[49]

At the same time movement mobilizations are often shaped in *response* to events that are globally reported by the media; movement intellectuals and groups are taking part in the struggle over the interpretation of the political implications of these events. For example the globally reported news reports from the war in Vietnam played an important role for the articulation of the anti-war movement politics in different places of the world.[50] Further, the reports on events in Sharpeville in 1960 and in Soweto in 1976 were followed by intensified mobilization against apartheid in different parts of the world. However, as I will show, a simple cause-and-effect analysis of the relation between 'media events' and political mobilization is deeply problematic. Further, studies have shown that the actual interpretation of global media events, and the way that international and global political issues are articulated and related to action strategies in different parts of the world, must be seen in relation to local, that is, often national, political traditions and institutional conditions.

Sharpeville and the role of media events

In this book, I will look at the role of the media and information in the context of the transnational anti-apartheid struggle, particularly at the development of what I will call media and information strategies. Through these strategies, the anti-apartheid movement took part of a struggle for representation that was played out on national arenas as well as in a transnational media space. However, the discussion on transnational media and media activism is particularly related to the national contexts of Britain and Sweden, two countries in which important actors in the transnational struggle against apartheid had their base.

An important focus in the analysis of the relations between the anti-apartheid movement and the established media in this book is the role of certain 'events'. 'Events' played an important role in struggle for media and information; for example Sharpeville and the protests against the tour in 1970 of the South African cricket team in Britain, which will be dealt with in Chapters 5 and 6; Soweto (Chapter 7), the shootings in Langa on Sharpeville day on the 25th anniversary of Sharpeville in 1985, and the release of Nelson Mandela (Chapter 8).

In the context of academic history as well as media studies, the definition of an 'event' has often been an issue under investigation and debate.[51] But whatever the definition, in a modern media society, an event is rarely an event if not reported by the media. Further, a clear-cut distinction between a 'real event' and a 'media event' risks reproducing a problematic view on the relation between 'reality' and 'media' – and a seldom-contested way of looking at the character of particular historical events and the role of collective action in relation to such events. For example, in the case of an established narrative of the role of 'Sharpeville' for the early emergence of a transnational anti-apartheid movement, a causal chain of events is constructed. It starts with the Sharpeville massacre, which is causing media to report on the naked brutality of the apartheid regime. This in turn gives rise to a moral outrage translated into public action and the emergence of a broad anti-apartheid movement. This chain of logic is based on the implicit assumption that 'the event in itself' is the fundamental reason for all the other things to happen. Thus, it is argued that the key to understand the event and its effects is the moral outrage caused by the sheer brutality of the South African police, as mediated in the news coverage.

However, as I will show in more detail in Chapter 5, a closer look at the processes occurring before, and partly leading to, Sharpeville, points to another way of understanding the role of the massacre as an 'event'. For certain occurrences to be reported in the media as an event, the media must be prepared for such reporting. Three months before Sharpeville, there was a massacre in Windhoek in which 11 people were killed and 44 were wounded. It was however largely neglected by the international media.[52] The wave of international mobilization often claimed to be caused by the Sharpeville massacre and the fact that it was reported world-wide, in fact originated before Sharpeville – *and prepared the ground for the media attention paid to the massacre on the 21 March 1960.* This pre-Sharpeville process of mobilization, which the protest in Sharpeville in fact can be seen as a result of, began inside South Africa, included as a crucial element the call for a boycott of South African goods, and culminated in the months before the Sharpeville shootings. At this time there was attention to, and debates on, the boycott in the media in both Britain and Sweden.[53]

Border thinking

During the last decades, a number of scholars from different disciplines have argued that the study of global or transnational phenomena requires a theoretical and methodological approach that is different from the dominant paradigm that equals the study of 'society' with 'national society'.[54] Attempts to think about power, territoriality, identity, structure and action beyond the 'nation state paradigm', or 'methodological nationalism', have often been centred on the concept of 'border'. Walter Mignolo has coined the concept of 'border thinking' in order to theorize present globalization in relation to the global history of colonialism.[55] It might also be used as a name for a 'transnationalist approach' shared by a number of scholars working in fields such as postcolonial studies, cultural studies, sociology, international relations and anthropology. Different from the images of a 'boundless world' of globalist ideology, 'border thinking' urges us to think in new ways about borders and boundaries, geopolitical as well as cultural or racial. It is an approach that pays particular attention to practices involving movements, mobility and diaspora – the crossing of borders and the construction of spaces across and in between institutionalized and relatively fixed boundaries – the latter understood in terms of 'borderlands' or 'third space'.[56]

Although I am arguing that 'border-crossing' is a key for understanding processes of organization and identification in the anti-apartheid struggle, it is just as important to focus and analyse the prevailing importance of old borders and the construction of new ones in this context. For example, as is stated in Michael Lapsley's account in the beginning of this chapter, not all people could travel. In fact, the South African borders were closed to a number of people, who wanted to leave or visit the country. And in the sense of cultural or 'racial' borders, not just the politics of the apartheid regime, but also the practice of solidarity work, involved constructing a number of borders between 'us' and 'them'. Such borders were often related to national identities and interests as well as national political cultures.

As this book shows, *globalization does not necessarily mean that the nation state, understood as a political space, is fading away. Rather, the nation state gains new meanings in the context of globalization, just as globalization has different meanings in different national contexts.* The different ways that international and global political issues are articulated and translated into political action in different parts of the world, are dependent on local, that is, often national, political traditions and institutional conditions. Thus, in order to find out about the implications of the process of globalization in different parts of the world, comparative approaches are necessary.

Empirically, my work has mainly been focused on two national contexts – Sweden and Britain, with complementary material collected in the United States and South Africa. Comparisons will be made, but this is not a comparative study in the classical sense. Britain and Sweden are not comparable units. Neither are they as nation states as closed entities as the classical comparative methodology presupposes. Rather, during the period of the anti-apartheid struggle, political (as well as other) practices in Britain and Sweden were increasingly related to worldwide processes. The main purpose of the book is to find out how transnational communication in the context of the anti-apartheid movement was carried out, what made it possible, and how transnational strategies, experiences and identities were articulated in the discourses of the movement. Consequently, I am interested in if and how organizations, groups and individuals based in the different countries were involved in transnational networks and processes of communication and identification. Comparisons between the two national contexts will thus be related to the context of transnational communication and political globalization.

Looking at the various national contexts of the global anti-apartheid struggle, both Britain and Sweden are, for different reasons, significant cases. As a 'postcolonial capital', London became an important centre of South African exile activists, organizations and activities. Further, two of the most important organizations in the transnational solidarity network, IDAF and the British AAM, had their base in London.

Looking at the case of Sweden, Southern Africa was the most important region receiving Swedish aid during the period of the anti-apartheid struggle.[57] The extensive financial support to the ANC from the Swedish State, under the rule of Social Democrats as well as non-socialist coalitions, could partly be understood in relation to contacts between ANC leaders and young Social Democratic and Liberal internationalists in the 1950s and 1960s. However, it was also the result of pressure from the Swedish anti-apartheid movement, which emerged in the early 1960s and continued to put pressure on the government until the first democratic elections in South Africa.

Notes on material and method

The empirical material and methods used in this study are related to the different sets of questions and analytical approaches reflected in the two major parts of the book. The first part looks at anti-apartheid as a social movement, focusing on different contexts and levels of action. While Chapter 1 focuses on the level of individual activism, Chapters 2 and 3 look at anti-apartheid in the context of global and national politics (Britain and Sweden). Chapter 4 specifically analyses some of the crucial aspects of the relations between the anti-apartheid movement and the media, nationally and globally. These chapters are mainly based on archival material and interviews with key activists. The anti-apartheid movement was a 'movement of movements', and this book does consider the broad context of organizations and networks involved. However the research has focused on the organizations *mainly* working against apartheid in Southern Africa. While the material on which the book is based includes interviews with members of the ANC, the PAC, IDAF and AAM, the latter is an obvious choice of particular focus, because of its major public role both in the transnational and the British anti-apartheid contexts. In the Swedish case, the key organizations were the South Africa Committees, the Africa Groups and the Isolate South Africa Committee (ISAK). While I have interviewed activists in all of these organizations, the Africa Groups is a relevant case for a particular focus, because it provides an example of how a relatively small key organization (in terms of membership) can play a crucial role in a broad social movement. Emerging out of the South Africa Committees and the student movement in the late 1960s, the Africa Groups established a national organization in 1975 (AGIS). In 1979, it initiated ISAK, aiming for a broad Swedish anti-apartheid umbrella organization. Through a number of tactical manoeuvres, AGIS both managed to get a number of established Swedish NGOs on board, including all youth sections of the political parties except Moderaterna (the Conservatives), and to get acceptance for a platform based on sole recognition of the ANC regarding its anti-apartheid solidarity work.[58] ISAK became the dominating Swedish anti-apartheid organization in the 1980s and 1990s. ISAK did not allow individual membership, but in 1989 it included 66 organizations with a total membership base of 800,000 people. While membership in the Africa Groups never reached far above 2000 during the anti-apartheid era, it kept its influence in ISAK as many of its leading members also were key activists in ISAK, and the activists of local committees of ISAK were also often members of the Africa Groups.[59]

The narratives of transnational activism in Chapter 1 partly focus on the individual level of action, but they also articulate different aspects of the collective organization of the transnational anti-apartheid movement. Through their reflections and narratives, the informants – retrospectively – constructed 'activist identities', defining one, often very important, aspect of their life history. They were thus accounting for an aspect of their personal biography and identity that was defined through their identification with the collective identity of the anti-apartheid movement.

For Chapters 2–4, the interviews, as well as the archival material and previous research on anti-apartheid, were used in order to gain knowledge about, and to analyse, the forms of national and transnational organization of the movement; the construction of its collective identities and major action strategies; and the major conflicts, internally as well as in relation to the movement's major opponents. Chapter 4 does not only focus on the media strategies of the anti-apartheid movement, including the construction of alternative media, but also on the interaction between the media strategies of the movement and the established media, as well as on the media strategies of the apartheid government. This chapter should also be seen as the bridge to the second part of the book, Anti-Apartheid Strategies and Public Debates in Britain and Sweden 1960–90.

Analysing debates on apartheid/anti-apartheid

The second part of the book consists of case studies, analysing the apartheid/anti-apartheid press debate in Britain and Sweden at five particular historical moments – with a specific focus on the presence or non-presence of the anti-apartheid movement in these debates.

Here, my approach is a form of discourse analysis that methodologically departs from Foucault and has been further developed in the context of British Cultural Studies.[60] This approach is integrated with a constructionist approach to social movements and media, in which media discourse is seen as 'a site on which various social groups, institutions and ideologies struggle over the definition and construction of social reality'.[61]

An important source of inspiration is Todd Gitlin's analysis of the role of the media for the New Left in the United States in the 1960s, *The Whole World is Watching*. Drawing on Stuart Hall's essay 'Encoding, Decoding', Gitlin uses the concept of *framing* in order to analyse how media discourse is implicitly structured:

> Media frames are persistent patterns of cognition, interpretation and presentation, of selection, emphasis and exclusion, by which symbol-handlers routinely organize discourse, whether verbal or visual.[62]

I also share Gitlin's emphasis on the relevance of a historical and detailed approach even when the purpose is to discern media frames that are relatively stable over a period of time. His account for the process through which a certain pattern of media representation was established in case of the US movement, is also true for the anti-apartheid movement, emerging at the same time:

> As movement and media discovered and acted on each other, they worked out the terms with which they would recognize and work on the other; they developed a grammar of interaction. This grammar then shaped the way movement-media history developed over the rest of the decade, opening certain possibilities and excluding others. As the movement developed, so did the media approaches to it, so that the media's structures of cognition and interpretation never stayed entirely fixed. The analysis must therefore attend closely to the precise historical experience.[63]

An important distinction in this form of discourse analysis is between the uncontested and the contested terrains of discourse.[64] The most important aspect of the debate on apartheid/anti-apartheid in this regard is that from 1960 and on, following the British Conservative Prime Minister Harold Macmillan's 'Winds of Change' speech in South Africa in

January and the Sharpeville massacre in March, an uncontested aspect of apartheid/anti-apartheid discourse in both Britain and Sweden (as well as in most parts of the world) consisted of a consensus that there must be change in South Africa. Because apartheid in such a profound way contradicted the values that were the cornerstones of the liberal hegemony of the Western world after the Second World War, the anti-apartheid movement always had an upper hand in public debates in Western countries. Anyone who contested the view that apartheid was wrong risked being excluded from the public arena, as for example happened with the extremist *Nordvästra Skånes Tidningar* in Sweden in 1960 (see Chapter 5). It was in this sense that the view that South Africa must change was an *uncontested* dimension of the discourse on apartheid/anti-apartheid during the period of this study. What was contested in the debate was *how* change should take place, *what* changes were possible and *when* they were possible. Further, and even more important, a major issue of contest concerned the means to put pressure on the South African government to initiate such change; this was the issue of *the legitimacy of the anti-apartheid movement* and its strategies. The fact that there was a consensus on that apartheid must change did not mean that the apartheid regime lacked defenders in public debates in Britain and Sweden. However, considering what defensible positions were available in the terrain of apartheid/anti-apartheid debate after 1960, those who wanted to defend the South African government and its policy would have to argue that South Africa was actually changing or that change was not possible at the moment – a position often claimed to be 'realistic'. The main emphasis of this strategy however, was critiquing or discrediting the anti-apartheid movement (rather than explicitly defending apartheid), arguing that the latter's demands for change were unrealistic, or that its claims to represent the public opinion was illegitimate – or in some cases even questioning the legitimacy of anti-apartheid protest *strategies*.

Thus, the debate on apartheid in Britain and Sweden to a large extent became a debate on anti-apartheid. It might even be argued that a major discursive strategy for those actors defending the South African government was to move the focus of the debate from a criticism of apartheid to a criticism of anti-apartheid. When the Cold War frame was put into play, it was even argued that the anti-apartheid solidarity movement, however good its intentions might appear on the surface, intentionally or unintentionally was playing in the hands of the Soviet Union. Further, from the early days of transnational anti-apartheid mobilization, there was also an internal debate on anti-apartheid strategies, particularly in the context of the solidarity movement.

As we will see in Part II of this book, different action strategies were in the focus of the debate at different periods of the anti-apartheid struggle. In case of the debate on the South African anti-apartheid movement, *the issue of violence/non-violence* was always on the agenda, particularly after the ANC abandoned its non-violent strategy in 1961. Regarding the solidarity movement, the focus was on the boycott in 1960, in the late 1960s shifting to direct action and civil disobedience as the student movement entered the struggle, while the sanctions issue was on top of the agenda in 1985 and 1990, after the release of Nelson Mandela.

The most important issue at stake in the discourse on apartheid/anti-apartheid was thus *prescriptions of strategy*, which ultimately defined the meaning of solidarity.

The analysis in part II is carried out in the form of case studies, focusing on moments of intensified debates, or 'critical discourse moments'.[65] The moments selected are related to events that have gained symbolic significance for the struggle against apartheid. The media reports on these events form, through their framing, a construction of reality, and the media thus initiates a process of symbolic struggle over the issue of apartheid.

In relation to an approach where the whole period is covered through a study of a few media, the advantage of the case study approach is that it is possible to include samples from a broader range of publications. This allows for a comparison regarding how issues are articulated in different publications and media institutions (established media, movement media) – and for an analysis of the relations between the different kinds of definitions and views that were produced. Because of the focus on debates, the main part of the material collected for the analysis consists of opinion articles in the major newspapers, with a particular focus on editorials.[66] However, because these debates were also influenced by the news reports of events, I have also studied news coverage, and in particular the front pages, of two major newspapers in each country, representing different ideological affiliations. While the *Guardian* and *Dagens Nyheter* represent a liberal position, *The Times* and *Svenska Dagbladet* are close to the conservative parties in the two countries. As we shall see, there were differences between the frames of the news reports and those of the editorial comments, but they were nevertheless connected to each other. Further, because of the focus on the presence of the anti-apartheid movement in the media, and the movement's own emphasis on the strategy of producing alternative media, I have also included publications of the major anti-apartheid organizations.[67]

Using the approach of Foucault to the 'order of discourse'[68] as a source of inspiration, the most basic questions for discourse analysis is to ask questions about who is allowed to speak (the subjects of the discourse), what is possible to say (and not to say) and what central objects are constructed in the discourse. Translating this approach more concretely to the debate on apartheid/anti-apartheid, I have focused on the main discursive strategies (or strands of argumentation) and standpoints in the debate. How is the conflict scenario of apartheid/anti-apartheid constructed? What are the most important frames structuring the conflict scenario and the debate? Who are the main actors in the discourse? To what extent are they objects/subjects of the discourse? When they speak as acting subjects, from which positions do they speak? Regarding normative statements on changes of apartheid and the strategies of anti-apartheid, what are the main arguments and positions? Where is the border drawn between what is possible to argue and what is not?

Thus, an important focus when analysing media discourses that construct conflict scenarios involving social movements is the representation of the different actors – in this case the anti-apartheid movement (in its broadest sense, in South Africa and internationally), the South African police and the government, other governments, international bodies such as the UN, corporations and established political parties in the different countries. The position of these actors in the narratives is not just related to whether they appear as objects or subjects in the discourse. Because of the strong claims to authenticity when actors appear in the media as subjects 'speaking in their own words', it is even more important to distinguish between different forms of constructions of such 'subjectivity' – or 'agency'. These constructions are related to the extent to which the actors are allowed space to define the situation 'in their own words', and to what extent they are able to control the context of their appearance. Looking at the representation of the anti-apartheid movement as an active subject in different types of media material, it is possible to distinguish between at least four different constructions of subjectivity; the movement can speak (anonymously or through named representatives) through quotations, statements or articles in the established media, and through the production of movement media. Quotations in news articles represent the lowest degree of control from the viewpoint of the movement, as the journalist provides not just the context for the statement, but also interprets and edits the statement of the interviewed person. A published or quoted movement statement means more control of the content of the statement, but not of the article providing the context. In cases where movement representatives publish letters to the editor or debate articles in the established media, they control the whole text, but not the context that is provided by the newspaper as the medium in which they speak (and most often not the headline, the introduction to, and the illustration of, the text). This kind of control is only achieved in the media produced by the movement itself. It must however be emphasized, that since social movements are in themselves processes involving internal struggles, movement media are also the result of a selection process reflecting power relations.

Finally, in discourse analysis, it is also important to look for and analyse silences and absences. In this regard the use of movement media has an important function in the analysis, as they, in relation to established media, are not just produced in order to provide different views on events, but often to 'speak' about subjects that are absent in the established media. This is not to say that movement media represent 'the truth' – rather they construct alternative interpretations of conflict scenarios and events, which might point to ideological closures in the representation of established media (just as articles published in the established media might point to ideological closures in movement media).[69]

Lastly, while my approach to the press material is basically analytical, I use a method of narration that includes a large number of quotations – resembling an ethnographic 'thick description' of the field under study. This is a consequence of the fact that my approach to media discourse analysis is both historical and emphasizes the importance of paying attention to the actual words and concepts used in order to analyse how meaning is constructed. Further, this form of narration is also intended to provide the reader with a sense of the atmosphere of the debates in the public spheres in Britain and Sweden at the particular historical moments.

Part I
Anti-Apartheid in Global Context

1
Narratives of Transnational Anti-Apartheid Activism

Introduction: transnational activists and historical experiences

Although networks, as well as social movements, are collective phenomena, it is important not to underestimate the role of individuals in the processes of their construction. Particularly in movements and networks that span over large distances, key activists play an important role through connecting different historical, cultural and political contexts. Through individual moves and movements they are connecting places, organizations and networks, carrying different cultural and historical experiences, that in the process of transnational communication get translated into new contexts.

The concept of learning process, introduced in the Introduction, highlights the role of the individual in the context of social movements and social change. However, it is important not to *equal* agency with individual action. As Keck and Sikkink state in their study on transnational activist networks, 'agency of a network can not be reduced to the agency even of its leading members'.[1] However, as a methodological approach, narratives of individual activists can be a useful tool not just to inquire into the role of certain key individuals; through narrated 'activist biographies', it is possible to grasp and analyse the significant historical experiences defining a social movement, as well as the meaning of its collective actions. Except for movement leaders, the role of individuals has often been neglected in research on social movements. One important exception is Ron Eyerman's and Andy Jamison's *Social Movements: A Cognitive Approach*, in which biographies of 'movement intellectuals' are used in order to 'place social movements in political historical context' and analyse the process of articulation through which a social movement comes into being.[2] I will use a similar approach here, although looking at a broader category of 'key activists' in the context of transnational activism. A key activist could be an intellectual or a leader, but this is not what defines her as a key activist. A transnational social movement like anti-apartheid may have a handful of leaders, but hundreds or even thousands of key activists. Key activists may be defined as nodes in movement networks, as they perform the function of co-ordinating, articulating and communicating the flows of information that constitute the everyday cultural praxis of a social movement.

In the following, I make a brief reconstruction of five biographies of transnational activism. They are based on the accounts of individuals that for a substantial part of their life took part in the anti-apartheid struggle. They belonged to the 'spiders' in the webs of transnational anti-apartheid activism. I have consciously chosen to focus on activists that belonged to a category of 'middle-range' activists in the transnational network, rather than to its top leadership. They were chosen because they, in relation to a larger empirical material, 'represent' different 'ideal types' of activists (or perform different roles within the movement), just as their 'activist biographies' reflect important dimensions of the collective experiences, the organization and the processes of identification of the social movement of which their individual actions constituted a part. Thus, just as their individual actions were part of the construction of the movement, their individual identities were partly constituted by their participation in the movement. The 'activist biographies' are used in order to inquire into (a) specific *historical experiences* that were translated into anti-apartheid activism (b) previously existing networks and movements that influenced and conditioned the transnational anti-apartheid movement (c) the *role of certain types of key activists* for a transnational social movement, and (d) the *meaning of the practices* that constituted the anti-apartheid struggle as a transnational social movement.

The story of Gunnar Helander highlights the importance of previously existing networks and of the *activist priest*, who brings the cultural, historical and organizational experiences of a previously existing network into the movement; in Helander's case the experiences of a network of church activists, which in the 1950s played an important role in the earliest phase of the transnational anti-apartheid movement. The narrative of Sobizana Mngqikana articulates the experience of an ANC *exile activist*, moving between different national contexts of the anti-apartheid movement, representing the 'the authentic voice' of the struggle.

The narratives of Margaret Ling and Mai Palmberg display the importance of the post 1968 student movement and its network, through which a second phase of transnational anti-apartheid mobilization was initiated. The story of Ling, representing *the movement organizer*, takes the perspective of a British activist, being 'politicized' through encountering exile activists at the university, as well as through reflections on the unfinished business of British colonialism, including the involvement of her own 'kith and kin'. The account of Palmberg represents the story of a *movement intellectual*, a concept that in Eyerman's and Jamison's terms denotes an individual that plays a key role in the knowledge production of a social movement. Similar to Antonio Gramsci's 'organic intellectual', emerging in processes of the historical formation of new social classes, the movement intellectual emerges in the context of a movement culture, challenging the dominant culture and its intellectuals.[3]

Finally, the biography of E. S. Reddy is not an activist biography in a strict sense, as it is the story of a UN official. However, as approaching and making connections with interstate and state organizations was an important part of the activities of the transnational anti-apartheid movement, an important role was played by the figure of *the activist public official*. In the case of Reddy, his narrative also articulates a historical experience of strong transnational anti-colonial links between India and South Africa.

The activist public official

On a number of occasions when I was interviewing anti-apartheid activists about their international contacts, 'Mr Reddy' was mentioned as a key figure. Enuga Reddy was born in 1924 in Gudur, a small village north of Madras (now Chennai) in southern India. Both of his parents actively supported the Indian national liberation movement. Since his father was a local chairman of the Congress Party, he was on the same platform as Mahatma Gandhi when the latter visited Gudur in the early 1930s, while Enuga went around and collected money from the audience in a Gandhi cap. Reddy's father also spent a short time in prison after performing civil disobedience. Reddy himself participated in activities organized by the student movement in Madras. After the end of the Second World War, in 1946, Reddy went to New York for postgraduate studies. In 1949 he got a position as a political officer in the UN Secretariat, doing research for the UN on Africa and the Middle East. When the UN Special Committee against Apartheid was formed in 1963, Reddy was appointed its principal secretary.[4]

Reflecting on an almost life-long commitment to anti-apartheid, Reddy told me that he always looked upon himself as an activist, but an activist that chose to work from within an institution. However, from this 'inside' position he could do a lot for activists on the 'outside', that is, for the people active in the liberation struggle in Southern Africa as well as the solidarity movements in other parts of the world that supported this struggle. At the time when the Committee was formed, NGOs did not have the kind of official recognition in the UN that they have at present. In this sense, The Special Committee against Apartheid was unique when it became, through activities initiated by Reddy, an important space of interaction for individuals, groups and organizations that were part of the network of transnational anti-apartheid activism which was created from the early 1960s and onwards. In this sense the Special Committee was a crucial facilitator in the process that, according to Jennifer Davis, key activist in American Committee of Africa (ACOA), 'mobilized civil society, even if we did not use that expression then'.[5] Here, information was exchanged, overall strategies were discussed, co-operation on campaigns, national as well as transnational, were co-ordinated, and friendships were made.

Since the 1970s, alternative NGO-conferences are regularly held 'outside' of the large official UN meetings.[6] Denis Herbstein, writer and journalist who left South Africa for London, and who has done extensive research on the role of the IDAF in the anti-apartheid struggle, states that it was Reddy who, through his work with the Special Committee, 'invented' the alternative conference.[7] Davis agrees: 'Reddy created a space for people to get together', as he 'pushed the limits of what people wanted to allow him to do, apparently in a very non-confrontative way'. Davis also states that the conferences organized by the committee were extremely important for ACOA, as well as for the international anti-apartheid movement.

Although the Committee, following the decision of OAU, supported both the PAC and the ANC, the Special Committees' contacts with the ANC might be considered as more close, and on a personal level particularly so between Reddy and the ANC exile leader Oliver Tambo. Accordingly, it was in dialogue with the liberation movements and the solidarity movements that the Special Committee developed the strategies that would guide its transnational anti-apartheid work.

In 1966, three main lines of action were agreed upon for the work against apartheid in the UN: (1) pressure on the South African government to abandon apartheid, and to seek a peaceful solution with 'the genuine representatives of all the people of South Africa' (2) appropriate assistance to the victims of apartheid and those who struggle against it, for a society in which all people would enjoy equal rights and opportunities (3) dissemination of information to focus world public opinion on the inhumanity of apartheid.[8]

Reddy states that the first two lines of action of course were fundamental, but since the first could not be made effective as long as sanctions were not agreed upon in the Security Council, and as assistance to the struggle against apartheid was also met by resistance from the dominant Western powers in the UN, the third aspect became increasingly important.

The activist priest

In the context of the global anti-apartheid movement it was the IDAF, formed in 1965, that more than any other organization developed an 'international' base. IDAF had strong connections to church and Mission circles.[9] The activities that subsequently led to the formation of the British Defence and Aid Fund in 1956 and to IDAF, was initiated in London by Canon Collins of St Paul's Cathedral in 1952, and was an outgrowth of Christian Action. One of the first national anti-apartheid organizations outside of England, Fonden för rasförtryckets offer (Fund for the Victims of Racial Oppression in South Africa), established in Sweden in 1959, later served as the Swedish chapter of IDAF. One of its two key initators, Gunnar Helander, who later also became vice-chairman of IDAF in London, was also a man of the church.[10]

For three generations, Gunnar Helander's forefathers had been priests in Falköping, a small town in the western part of Sweden.[11] When Gunnar Helander, born in 1915, with the intention to follow his family track, went to Lund University to become a priest, he began a journey that would lead him far away from his family, its location and its outlook on the world. In 1937, when he had finished his exams, he was asked by the Director of the Church of Sweden Mission (CSM) if he wanted to go on a mission to South Africa.

To improve his English and to learn more about South Africa, he first went to study for a semester at Kingsmead College in Birmingham, England. Here, he became close friend with Kassim Lakhi, an Indian student from South Africa. He noted that his friend, as well as the black African students, was met by formal respect but also with a subtle form of racism in the British university environment. Although the practice of segregation in the British colonies in Southern Africa was hardly mentioned in the lectures that he attended or the books that he read at the university, he knew that racism was much worse in South Africa than in Britain. Still, the reality of segregation came as a shock to him when he arrived in South Africa in 1938. From Helander's account of his encounter with South African society, it is evident that his commitment against apartheid first and foremost started from the experience of socialising and identifying with his Indian friend:

> As an Indian he was mainly treated as a black, everywhere there were signs saying 'only Europeans/only non-Europeans, and since he was 'non-European' we could not sit on the same park bench, or go through the same door at a railway station, or go to a restaurant or a cinema together ... We could socialize at his place or mine. But it could happen at my place that whites came in and refused to shake his hand, and then I had to say, either you shake his hand or you leave! I became furious.

Helander started to express his criticism in articles that was sent to Swedish newspapers. As the apartheid legislation of 1948 was enforced and segregation in South Africa became more widely known, Helander continued his critical writing, publishing articles in Swedish as well as British newspapers. His articles were more often accepted after he had published *Zulu Meets the White Man* in 1949, the first of ten novels in ten years, all of them expressing criticism against apartheid. His books were originally written in Swedish but were subsequently translated to English and eight other languages.[12]

However, this was still far from uncontroversial in church circles. In Swedish mission circles, Helander was one of a few critical priests forming a small group that was in opposition to the society of Swedish Missionaries in Southern Africa as well as to the CSM board in Sweden. The general attitude of the Swedish missionaries was, according to Helander, a form of paternalism towards the black South Africans, including an 'apolitical' view that 'apartheid is regrettable, but we have to accept it, our mission is not to participate in any revolution or struggle for civil rights'.[13] However, the Swedes that were in opposition to this view were part of an international community of 'critical priests' that, in alliance with local churchmen, was large enough to become a significant anti-apartheid actor within South Africa. In this context Helander became a friend of Trevor Huddleston, later President of AAM in England, as well as with the chief and church leader Albert Luthuli, who was elected as ANC president in 1952. In 1941, Helander participated in the Ecumenical Natal Missionary Conference in Durban that elected Luthuli as chairman. Helander also played an important role for promoting Luthuli as a candidate for the Nobel Peace Prize (which he was awarded in 1961).[14]

When Helander in 1957 was going back to South Africa after a holiday in Sweden, he was refused a visa. This meant that Helander's new mission became the one of a public speaker on the conditions of apartheid in the Swedish public arena. Through articles and lecturing tours around the country, he became a leading 'anti-apartheid' public profile in Sweden in the early 1960s, and was one of the founding members of the Swedish Defence and Aid Fund in 1959, and the Swedish South Africa Committee in Stockholm in 1961.[15]

Helander continued his anti-apartheid involvement until 1994, both nationally and internationally. However, as a leading public figure he was most influential in the 1950s and early 1960s. As the anti-apartheid movement, under the influence of the student movement in the North as well as of the anti-colonial movements in the South, was radicalized in the years of post-1968, and tensions and conflicts within the movement arose around the issue of sanctions, Helander followed the line of the Swedish Churches.[16] When the World Council of Churches (WCC) in a meeting in Utrecht in 1972, following the UN General Assembly's call for isolation of South Africa, adopted a policy of disinvestment some Evangelical Lutheran churches, among them the Church of Sweden, expressed a 'minority position' in the final resolution. This position, that advocated a policy of 'constructive involvement' in order to improve the conditions for black workers in the foreign owned companies, was in Sweden called 'the new strategy' and was formally adopted by the Swedish Ecumenical Council in 1974.[17]

In this matter, it is relevant to mention the close contacts that the Swedish Church Mission had with Mangosuthu Buthelezi, Chief of KwaZulu – a link going back to the late nineteenth century when the Mission started its South African adventure in Zululand.[18] Buthelezi was in 1974 launching a campaign that defied ANC's call for sanctions. Together with three other homeland leaders, in a full-page advertisement in *The Economist* in England, Buthelezi invited foreign investors to South Africa, stating that: 'South Africa has the most stable government on the African continent', that 'we do not suffer from militant trade unions' and that the homelands could provide 'problem-free labour resources'.[19] The Swedish Church Mission also several times invited Buthelezi to Sweden. At one occasion, in 1977, he held a secret meeting with the ANC leader Oliver Tambo. Another meeting was going to be held at Gunnar Helander's residence, which hosted Buthelezi during his visit in 1978.[20]

If many of the influential individuals of the 'first generation' of transnational anti-apartheid activists had their base in the churches and its international networks, that is, people like Gunnar Helander, Albert Luthuli of ANC, Trevor Huddleston of AAM, Canon John Collins of IDAF and George Houser of ACOA, the second generation came out of the international student movement of the late 1960s.

The exile activist

Sobizana Mngqikana was born in East London, South Africa in 1938. As many other ANC leaders and activists he went to study at the University of Fort Hare. In 1961, a year after the ANC was banned, he became active in the underground structures of the organization. His anti-apartheid activities led to his expulsion from the university in 1962, and in 1963 he was arrested and sent to jail. This experience was important for his life-long commitment to the ANC:

> It was a bitter experience although it was just a year, I mean I admire people who could sit there for 27 years like Mandela, and not be bitter ... And of course it was an eye-opener to see the ruthlessness of apartheid, brutally implemented on the micro-cosmic level in jail, where you saw the brutality that was admitted to prisoners, especially black prisoners.[21]

When he was released, he saw an advertisement in the *Cape Times* about a scholarship sponsored by the University of London. He applied, succeeded and arrived in London in 1964. A couple of minutes walk from the student hostel in which he was staying, the British AAM had its office. When Mngqikana visited the office, he learned that there was an ANC office in London. The ANC representative, Raymond Kunene, put Mngqikana in touch with a group of his own age, among them Thabo Mbeki, who became a close friend. The group formed what they called the ANC Student and Youth Section, its task being mainly political education in the context of the black South African exile community. Members of the group were also often invited by the AAM to address public meetings, in order to represent 'authentic voices' of South Africa. After finishing his studies he joined the ANC staff full time in 1969. In 1973 a decision was made that the ANC should open a mission in Sweden (the second in Europe).[22] By this time the ANC had established close contacts with the Social Democratic government, and had begun to receive financial support.

There were many contrasts between living and working as a black and as a political activist in London and Stockholm respectively. In terms of working as an anti-apartheid activist in England in the 1960s,

> there was a lot of hostility, we were called terrorists you know, and there was a strong opposition from the government, the Conservative Party, so it was not easy there, it was a challenge to penetrate British Society, whereas in Sweden, there was an understanding, a revulsion against racism and apartheid. But of course there was a difference as how to tackle the issue, and that was where the problems started between myself and some of the people who were working here.

The problems that Mngqikana is referring to started soon after he had arrived, as he felt caught in the web of conflict-ridden relations of the Swedish political arena of the early 1970s. If the churches, the unions, the Social Democratic Party (SDP), Folkpartiet (the Liberals) and the Africa Groups all expressed a commitment to the anti-apartheid struggle, it was also affected by their different and conflicting agendas in relation to national as well as international politics. Much of the tension was related to the Cold War divide. In certain circles to the right as well as to the left, the ANC was regarded with suspicion because of its alliance with the South African Communist Party, as well as its contacts with the Soviet Union, and was even in some cases perceived as a 'pro-Soviet force', steered by Moscow.

In the 1970s even old supporters from the early 1960s were criticizing the ANC for its Soviet contacts. In 1977, Mngqikana got involved in a public debate about the issue with Per Wästberg, the leading anti-apartheid journalist and writer in Sweden since the early 1960s, and at the time chief editor of the liberal *Dagens Nyheter*, Sweden's largest daily.[23]

Mngqikana's mission in Sweden was, in line with the ANC's 'broad church approach', to seek to broaden the ANC's support in Sweden. The model was the co-operation between the ANC and the inclusive and broad anti-apartheid coalition in Britain. One of the tensions that Mngqikana encountered in this work was related to an internal divide within the labour movement regarding its strategy in relation to the anti-apartheid struggle.[24] While the SDP leadership under Olof Palme had decided to give the organization full support, the unions were more sceptical towards the ANC and its call for isolation of South Africa. In fact, in the debate on isolation versus involvement ('the new strategy') in the early 1970s, the blue collar Landsorganisationen i Sverige (LO) and the white collar Tjänstemännens Centralorganisation (TCO) – under the umbrella of ICFTU (International Confederation of Trade Unions) – 'embraced the "new strategy" '.[25]

The position taken by LO and TCO at this time must be related to international conflicts as well as national interests. *First*, the strong 'anti-communism' within ICFTU did not make the ANC popular, since its main union ally at this time was SACTU (South African Congress of Trade Unions), that was affiliated to the communist-dominated WFTU (World Federation of Trade Unions). *Second*, support for isolation might have been limited by the fact that it could be seen to contradict the 'self-interest' of the organizations, since it could have the consequence of creating unemployment in Sweden.

However, since this position was not uncontroversial, in 1974 LO and TCO, following the example of the British Trade Union Congress (TUC), decided to send a 'fact-finding mission' to South Africa. As soon as the mission was publicly announced it was heavily criticized. Mngqikana, for the first time making himself known to the Swedish public in an interview in public radio, argued that the mission would serve as recognition of the apartheid regime and denounced the trip as a 'propaganda stunt'.[26]

In this criticism against the unions, Mngqikana got support from the Africa groups, which also protested publicly against the trip. However, this did not mean that *the relations* between the ANC representative and the Africa Groups were easy – at least not in the beginning. Through the small but politically active South African exile community – also ridden by conflicts between supporters of the PAC, the ANC and the Unity Movement – Mngqikana soon after his arrival got in contact with the Africa Groups. The Africa Groups was part of a young and fervent, marx-ist oriented left wing political culture, that had come out of the student protest of the late 1960s, now forming different ideological and party fractions, and solidarity organizations focused on different parts of the world.[27] When Mngqikana arrived, the Africa Groups had mainly been focusing their work on the Portuguese colonies and had not yet recog-nized the ANC as a leading force in the South African struggle (which they did in November 1974).[28] As Mngqikana soon after his arrival was invited to a meeting with a few people in the Africa Groups, he was confronted with the statement that ANC was 'run by Moscow'. The speaker referred to a study book titled *Afrika: Imperialism och Befrielsekamp* (*Africa: Imperialism and Struggle for Liberation*), written and published by the Africa Groups. In the book, FRELIMO, MPLA and

PAIGC were referred to as the avant-garde organizations of the African struggle for liberation, praised for their 'successful struggle for liberation since the early 1960s'. ANC, on the other hand, was criticized both for their non-violent strategy in the 1950s and for being too close to the Soviet Union.[29]

This was, according to Mngqikana, 'the beginning of my fights with them, sort of clashes'. These clashes were however not so much about ideology as about *strategy*, as is shown in the following example on how Mngqikana argued in relation to the issue of defining the struggle in public space:

> Someone would come up with some silly idea that if they are going to organize a demonstration, it must be on the basis of anti-imperialism. Any organization that would not support anti-imperialism would not be welcome. I said no, that is not acceptable to us, we want a broad support from the Swedish people. If you want to talk about anti-imperialism, we can discuss that with you ... We can not put conditions to people, ... why are you not trying to focus the whole Swedish community towards the goal of dismantling apartheid?

In spite of these differences, the young leftist political culture that the Africa Groups was part of was familiar to Mngqikana. In fact it was a transnational political culture born out of the global student activism of the late 1960s. The activists belonged to his generation, they were all marxists of some kind and Mngqikana did not mind discussing how to fight imperialism. However, the fact that Mngqikana was seen mixing in these circles awoke criticism in other political camps. On one occasion Oliver Tambo told Mngqikana that he had received a letter from a Swedish MP for the Social Democrats, complaining that the ANC representative was 'flirting with people who are attacking us' ('us' referring to the Social Democrats), indicating that if this continued, it could mean that the support to the ANC would be withdrawn.

However, at the end of the 1970s this situation would start to change, partly as a consequence of Mngqikana's effort to bring together the conflicting camps of the Swedish anti-apartheid movement. In 1979, the same year that Lindiwe Mabuza replaced Sobizana Mngqikana as the ANC chief representative in Stockholm, AGIS initiated a new organization, ISAK (The Isolate South Africa Committee), quite similar to the British AAM. It was a broad umbrella organization, including solidarity organizations, churches, the youth sections of all the political parties except the Conservatives and a few unions (see Chapter 3).

The movement organizer

Margaret Ling came from an English liberal minded middle-class family with an international orientation.[30] One of her relatives was a missionary in India, and another was involved in the International Alliance of Women, which grew out of the suffragist movement. Ling states that she was always aware from a small child of international issues and conferences, and remembers people from different parts of the world that were coming to stay in her aunts' house. She clearly remembers the 21 March 1960, the day of the Sharpeville massacre. At the time, her father was a teacher in a public school, and was also Housemaster of one of the boarding houses. By coincidence, Bishop Trevor Huddleston was staying in the boarding house where Margaret Ling and her family lived, after preaching in the school chapel. The year before, Huddleston had been invited as one of the speakers at the founding meeting of the organization that subsequently was called the Anti-Apartheid Movement. He was one of the front men of the organization until its dissolution in 1995. As the news about what had happened in Sharpeville was reported around the world, the editor of *The Times* rang Huddleston up to get a quote on the massacre. This was the first time that Margaret Ling, then 12 years old, was aware of apartheid, but it would be more than ten years until she would become involved in AAM and IDAF in London, becoming one of the key anonymous communicators and organizers of the everyday life of anti-apartheid activism. This was a full time commitment that lasted for two decades.

In 1972, after a trip to India, Ling became a sociology student in Oxford. Here, she got involved in solidarity organizations such as Third World First, which was campaigning on issues of global poverty and the North–South gap. She also met and became friends with South African exiles Frene Ginwala (who after the democratic elections became Speaker of the House of parliament in South Africa), and Ethel de Keyser, who at the time was executive secretary of AAM. Ling states that Keyser had a strong influence on her and when an anti-apartheid group was being formed in Oxford, her involvement with the AAM started.

Reflecting on how she became an anti-apartheid activist, she accounts for a complex process that had started during her trip to India, and that was a result not just of encounters with exile South Africans, but also included theoretical reflections coming out of her university courses, as well as personal reflections on her family history:

> I wouldn't say that I was politisized in India, but that gave me an awareness of the situation in the so called Third World and the gap

between the North and the South ... I was quite late to be politisized ... I was doing a course in Sociology and I remember coming across apartheid as part of that, looking at sociological theory. And then the experience of having been in India and visiting a member of my family whom had gone out to be a missionary, who was continuing to be supported by my family, who had a business, which at one time had a subsidiary in South Africa. I started to put things together and really began to understand where I stood in the British class system, and the relationship of that class system to what was going on in South Africa. So there was both a politization through friendships and emotional involvement, and through theory and through beginning to understand a bit more about of whom I was and where I fitted in.[31]

When Ling had finished her university studies, she moved to London, where she became a full-time activist. Being an AAM activist, she was offered a job in IDAF, working in the research and information department, a position she held for nine years. For a period, she was also the editor of AAM's magazine, *AA News*.

As an activist, she spent her everyday life in the context of the 'movement culture'. As Ling (today) recognizes that the AAM was part of such a culture, she emphasizes the importance of the labour movement:

Anti-apartheid was located within that whole galaxy of left or progressive movements, and that's how it was organized ... this whole context within which AAM was organizing. Without the support of the organized trade union and labour movement, it would never had got the strength that it did in Britain, and funding without the trade movement would have been very difficult.

As the women's movement was increasing its influence in the context of the new movement culture in the late 1970s and early 1980s, gender became an issue in AAM, partly expressed in terms of solidarity with black South African women, emphasizing gender aspects of the apartheid system. But it was also raised as an issue of male dominance within the anti-apartheid movement. In 1980, the same year that 30,000 women gathered at a peace camp in Greenham Common, an AAM women's committee was formed by some of the activists, including Ling.[32]

A movement culture is not just defined by networks of groups and organizations; it is also a context in which people perform 'life politics', constructing their personal identities through different processes of identification.[33] This means identifying with collective images and symbols created by the movement, and also identifying with other people in the context of personal encounters. For some people, like Margaret Ling, participation in this cultural process came to define a large part of her everyday life:

> Your whole social life gets wrapped up in it, which was very very important for the anti-apartheid movement. That became our social life, going to meetings, and then not just political meetings but also social events and people in the region became friends and there were relationships and marriages.

For others, participating in a movement culture might have been limited to occasional visits to collective events, such as going to demonstrations, wearing a 'political T-shirt', and boycotting South African goods when shopping in the local supermarket. Further, 'life politics' politicizes consumption, as in the boycott. When Margaret Ling set up the independent AA Enterprises in 1985, the idea was to take the boycott campaign a step further. As a way of supporting the frontline states in their solidarity against apartheid, anti-apartheid activists and supporters should be buying goods from the frontline states. She says it was a 'concept of positive purchase, of using your power as a consumer, in a positive sense – boycott apartheid, buy from the frontline states, that was the slogan'. AA Enterprises was part of a merchandising co-operative whose purpose was to create and disseminate the products.

Comparing the activities of the British AAM in the early 1970s and in the mid-and late 1980s, when the anti-apartheid movement was at its peak with regard to public support, there is no doubt that the practices of the movement culture that it was part of were affected by wider societal changes taking place predominantly in the 1980s. On the one hand, the AAM was largely perceived as having a leftist profile and even became a major forum for extra-parliamentary criticism of Thatcherist politics. On the other hand, the economic, political and cultural climate of the 1980s was clearly reflected in its new strategies for getting a message across to a wider public. AAM, as well as the ANC, developed new skills in Public Relations, improving its media strategies, and got involved in merchandise on a scale different from earlier periods (see Chapter 4). These changes, as well as its paradoxes, is quite well expressed by Ling as she reflects on her involvement in AA Enterprise, as well as on the functions, meanings, and the context of, 'movement merchandising':

> I think merchandise was also extremely important in conveying a message, in creating and sustaining a sense of identity of the movement. It was also a way for people to identify with the movement through wearing t-shirts, buying the merchandise ... Getting involved in merchandising myself, I certainly saw that very much as a contribution to the AAM campaigns, and in building a movement and at the same time raising money for it. And in that time, the late 80s, it was a period in this country when merchandise was very important for political activism, all the campaigning organizations had merchandise, and wearing a political T-shirt was very much of a fashion thing. Marxism was quite fashionable, I suppose it was partly a reaction to Thatcherism.

In the late 1980s and early 1990s, enterprising anti-apartheid became an extremely successful adventure for AA Enterprise, and even more so for the ANC. Not just because all of the nearly 200 local AA groups in Britain sold the products, but also other organizations and groups in the transnational anti-apartheid network. At the time when the BBC in April 1990 broadcast the second Mandela concert organized by the AAM, anti-apartheid t-shirts were 'being worn from New York, to Vancouver, to Moscow, to Sweden, to South Africa', to quote an ANC public relations officer.[34]

The movement intellectual

In 1976, AGIS commissioned one of its members, Mai Palmberg, to write a study book on the situation in Africa for the organization's prospective members.[35] The first edition of the book, titled *Befrielsekampen i Afrika*, came out in 1978. By chance Palmberg brought a fresh copy of the Swedish original when she represented AGIS at the first MPLA congress in Luanda in December 1977. Staying at the same hotel as delegates of all the liberation movements in Southern Africa, she displayed the book and was asked to bring out an English translation. With financial aid from the Swedish International Development Agency (SIDA), which funded the printing of 1000 copies each to the ANC and SWAPO and 500 to SACTU, the book was published as *The Liberation Struggle in Africa* by Zed Press in 1983. The South African government immediately banned the book and it became a sought-after item.[36]

In 1962, Mai Palmberg, who was born in Åbo in Finland 18 years earlier, went to the United States for two years of college studies in Massachusetts. According to Palmberg, this trip was a 'clear impulse' for her life long commitment to anti-apartheid, as she in the United States encountered racism, anti-racism as well as an 'almost euphoric' support for the de-colonization process in Africa. While the college was for white women only, she actively sought contact with the black community and its cultural and political expressions. A concert at the University of Maryland in 1964, during which the South African singer Miriam Makeba performed in front of a mixed audience, made a strong impression. Further, during a course in urban sociology, the lecturer taught about Malcolm X and the emerging black urban political activism. Through a guest speaker at the college, Zelma George, she also got the opportunity to meet Malcolm X in person. George, a black Republican, had been part of the US UN delegation when the UN General Assembly passed the important resolution on de-colonization in 1960. While the US delegation decided to abstain, George expressed her protest against this decision publicly when she rose and applauded as the resolution was passed. During a visit in Cleveland, George offered to pick up Palmberg and bring her to a party to which Malcolm X also was invited. When Palmberg came back from the party, the mother of the college class mate she visited got furious. Palmberg still remembers her words:

> She said 'have they come that close?' It was that kind of episode when I suddenly was hit by racism straight in the face. In a homogenous society like the Finnish, you don't have that kind of experiences, although racism might still be there.

Coming back to Finland to study political science at the University in Åbo, her Professor proposed to his students that they write their papers on Finnish law on local government. However, as this seemed petty after her American experience, Palmberg ended up in the Nordic Africa Institute in Uppsala, Sweden (NAI, a research institute funded by the Nordic governments), writing an MA thesis about African socialism. Here, she also joined the local Africa Groups after they had made her 'mighty impressed' when protesting against the President of Senegal, Leopold Senghor, in 1970 during his visit to Uppsala. As news had spread that Senegal had closed the border to Guinea-Bissau, blocking the movements of the liberation organization PAIGC, whose liberation struggle was actively supported by AGIS, activists prevented Senghor from speaking by taking over the platform. Placards were raised and leaflets were distributed. A member of the Africa Groups in Lund managed to publish an article in *Aftonbladet* (the largest labour daily) in which Senghor's writings on Négritude were criticized for being a form of 'black racism'.

As an activist Mai Palmberg continued to travel, representing AGIS at different international conferences. In this context, she met Basil Davidson, British historian and author of several books on Southern Africa, and Ruth First and Joe Slovo, both members of the South African Communist Party (SACP), married and influential figures in British anti-apartheid exile circles. They became both friends and intellectual mentors and taught her that the issue of apartheid/anti-apartheid 'was not just about whites against blacks'.[37]

The many changes occurring in Southern Africa during the first half of the 1970s, and the fact that AGIS now supported both SWAPO and the ANC, required a new version of its study book. The book firmly rested on a version New Left marxist analysis of world politics, motivating its emphasis on the southern part of Africa by explaining that 'this is where the conflict on the African continent is the sharpest'.[38] Second, it argued the armed struggle in the region 'is where the real significance of the struggle for Southern Africa lies, not only for Africa but for development in all Third world countries and thereby for the whole world'.[39]

Although Palmberg's condition on accepting to write the book was that she should have the final say about the content of the manuscript, it was largely a collective enterprise and the Swedish version was listed as a publication by AGIS, while she was presented as the editor on the cover of the English version. Further, the offices of SWAPO and the ANC in Stockholm were shown the English version of the manuscript for information and comment. Palmberg nevertheless made herself a name through her continued writing, moving across borders not just geographically but also intellectually, pursuing an academic career at the NAI, contributing with articles to AGIS publications and occasionally also writing about Southern Africa in the daily press. Thus, as is the case with any movement intellectual, her activist writing provided her with a platform from which she could address a broader public than the movement's supporters.

Conclusion: transnational activism and its contexts

Collective action against apartheid came out of, and involved, a number of different historical experiences, related to different historical processes and structural contexts. On the level of sustained personal commitment, the process of becoming a transnational activist could involve direct experiences of the brutality of the South African apartheid system, as in the case of Sobizana Mngqikana, or the experience of witnessing a close friend being exposed to apartheid, as in the case of Gunnar Helander. In the case of solidarity activism it could develop through the participation in other social movements, which through processes of political articulation became linked to the anti-apartheid movement, such as the North American civil rights movement (Palmberg) or the Indian anti-colonial struggle (Reddy). Sustained solidarity commitment could also, as in the case of Ling, emerge out of a process including encounters with exiles, and theoretical reflections on the legacy of colonialism in contemporary society as well as on the personal level of family relations.

Linking the inside and outside of the movement, individual experiences of anti-apartheid activism could partly be seen as articulations of the conditions of the historical and social *contexts* that conditioned its action space. The activist biographies of this chapter point to *the condition of postcoloniality, the Cold War and the latest phases of political, economic and cultural globalization* as crucial contexts for the anti-apartheid struggle.

Regarding *postcoloniality*, the different activist narratives of this chapter show how the legacy of colonialism and racism in different contexts and through different practices could be reproduced, negotiated or transcended.

As the cases of Reddy and Mngqikana also shows, globalization of politics during the post-war era was also to a large extent a matter of the division of any significant political field, national as well as international, along *the Cold War* lines. The Cold War was a crucial factor in the circumstances that made it possible for the South African apartheid government to sustain its position internationally.

Further, the final phase of the anti-apartheid movement, in which it reached its peak in terms of public mobilization, coincided with an intensified globalization of media and economic relations, developments that were related to the politics of neo-liberalism led by the Reagan and Thatcher governments. As the biography of Ling show, these developments in different ways influenced the practices and strategies of the anti-apartheid movement. Through symbolic actions and media oriented campaigns like Sun City and Free Nelson Mandela, it used the space opened up by the global media in order to articulate an anti-apartheid message and facilitate collective solidarity action in a global context. Through activities like AA Merchandise, it initiated forms of economic practice, which attempted to rearticulate the concept of international trade. Thus, through these practices, transnational economic relations and global media became embedded in the context of a movement culture in which solidarity was constructed as a fundamental value. In relation to the activities of global corporations, it meant that the meaning of 'globalization' in this context was redefined, facilitating global solidarity rather than reproducing commodification.

However, within this very general frame of meaning, 'solidarity' could be defined in various ways in movement discourses, and it could refer to many different, and sometimes conflicting, practices. Internal divisions was an integral part of anti-apartheid activism, sometimes even leading to the construction of relatively permanent borders between 'us' and 'them' *within* the movement, sometimes leading to exclusions of groups and individuals. Following my argument about the interconnectedness of 'the inside' and 'the outside' of the movement, these 'inner' tensions and differences of the anti-apartheid struggle largely were articulations of conflicts defining the historical and social *contexts* of the movement.

However, in spite of the many structural and historical conditions *constraining* opposition against apartheid, anti-apartheid collective action, at certain moments transgressing boundaries and borders – national, racial and cultural – did take place, and was sustained for four decades. This was made possible through a set of practices and strategies that were taken over from previous networks or movements, or were invented in the movement. In the different waves of anti-apartheid mobilization, the churches, the labour movement, including its socialist and communist wings, and the student movement were particularly important influences, also bringing particular historical legacies, political and cultural learning processes and ideological commitments, as well as conflicts, into the movement.

To conclude, one of the important structural changes facilitating anti-apartheid activism across borders was obviously the increasing role of media during period of the anti-apartheid struggle. However, the role of the media must not be over-emphasized, as is so often the case in studies of transnationalism and globalization. As we have seen, travel, or mobility, was also a crucial aspect of transnational activism. As the narratives of the activists show, the existence of a transnational network of political exiles seemed to have played a particularly important role for the emergence of solidarity groups and movements in different parts of the world. Thus, face-to-face interaction with 'distant others', was an integral part of sustained global anti-apartheid activism.

2
The Globalization of the Anti-Apartheid Movement

Introduction: transnational collective action and globalization

During the last decades of the twentieth century, the process of globalization started to change the meaning of politics. The action spaces of states opened up and collective action in the context of civil societies was increasingly stretched across borders. As a consequence, political action became an increasingly complex and multi-dimensional activity. The mobilization of transnational collective action was facilitated as actors had access to new resources, including new means for electronic communication as well as cheap air travel. Influential social movement researchers have however been sceptical to the thesis put forth that this development has resulted in the emergence of transnational social movements and a global civil society. For example Sidney Tarrow has argued that:

> it is hard to find, combined in the same movement, the conditions necessary to produce a social movement that is, at once, integrated with several societies, unified in its goals, and capable of sustained interaction with a variety of political authorities.[1]

I would like to argue that the transnational anti-apartheid movement fulfilled these criteria. In this sense the anti-apartheid movement was part of the construction of a global civil society during the post-war era. Collective action against apartheid thus constituted a political globalization from below; a process partly opposed to but also dependent on, political globalization from above. There is no doubt that national policy, national organizations as well as national political cultures played

48

.

a significant role in shaping the anti-apartheid struggle in different parts of the world. However, the anti-apartheid movement is also a significant example of the fact that issues and networks of new movements have become increasingly global during the post-war era. Further, the structural processes that have created the preconditions for the emergence of new forms of collective action have been transnational, rather than bound to any *specific* nation states.

Transnationalism and its tensions: liberation movements, solidarity networks and 'the struggle within the struggle'

Social movement studies have emphasized the importance of previously organized networks for the mobilization of a social movement.[2] Since networks are carriers of values, previously organized networks bring a historical legacy into the formation of a new movement. In the context of the anti-apartheid movement, the churches, the labour movement and the anti-colonial movements provided such networks. As discussed in the Introduction, the forming of the transnational anti-apartheid movement as a space of intersection for a wide range of actors, a 'movement of movements', included both internal negotiation and struggle. While the identification of a common ground was necessary in order to bring about collective action, internal relations were also constantly defined by conflict, partly related to the historical legacies brought into the movement by the different networks. In the movement's own terms it was a 'the struggle within the struggle' – ultimately a conflict over hegemony of the movement.

In the following, I will discuss a number of overlapping tensions that at different moments were defining internal relations of the transnational anti-apartheid movement. As discussed in the Introduction, conflicts related to apartheid/anti-apartheid were largely articulated in terms of debates over strategy. In the following discussion on the emergence of the transnational anti-apartheid movement, I will point to a number of issues that were all articulated as conflicts regarding anti-apartheid strategy: (1) ANC versus PAC, including a tension between 'multi-racialism' and 'Africanism' (2) armed struggle versus non-violence (3) isolation of South Africa through sanctions versus 'constructive engagement', including a tension regarding the role of Buthelezi's Inkatha movement (4) cultural boycott versus cultural exchange (5) the role of the Black Consciousness Movement (BCM), involving a conflict between two economically powerful organizations within the transnational movement, IDAF versus IUEF (International University Exchange Fund). In addition, there was tension around the naming of the struggle, connecting the definition of anti-apartheid to wider ideological conflicts. Finally, these specific anti-apartheid conflicts were always connected to the more over-arching political conflicts of postcoloniality and the Cold War divide that overshadowed the anti-apartheid movement and the emerging global civil society it was part of. It was not just through its impact on interstate relations that postcolonial and Cold War tensions, ambivalence and conflict conditioned the anti-apartheid struggle; these contexts were also structuring the movement's internal organization, its debates and action strategies. In particular, there was always an element of Cold War division in the more specific anti-apartheid conflicts. The outcome of the internal anti-apartheid conflicts at different moments was also largely dependent on ideological conjunctures and power balances in this wider global context.

ANC, PAC and the armed struggle

The globalization of the anti-apartheid struggle was initiated by South African organizations and the transnational solidarity movement was always dependent on, and influenced by, the actions of South African organizations and networks – working inside the country or in exile. On the other hand, South African anti-apartheid organizations, whether mainly working on the inside or on the outside of their home country, were always heavily influenced by transnational processes. The South African Native National Congress (formed in 1912), that subsequently became the ANC, was under a certain influence of the anti-colonial struggle led by Mahatma Gandhi, who lived in South Africa between 1893 and 1914. Also during the following decades South African political resistance would largely continue to be defined by the ideology of non-violence and its major action strategies, manifested in collective action gaining international attention and support, such as the Defiance campaign in 1952, engaging in civil disobedience against the pass laws, and the call for an international boycott of South African goods at the All-African People's Conference in Accra in 1958.[3] The ANC also attracted international support because of its 'broad church approach'. Although it did not allow for white membership until 1969, it sought alliances with a wide range of organizations and groups that were willing to challenge apartheid, including the multi-racial political parties of the South African Liberals (LP, which dissolved itself in 1968 in response to South African legislation that made multi-racial parties illegal) and the Communists (SACP). This broad, 'multi-racial' approach was manifested in the Congress Alliance, formed in 1954 and in its central movement text, the Freedom Charter, which was adopted at a large public meeting in Kliptown outside of Johannesburg in 1955. Except the ANC, the Congress Alliance included the South African Indian Congress (SAIC), Coloured People's Congress (CPC), the South African Congress of Democrats (SACOD, dominated by white members of the SACP) and from 1955 SACTU (the Congress of South African Trade Unions). Further, through an early international orientation, including presence at different international conferences, the ANC managed to link itself to a broad transnational network even before the transnational anti-apartheid movement took off in the early 1960s. For example, links in Britain leading to the formation of AAM, as well as personal contacts that laid the base for the substantial financial support from the Swedish government, were all established already in the 1950s.

The broad church approach did however also lead to internal friction between 'Charterists' and 'Africanists', finally causing a split in 1959, when a group of Africanists left the ANC to form the PAC. Connecting to the broad Pan-African movement that swept the continent at the time, the PAC argued that South Africa was not different from other colonized societies in Africa. Its basic conflict was the one between the African people and its white colonial oppressors and the goal of the struggle was government of South Africa by the Africans. Later it invented a new name for South Africa, Azania, derived from an Arabic expression, in order to construct an alternative black South African identity. Initially the PAC, through its charismatic leader Robert Sobukwe, articulated a rather sophisticated criticism of racism, including a critique of ANC's 'multi-racialism', manifested in the representation of 'ethnic groups' through different organizations in the Congress Alliance. According to Sobukwe, this mode of organization reproduced the idea that there were different races, while 'there is but one race, the human race'.[4] The major PAC criticism of the ANC was however that the latter allowed for too much influence of whites, something that risked alienating the black South African population, whose everyday experiences of whites were different from the ANC elite, who were mixing with a tiny minority of white anti-racist radicals. The PAC thus came to emphasize an appeal to black African identity as the key mobilizing instrument – its rhetoric, in spite of Sobukwe's theoretical sophistication, affirming the idea of the existence of different races. The PAC's criticism of white influence in the ANC was however not just about racial power structures. As the most influential whites in the Congress Alliance were members of

the SACP, who had contacts with Moscow, it was also a matter of anti-(Soviet) communism. The Communist Party of South Africa had been disbanded in 1950, just before the Suppression of Communism Act came into force. In 1953, it re-emerged as the underground SACP. Adding to this the young intellectual generation emerging in the ANC in the 1950s, who would dominate the struggle internationally until its final phase, was attracted to marxism and showed a great interest in what the leaders of SACP had to say.

Tom Lodge also emphasizes that an important matter of division between the PAC and the ANC was the issue of spontaneity. While the ANC emphasized organization and education, the PAC argued that all that the party needed to do was to 'show the light and the masses will find the way'. This issue was also present in the conflict between the two organizations around the campaign against the pass laws in 1960 (see Chapter 5). Both Sharpeville and Langa, where the South African police opened fire against demonstrations on the 21 and the 22 of March, were PAC strongholds, and PAC leaders and activists would later refer to the international symbolic significance of 'Sharpeville' as a successful outcome of its strategy of mobilization.[5]

The South African government's banning of the ANC and the PAC in 1960 in response to the spontaneous uprisings in various parts of South Africa that followed on the shootings in Sharpeville and Langa, was a turning point for both organizations. It marked the beginning of the turn to armed struggle and a long period of exile, in which the two organizations through extensive transnational networking competed for international support. While the ANC initially had an upper hand because of the contacts it had established previously, the PAC quickly established a relatively strong presence internationally during the early 1960s, perhaps at this time even seeming to be more successful than did its rival, particularly on the African continent.[6]

During the conference of the Pan-African Freedom Movement for East, Central and Southern Africa (PAMFESCA) in 1962, a number of African leaders were sceptical of the multi-racial character of the Congress Alliance. Large sums of money were however promised both to the PAC and to the ANC by Nigeria, Ethiopia, Morocco and Liberia. The Algerian Front de Liberation de Nacionale (FLN) declared that their military training camps were open to both organizations. The fact that the Organization of African Unity (OAU) the following year recognized both the ANC and the PAC as legitimate representatives of the South African people was important for both organizations, since it established a praxis that later was followed by the UN Special Committee Against

Apartheid, the UN General Assembly and by many solidarity organizations, including the British AAM.[7]

Poqo, the armed wing of the PAC, later renamed as the Azanian People's Liberation Army (APLA) in 1968, was the first South African organization to adopt the strategy of violence directed at people, basing its guerrilla operations in Lesotho until 1965. Further, in the 1960s it engaged in alliances with other liberation organizations in Southern Africa that were carrying out an armed struggle: ZANU in Rhodesia, UNITA and the FNLA in Angola and Coremo in Mozambique. Uganda and Libya also subsequently provided military training facilities.

In 1962, the PAC established its headquarter in Maseru (in 1964 moved to Dar Es Salaam, then to Lusaka in 1967, and then again to Dar Es Salaam in 1973) and offices in London, Accra, Cairo, Francistown and Leopoldville – and later also Algiers and Lagos. PAC's combination of Pan-Africanist anti-racism and anti-Soviet communism also led PAC activists to seek support not just in the independent states on the continent and in Europe, but also in the United States and China. In 1963 a small PAC delegation toured the United States to ask for recognition and support from the UN headquarters in New York, the leading American labour union AFL/CIO, the churches, Congressmen, and Department officials. The PAC always had a better position in the United States than in Europe. First, because of ideological affinities, it was easier for them than for the ANC to link up to the emerging Afro-American movement. Because of their criticism of the ANC's alignment with the SACP, they were supported by organizations that strongly emphasized anti-communism (in spite of PAC's connections to China), particularly by AFL/CIO, who were a leading force in the ICFTU. This support, and the frequent trips to the United States, also led to constant allegations that the PAC was receiving support from the CIA.

In 1964, a PAC delegation went to China, who, after the ANC had supported the Soviets in the Sino-Soviet conflict the same year, was also willing to provide military training and financial support to the PAC. This led to an ideological re-orientation; the PAC would hereafter artic-ulate their criticism of apartheid, as well as its strategical manoeuvres, in a maoist framework. Its anti-Soviet communist position also meant that the maoist and trotskyist factions in the New Left that emerged in the late 1960s and early 1970s supported the PAC. This did not however help the PAC to much influential support from the student left in Europe. The maoists were mainly preoccupied with the anti-Vietnam war movement, while in the in solidarity work with Southern Africa the trotskyists (who also had its own South African anti-apartheid organization, the Unity Movement) were often defeated by those who were closer to Soviet communism.

ANC's forming of a military wing, the Umkonto we Sizwe (Spear of the Nation) in 1961, under the leadership of Nelson Mandela, meant the end of the carefully built international image of the organization as 'the moderate alternative' in black South Africa (see Chapter 5). Ever since the forming of the ANC, it had had a strong Christian element that, combined with the Gandhian commitment to non-violence, had made it a popular ally of the radical wings of churches all over the world. Many of these Christian circles did not welcome the turn to armed struggle. The launching of ANC's President Chief Albert Lutuli as a candidate for the Nobel Peace Prize by Scandinavian anti-apartheid supporters, among them the activist priest Gunnar Helander (see Chapter 1), might even be seen as a strategy to support the strategy of non-violence at a moment when it was losing support within the organization. But when Lutuli finally got the prize in December 1961, it was already too late. In that year, Nelson Mandela had been travelling to a number of capitals in Africa and Europe to ask both for diplomatic and military support, also spending time in an FLN guerrilla training camp. At the same time Arthur Goldreich (a leading member of SACP) led a delegation to the Soviet Union to ask for support from the Eastern bloc on behalf of Umkonto we Sizwe. ANC also sent members for military training in China in 1961. After the Sino-Soviet conflict it was however the Soviet Union that was ANC's main ally in the communist world, and for the coming decades the Eastern bloc would provide the ANC with both arms and military training.

Thus, the launching of Umkonto We Sizwe, which, different from the ANC at the time, was open to white membership, did strengthen the influence of SACP in the ANC. During the state of emergency in the wake of Sharpeville in 1960, SACP had issued a statement calling on its members to engage in the Congress Alliance, and in December the same year it had urged its members to engage in a campaign of sabotage. The architect behind the sabotage campaign was Joe Slovo, SACP member with military experience from the Second World War. In 1962, the ANC established links with CONCP, the alliance of multi-racial and marxist liberation movements, including FRELIMO, MPLA and PAIGC. As the Tanzanian foreign minister, Oscar Kambona, became chairman over OAU's African Liberation Committee, Dar Es Salaam became a centre for guerrilla activity, and the ANC established four camps in Tanzania during the following years. The ANC also formed an alliance with Zimbabwe African People's Union (ZAPU), trying to infiltrate South Africa from

Rhodesia and participating in joint operations against the Rhodesian army. This operation did however collapse in 1970.

Adding to the armed struggle, the support from the Eastern bloc was yet another factor contributing to the fact that the ANC lost influential supporters in the Western world. Those international organizations for which anti-communism was an ideological fundament, such as the ICFTU, even actively worked against the ANC, pursuing other alternatives in the context of the transnational anti-apartheid movement. Further, internal divisions concerning the organization's position on communism and white membership had not come to an end with the forming of the PAC. In 1969, an important conference was held in Morogoro, in order to settle internal divisions that were threatening to tear the organization apart. It was decided that white members would be allowed in the ANC, but not in the national executive. Tensions did however continue to be present. For example in 1975 the famous poet Breyten Breytenbach returned to South Africa from his exile in Paris, and travelled around the country on behalf of 'Okela', a white anti-communist faction that supported the ANC. In 1975, eight leading members of the ANC in London, led by Tennyson Makiwane, were expelled because of their attack on the white Communist influence in the leadership of the ANC.

In the 1970s, the ANC did however begin to re-emphasize its 'broad church approach' internationally. It also started to receive support for 'non-military purposes' from the Scandinavian and Dutch governments. This coincided with a new wave of mobilization in South Africa, beginning with the Durban strikes in 1973 and reaching a peak with the Soweto uprising, which marked the beginning of the end of the long and difficult period for the anti-apartheid struggle, both inside of South Africa and internationally (see Chapter 7). The internal force that managed to awake a slumbering international anti-apartheid opinion was the Black Consciousness Movement, ideologically being closer to the PAC than the ANC. Nevertheless, it was the latter that came into the 1980s with a new strength, as it slowly but firmly managed to link up both with the internal mobilization that led to the forming of the UDF, which represented 500 organizations, and to the increasing international attention to apartheid.

The PAC did however also manage to establish links with the internal movement in 1983, when the National Forum (NF) was formed. The NF was led by Africanist groups associated with, or close to, the PAC and BCM and its most important organization was AZAPO. Further, at this time the Inkatha movement, formed by Mangosuthu Buthelezi, increasingly profiled itself as a national political organization rather than just a Zulu movement. It was however the UDF that became the most important political actor in the 1980s as it succeeded in articulating an inclusive collective resistance identity, and an organization representing a broad spectre of South African society.[8] In November 1985 the position of the UDF was further strenghtened by a powerful ally, as the Confederation of South African Trade Unions (COSATU) was formed – being the largest federation as it gathered unions with 500,000 members – and declared that it would take part in the broad political struggle.

In this process, transnational connections played an important role. Through its links with the ANC, the UDF could benefit from the international network that the latter had established since the late 1950s, while Buthelezi developed international links with Conservative leaders, supporting 'constructive engagement'. The contacts of NF and AZAPO were mainly the ones developed by the PAC, and it to a large extent suffered from the relative weakness of these links in comparison with those of its rivals. Outside of Africa, it was among black political activists in the United States that the Africanist National Forum had its strongest support. However, after demonstrations against Kennedy's visit in January 1985, the NF lost an internationally important supporter in Desmond Tutu, who had made strong efforts to mediate between the Africanist and the Charterist wings of the South African anti-apartheid movement.[9] Tutu was awarded the Nobel Peace Prize in December 1984 and emerged as a key figure linking the South African anti-apartheid movement with the solidarity struggle outside of Africa, particularly the anti-apartheid movement in the United States (led by organizations such as TransAfrica and ACOA), who at the time began to play a more important role internationally than previously.

When the internal insurrection was initiated in 1984, the ANC was, thanks to its coalition with the UDF and COSATU, for the third time of major benefit from a wave of mobilization inside South Africa that it had not initiated. However, it must be underlined that black people in South Africa still had strong confidence in the organization because of the presence of its underground structures, including the 'above ground' radio broadcasts, as well as its armed presence in the region, which were also important reasons as to why it made the important links with the new organizations. In June 1985, an ANC conference was held in Zambia, and 250 delegates from abroad, including 21 missions, as well as from inside the country, participated. The declaration of the conference, building on the policy review made in the wake of Soweto in 1978, assured that the ANC would seek no other settlement with Pretoria than transfer of power after the apartheid government was defeated. Relating to the ongoing insurrection, it further declared that it would promote 'the peoples war'.[10]

Ten years after Soweto, the ANC was appearing on the front stage of world politics. In 1986, ANC leaders met with the Eminent Persons Group of the Commonwealth, and the ANC President Oliver Tambo was invited to a meeting with the British Foreign Minister. In January 1987, Tambo met with the US Secretary of State, George Shultz. When South African business leaders grew impatient with the lack of reforms of the South African government in the late 1980s, they contacted the ANC for informal talks.

The PAC did have a period of re-emergence both internationally and in South Africa in the late 1980s. In 1988, there were reports of PAC guerrilla activities inside the country and the same year the organization was invited to the Soviet Union. Further, mainly because of its connections with Libya, the PAC at this time managed to link up with the emerging political Islamism in the Western Cape, and in Johannesburg young political activists were seen wearing T-shirts with the famous PAC-slogan 'One settler one bullet'. As an attempt to respond to the ANC-allied UDF, the PAC launched the Pan Africanist Movement (PAM) in 1989. Nevertheless the election results in 1994 spoke in a clear language: while the ANC internationally was widely treated as the legitimate voice of black South Africa and received 62.6 per cent of the votes, international attention to the PAC was marginal and it got 1.25 per cent of the votes.[11]

How is one to account for the outcome of the struggle within the struggle between the ANC and the PAC, a struggle that was largely played out on a transnational political field, and an outcome that was far from easily predictable when the two movement organizations began their long journey in exile in the early 1960s? While it is impossible to make a clear distinction between the internal factors (meaning the internal dynamic of ideological and organizational development) and external factors (meaning the influence of the context in which they acted, particularly the support of international actors of various kinds) in this matter, such a distinction could nevertheless provide some clarification regarding this important question, particularly if the interplay between internal and external factors is considered.

If the PAC managed early to link itself to a broad transnational network, it did also quite early get an international reputation of being ineffective and of having an appetite for serious internal factionalism. One of the most important achievements of the PAC on behalf of the whole anti-apartheid movement was its relatively successful communication with the UN and the OAU. It is however significant for the constant state of internal division that David Sibeko, the highly charismatic Director of PAC's Foreign Affairs that played a crucial role for its international moves in the 1970s, was assassinated by fellow activists in Dar Es Salaam in 1979 in an internal insurrection which also resulted in the expelling of its leader since 1962, Potlako Leballo (three years earlier, Leballo had managed to get six of the eight exile members of the original executive expelled).

The PAC's emphasis on spontaneity and charismatic leadership contrasted sharply to the ANC's devotion to the building, and sustaining, of organizational structures reaching across borders. According to Tom Lodge and Bill Nasson, authors *of Black Politics in South Africa*, it was a successful strategy:

> From a cluster of shabby backstreet offices in Lusaka, the capital of Zambia, the ANC's leadership managed to build an extensive bureaucracy across half-a-dozen African countries and to conduct a world-wide diplomacy. ... The external ANC maintained an army, administered schools and vocational training centres, ran farms and workshops in Zambia and Tanzania, exercized juridical authority over its members, and received quasi-diplomatic recognition from governments and international agencies.[12]

At the time of the Soweto uprising in 1976, the PAC's underground presence in the country was practically non-existing and its exile organization was weak. Although the ANC had little to do with the uprisings it did have a presence in the country through underground structures, and – more important, when thousands of potential recruits came out of South Africa in the wake of Soweto, it was the ANC that was able to receive them for military training.

While the failure of the PAC might be explained by internal factors, such factors are not sufficient to explain the success of the ANC. Even more important than organizational strength was the fact that the ANC won the struggle for international support. Although the ANC's alliance with ZAPU did not turn out to be particularly successful, the regional alliance with FRELIMO and MPLA, who came out as victors in the Portuguese colonies, were more fortunate than the PAC's alliances. More important, while the promised financial support from the OAU (to both organizations) and China (to the PAC) came to very little, the support to the ANC from the Eastern bloc and Scandinavia was sustained and included funds, military equipment (including arms), training and diplomatic support. Still, the ANC's return on the international political stage in the West in the late 1980s as a 'respectable' alternative might in retrospect may appear as unexpected, considering that this happened before the end of the Cold War, when anti-communism was still a highly significant global political force.

The fact that the ANC actually escaped from being entirely trapped in the Cold War bipolar political logic might still be explained in Cold War terms. The re-emergence of the ANC internationally from the late 1970s and on was supported by the European, and more particularly, Scandinavian Social Democracy. Supporting the ANC (and other liberation movements) was part of a strategy in which the Socialist International intended to carve out a political space for itself between the two power blocs.

This was also a development that was initiated around the time of the Soweto uprising. In the Spring of 1976, before Soweto, Henry Kissinger had gone on a journey to Southern Africa to emphasize a stronger US presence in the region, in order that it should not fall into the hands of the Soviet Union. In August the same year, Swedish Prime Minister Olof Palme, referring to the wave of international protest following Soweto, made an attempt to strengthen the position of Social Democracy's 'Third Way' in relation to Southern Africa. In a speech that was part of a national election campaign (see Chapter 7), Palme addressed Social Democracy in Western Europe, appealing that the Socialist International should engage in a high-profile support to the liberation movements in Southern Africa. And as the Social Democrats lost the election, Palme devoted a large part of the coming year seeking support for his cause, making a number of international journeys, including his leadership of a visit to Southern Africa by the Socialist International.[13] Reflecting in retrospect on the role of the Swedish government in the context of interstate anti-apartheid mobilization, AAM Executive Secretary Mike Terry, centrally placed in the anti-apartheid networks at the time, states that 'one sensed that behind of it all was a kind of battle between Swedish Social Democracy and the Soviets, trying to have its influence in the Frontline states, within the ANC and the liberation movements'.[14]

The sole recognition of the ANC as the receiver of support from Swedish Social Democracy, who in the early 1970s initiated a financial support from the Swedish government that finally amounted to around two-thirds of the ANC's civil budget, was not uncontroversial. I argue that an important reason for the fact that it did happen, was that among the early contacts made at international meetings made by representatives of the ANC in the 1950s and early 1960s, were young Swedish politicians that would later play a leading role nationally (see Chapter 3).[15] As we saw an example of in Chapter 1, although both Liberals and Social Democrats who had made early contacts with the ANC were often highly critical of the links to the SACP and the Eastern bloc that the ANC developed, they nevertheless kept supporting the organization.

These contacts points to an additional important difference between the ANC and the PAC, highlighted by Tom Lodge; that the class background of the leadership of the ANC and the PAC generally differed. As the former came from a more privileged background than the latter, they more easily moved in the international networks of individuals that were later to become national political elites.

Sanctions, boycotts and constructive engagement

Economic, cultural and sports boycotts and sanctions – disinvestment, and divestment – represent crucial strategies of the transnational anti-apartheid struggle. Activists ascribed different meanings to these forms of action, and linked them with each other in different ways. They were also subjects of intense debates within the movement. The positions in such debates were not just related to different opinions about the efficacy of the different strategies, but they also reflected links to different political alliances and contexts. Further, these positions were also based on conflicting analyses of the political and economic situation both globally and in South Africa.

From one point of view, these strategies were all intended to put pressure on South Africa through economic or cultural isolation. At the heart of the conflicts that surrounded many of the campaigns was however a contradiction inherent in the strategy of organizing across borders in order to put a massive global pressure on South Africa by isolating it from the world community. Critics of the strategy of attempting to isolate South Africa argued that while the government in South Africa through its system of apartheid isolated itself from a world community that emphasized racial equality and human rights, it was rather through the
presence of international forces in the country, than through isolation, that apartheid was most effectively fought.

The different types of boycotts and sanctions also represent different ways to approach transnational politics and mobilization, as they empha-size different channels of political influence. While sanctions as a policy of disinvestment of a state (that through legislative measures enforces a withdrawal of companies from South Africa) emphasized the power of the nation state as the ultimate instrument for putting pressure on South Africa, boycotts and divestment (the sale of stock in multinational companies with subsidiaries in South Africa), represented forms of political pressure that by-passed the nation state. The consumer boycott and the strategy of disinvestment emphasize the power of collective action of consumers/clients, and therefore seems to be a political strategy well suited for a phase of the globalization process in which increasingly mobile transnational corporations more and more easily escape the political control of states.

As already discussed, the first co-ordinated transnational anti-apartheid action was a boycott of South African goods. It was initiated by the South African Congress movement, who linked up with an anti-colonial boycott strategy and, further back, with the abolitionist movement. The ultimate aim of the economic, cultural and sports boycotts was of course to put pressure on the South African government through isolating the country culturally and hurting it economically. However, as several activists that I have interviewed have pointed out, the anti-apartheid organizations also viewed the boycott as an important tool for mobilization and 'consciousness raising' of large numbers of people. Through the launching of boycott campaigns, the organizations offered people an opportunity for 'everyday' participation in solidarity action. It was argued that in the long run such active participation would generally raise public consciousness about the issue, and eventually increase the pressure on national governments and international organizations, like UN or EEC, to impose sanctions. From this point of view, to participate in a boycott could also be seen as 'voting' for sanctions (the British AAM called boycott action 'people's sanctions').

In the US anti-apartheid movement, a consumer boycott was never a big issue, because there were hardly any South African goods to boycott. An exception was however the boycott campaign against Shell, launched in 1986, and led by the Dutch, the British and the US anti-apartheid movements in co-operation. Otherwise, *divestment* became the crucial anti-apartheid strategy in the country where a significant number of the transnational corporations present in South Africa had their headquarters. George Houser, veteran activist in ACOA, argues that this form of action, now widely used by the environmental movement and the global justice movement, was invented by the anti-apartheid movement.[16] It had a strong support base in the student movement and began in 1965, when the Students for a Democratic Society (SDS) initiated a protest against

Chase Manhattan Bank's loans to South Africa, an action that was followed by protests against a number of universities, demanding that they sold their shares in companies with subsidiaries in South Africa. A third form of divestment campaign was directed at local governments, demanding a restricted municipal contracting with companies with links to South Africa.[17] The strategy of divestment quickly spread around the world – for example British AAM in 1969 launched a campaign against Barclays Bank – the actions mainly carried out by students. The single most visible and important effect of the divestment campaigns was that Chase Manhattan Bank, who was being put under pressure by institutional investors, such as New York City and a number of universities, announced that it would not grant South Africa any further loans. However, just as in the case of the boycott strategy, divestment had several functions; according to Meg Voorhes it 'directly influenced corporate policy, reinforced grassroots anti-apartheid mobilization, and contributed to the dramatic public shift in favour of sanctions against South Africa'.[18]

Sports had been on the transnational anti-apartheid agenda since the late 1950s. It was a highly relevant target for several reasons. First, sports was an important part of an increasingly mediatized global popular culture. Thousands, and sometimes millions of people, followed sports games in real-time through radio and television. Sports campaigns, and particularly demonstrations or direct actions carried out during a game, thus automatically reached out to a large public. Although South Africa did not get public television until 1976, white South Africa was no exception regarding the popularity of sport. Particularly big Commonwealth sports as rugby, cricket and tennis were extremely popular among the whites. Further, sports had an important ideological function in apartheid society. This was for example indicated by *AA News* in 1970, when it quoted the South African newspaper *Die Transvaler*, which stated that 'sport has become a matter, which is directly concerned with the maintenance of white civilization'.[19] Thus, the South African government put a large amount of prestige into showing off successful all-white teams internationally. When there finally was an almost complete international boycott on South African sport, it was a great blow to the apartheid regime.

In Britain Trevor Huddleston initiated the Campaign Against Race Discrimination in Sport in 1958. In 1962 the South African Non-Racial Olympic Committee (SAN-ROC) was formed. It was soon forced into exile but succeeded in getting South Africa suspended from the Olympic Games in 1964. In January 1968, the Olympic Committee once again decided not to allow South Africa into the Olympic Games. Further, the successful campaigns against the South African rugby and cricket teams' British tours during the late 1960s and early 1970s pretty much put an end to apartheid South Africa's presence in international sport. The sports boycott was never really controversial within the movement, although it caused internal debates on the *methods* of protest. The sports protests did however cause heated political debates in the public spheres of different national contexts, as local defenders of South African sports teams argued that sports was not be mixed with politics (see Chapter 6).

An early cultural boycott was initiated in Britain when the Musician's Union forbade its members to perform in South Africa in 1961.[20] AAM also initiated its long-lasting campaign for a global cultural boycott of South Africa in the early 1960s, being supported by trade unions of cultural workers both in the United States and Britain.

Having varied success in different cultural fields during the 1960s and 1970s, AAM's cultural boycott was strengthened when a UN General Assembly resolution condemning cultural collaboration with South Africa was passed in 1981. Further, the publication of a register of artists who had performed in South Africa by the UN Special Committee Against Apartheid contributed in putting further pressure on cultural workers. In 1986 the Artists Against Apartheid (AAA) was formed in Britain, an organization that was an important force in pursuing the cultural boycott in its final phase. AAA was also instrumental for the organization of the Mandela concerts at Wembley in 1988 and 1990.

That the cultural boycott clearly had an effect was confirmed by responses from the South African government, such as the legalizing of the pirating of plays and the permission to allow mixed audiences at certain performances. But AAM's aim of a total international cultural boycott of South Africa was never close to being realized. For example, while some internationally well known artists like Elton John and Rod Stewart were persuaded to cancel their South African tours, others like Cilla Black, Eartha Kitt and Status Quo at different moments ignored the boycott.

In the 1980s, the cultural boycott also became a matter of conflict within the transnational anti-apartheid movement, as the ANC and AAM had different opinions on what it meant and how it should be organized. Part and parcel of the broad internal anti-apartheid mobiliza-tion out of which the Mass Democratic Movement (MDM) and the UDF was born in the 1980s, was a cultural movement emphasizing music, poetry, dance and theatre as vital elements of the struggle. The ANC basically supported the view put forth by the movement in South Africa (although there was also tension between the ANC and the UDF on this issue) that it was important that South African cultural groups that took part in the struggle should also be able to tour abroad. Further, in order that South African artists could be part of international cultural exchange, being influenced by and influence global cultural developments, the ANC argued that certain cultural groups should also be exempted from the boycott's rule that no cultural groups should tour in South Africa.

The AAM, who had put a lot of its energy and prestige into persuading individual artists and unions of cultural workers to follow the boycott, felt that it was an impossible task to organize a selective cultural boycott, as it would be extremely difficult to decide and motivate who should be exempted from the boycott. As it wrote in a sharp tone in a Memorandum to the ANC in February 1987:

> We should appreciate knowing what criteria are used in taking such decisions. ... What is the rationale for such exemptions? More importantly, how would such a policy work in practice? What mechanisms/ structures will exist? How will people be advised of who has been exempted etc.?[21]

Parallel to the demand for an international boycott in the late 1950s, key anti-apartheid activists initiated a discussion on whether economic sanctions by national governments would be the most effective way of putting international pressure on South Africa. One of them was Ronald Segal, the South African editor of *Africa South*, who had fled the country together with Oliver Tambo and settled in London, where he was active in British AAM. Segal felt that while economic sanctions had been discredited because they had failed when tried against Italy during the 1930s, they deserved to be given a new chance in the context of anti-apartheid.[22] In 1964, Segal organized an international conference in London in which independent academics, lawyers and journalists presented 'expert papers'. It was attended by around 250 delegates, including official delegations from 30 countries and 5 observers from the UN Special Committee Against Apartheid.[23]

Putting pressure on governments and international organizations to introduce economic sanctions was on top of the agenda of the transnational anti-apartheid movement for most of the period in which it was active. There was positive response on the campaign from the UN Special Committee, and 1982 became UN's 'International Year of Mobilization for Sanctions Against South Africa'. However, when resolutions on sanctions were put forth in the UN Security Council, they were always vetoed by Western members such as the United States, Britain, and sometimes also France. It was only in the mid-1980s that the sanctions campaign started to have a significant effect internationally. Between 1985 and 1987, Britain, France, Spain, Panama, Portugal and the United States introduced economic sanctions, while the Nordic countries further sharpened the legislation previously introduced. As with all the other campaigns to isolate South Africa however, it also had strong mobilizing effects, broadening the collective identification with the movement both nationally and transnationally. For example, at the Commonwealth meeting in Bahamas in 1985, Abdul Minty of AAM presented a declaration urging sanctions that was signed by representatives for organizations that represented 18 million people. In December the same year, more than 100,000 people demonstrated in London (see Chapter 8).[24]

While sanctions have always been criticized for being a measure that might hurt the people of a country more than those in power, proponents of sanctions against South Africa could refer to support from the ANC as well as the PAC. While critics responded that these exile organizations had lost touch with their home country, the Inkatha Freedom Party (IFP), led by Mangosuthu Buthelezi, was the only significant anti-apartheid force within South Africa that was opposed to sanctions. Nevertheless, the issue of sanctions versus different versions of 'constructive engagement' was the most important conflict within the broad transnational anti-apartheid movement. The conflict was also linked to the issue of anti-communism; those who searched for an alternative to the ANC because of its communist links tended to favour constructive engagement. As already mentioned in Chapter 1, constructive engagement was in an early phase supported by the unions affiliated to the ICFTU, who argued that an international economic presence in South Africa would strengthen the emergence of a labour union movement. Further, it was also linked to the issue of violence/non-violence as Buthelezi at the time when he declared his support for constructive engagement, also claimed that IFP advocated non-violence, something that rendered him support from influential actors in the transnational church network (although it would be sharply contradicted by the actual practices of the Inkatha Movement). Constructive engagement also got support from governments as well as from influential transnational corporations. In 1974, the British Labour government introduced 'codes of conduct' for British firms in South Africa, and similar codes were introduced in the EEC in 1977. The same year Leon Sullivan,

Baptist Minister, successfully launched principles for US Firms with affiliates in South Africa ('the Sullivan Principles'), an act that subsequently earned him a position as the first black director of General Motors.[25]

The conflict of constructive engagement versus sanctions was at the heart of the definition of the collective identity of the anti-apartheid movement; it was a struggle located right at the border of the demarcation line that divided those who were considered to be part of the movement and those who were not. While 'constructive engagement' was certainly used as a cop-out by certain forces that were more interested in status quo than in structural change in South Africa, it was also advocated by a number of individuals and organizations who performed a commitment to anti-apartheid. Nevertheless, key anti-apartheid individuals and organizations felt that they were betraying the movement. As Christabel Gurney, AAM activist and editor of *AA News*, puts it:

> Constructive engagement, code of conduct – AAM felt that that was not fighting apartheid, it was not part of the anti-apartheid movement. That was a great difficulty, and a lot of tension and emphasis was put in promoting the idea of sanctions ... so that was the main tension.[26]

Black Consciousness Movement, the IUEF and 'Operation Daisy'

In spite of the severe repression of black politics by the apartheid regime during the 1960s, including its attempts to prevent political communication across its borders, the rise of the BCM was linked to a transnational wave of mobilization in the 1960s. The process of black student mobilization that lead to the forming of the South African Student's Organization (SASO) under the leadership of Steven Biko in 1969, occurred in interaction with international developments, particularly with the diverse US movement culture involving the civil rights movement, student activism and Black Power. Steven Biko showed a strong interest in the Black Power movement as well as in the Black Theology developed in the United States.[27] The influence from black politics in the United States was also manifested in SASO's adoption of 'black' as the central identity concept of the movement; a concept that in its political articulation included all people's experiencing oppression based on race. It was also in the United States that the BCM had its strongest support base outside of South Africa, and the news that

Biko was killed in detention in 1977 further fuelled the US solidarity movement.

In many other parts of the world however, and particularly in those key organizations in Europe that were close to the ANC, the BCM was regarded with a certain scepticism. Ideologically, the BCM was perceived to be based on the same mode of Africanist thinking as the PAC, and in 1976 an article in ANC's publication *Sechaba* dismissed the BCM's anti-racist discourse as 'wrong ideological teaching'.[28] Key anti-apartheid activists also feared that the BCM would replace the ANC as the main receiver of international support.

These fears were not groundless, as forces within the solidarity network that emphasized anti-communism supported BCM. The economically most important support in this respect came from the IUEF, reputed for its involvement in the most famous 'spy-story' in the history of the anti-apartheid movement. This story shows that the internal conflicts of the transnational anti-apartheid could have far reaching political implications and serious consequences in the context of the Cold War.

IUEF was an international NGO formed in 1961 and based in Geneva. Its financial support came from the Scandinavian countries, Canada and Holland. Its objective was to support the needs of education of refugees, particularly related to Southern Africa (and at a later stage also Latin America). From 1964, its largest donor was the Swedish Development Agency (SIDA), and in 1966 Lars-Gunnar Eriksson, a Swedish Social Democrat, became its director.[29] Under Erikssson's leadership the IUEF started educational assistance to South Africa, which included a rapidly increasing support to the BCM in the 1970s. This happened at the same time as the Swedish Social Democracy followed the advice of SIDA's Consultative Committee of Humanitarian Assistance (CCHA), including members from all of the major Swedish political parties, not to provide official support to the BCM, but to continue to favour the ANC.

Being dissociated from the Swedish political culture of consensus, Eriksson continued to take the IUEF in the direction he had previously laid down. The support to the BCM also created tensions in relation to IDAF, the other international key organization for channelling money to South African anti-apartheid organizations from governments and international organizations. While the IDAF was close to the ANC and the British AAM, Tor Sellström has argued that Eriksson's agenda was clearly to promote BCM as an alternative to the ANC, as he belonged to a section in the worker's movement who had a strong commitment to anti-communism.[30]

The apartheid regime's fear of BCM as an internal political force also led the South African Bureau of State Security (BOSS), to IUEF and Eriksson. Eriksson's eccentricity and appetite for adventurous political games and intrigue – in an article in Sweden's largest daily he was described as 'a combination of James Bond, Robin Hood and Don Quixote', who considered himself 'an anti-communist crusader in Africa' – included a mismanagement of the IUEF, which opened up the organization for infiltration.[31] The person selected by BOSS for this mission, termed 'Operation Daisy', was Craig Williamson, a white South African doing intelligence work for the apartheid state already when he was appointed as Vice-President of National Union of South African Students (NUSAS) in 1975. Williamson became a key figure in the series of cross border operations that were initiated by the apartheid State at this time, and that lasted for more than a decade. He later admitted that he was part of the group that bombed the ANC's London office in 1984 and prepared the parcel bombs that killed the ANC members Ruth First in Maputo in 1982 and Jeanette Schon (and her eight-year-old daughter) in Lubango in 1984. Further, he organized the infiltration of the Spanish anti-apartheid movement, whose leading figure in the 1980s was an apartheid agent.

Faking an 'escape' from South Africa, Williamson arrived in Geneva in 1977 and was assigned 'special responsibilities' for IUEF's internal programmes in South Africa under Eriksson's wings. Operation Daisy, as well as other BOSS's foreign operations, were revealed in the *Observer* in January 1980 by Arthur McGiven, former colleague of Williamson. Before this, Williamson did however manage to get IUEF to change its direction of support to South African organizations; in the wake of Biko's death in 1977, it recognized the ANC as the main liberation movement – thus making it susceptible for monitoring by Williamson.

Naming the movement

How should one conceptualize the internally diverse transnational anti-apartheid movement? Was it a social movement for human rights? I would argue that 'human rights' does not sufficiently conceptualize the articulation of the anti-apartheid struggle. Although human rights was an important element in the discursive repertoire of the movement throughout the anti-apartheid struggle, the issue was also articulated through discourses with different ideological implications – for example as anti-imperialism, national self-determination, de-colonization, anti-capitalism, or Pan Africanist anti-racism. This discursive diversity could partly be explained by the fact that movement actors sometimes strategically adjusted their terminology to different contexts. In the context of transnationalist politics, political actors capable of moving across borders could choose to appeal to the institutions or political arenas that are the most likely to be the most receptive to a specific issue, a practice that has been termed 'venue shopping'.[32] Each venue is dominated by a specific political discourse, and addressing different venues could thus imply using different political languages. For example, in the context of the UN General Assembly, the dominant discourse emphasized human rights and national self-determination, while in the Security Council the issue tended to be brought up as 'a threat to the maintenance of international peace and security'.[33] In the communist-dominated WFTU, anti-apartheid was articulated as an issue of anti-imperialism and anti-capitalism, while in postcolonial organizations like the OAU and the Commonwealth the issue was primarily related to a discourse emphasizing anti-racism, pan-Africanism and decolonization.

However, although particularly the ANC at an early stage developed high skills in such 'venue shopping', it can only provide part of the explanation of the different ways of naming the anti-apartheid struggle in different public spaces and at different moments. As I have tried to show in this chapter, the fact that the transnational anti-apartheid movement was a 'movement of movements', consisting of an extremely broad alliance of groups and organizations involving varying ideological commitments and collective identities, made the struggle within the struggle a fundamental aspect of the movement's activities.

What then, united the different actors struggling against apartheid? They were of course united in the common goal of ending the apartheid system in South Africa. However, a common goal is not enough for a constellation of actors to compose a social movement. *What is required is a shared collective identity*, which is a fundamental aspect of the definition of a social movement that I use here.

In terms of collective identity, sustained transnational anti-apartheid action across borders was made possible through the construction of *an imagined community of solidarity activists*. In this sense, the anti-apartheid movement was part of a *globalization from below*. However, this does not mean that the movement was separated from political globalization from above. Rather it interacted, and partly intersected, with a number of international communities that emerged in connection with the rise and consolidation of new 'global' political discourses and institutions.

Political globalization from above

The norm that guided the foundation of the interstate system, the principle of national sovereignty, has continued to be dominant in the context of the complex interstate system, where states increasingly bind themselves to supra-national agreements. This is to a large extent confirmed when looking at how the issue of apartheid was articulated in the field of interstate relations. As South Africa claimed that any criticism of apartheid was an intervention in its 'internal affairs', this argument was countered in 1973 in the UN General Assembly by a resolution stating that it was the liberation movements (the ANC and the PAC) that were the authentic representatives of the (*national*) people of South Africa.[34] The resolution thus confirmed the principle of national sovereignty, however altering its subject in the specific case of South Africa.

However, membership in interstate organizations also meant increasing dependence on relations with other states during the Cold War era. Depending on the relative strength of a state internationally, this could mean less autonomy and even pressure on state governments to abandon its national sovereignty, as the South African government experienced in the context of the UN and the Commonwealth. It is important to emphasize that this increasingly complex international system is not just composed of formal institutional arrangements. It should be conceived as a conglomeration of overlapping *international communities*, understood as 'sites of identity and interest'.[35] Such communities may be formed for various historical reasons, and their identities may change as a result of historical change and shifting power relations between its members. In order to understand and analyse the significance and changing roles of these communities in global politics it is thus important to locate their identities and interests in relation to wider historical contexts and changes in power relations.

When looking at the political context of the global anti-apartheid struggle, a number of international communities were important. For the European anti-apartheid movement, the EEC was of course important. For example, AAM built relationships with members of the European Parliament and met the European Parliament Socialist Group. In April 1985 EEC agreed to partial sanctions, which were extended in 1986.[36] Globally, even more important were however particularly the OAU, the Commonwealth, and the UN, being the largest and most complex of international communities during the post-war era.[37] The foundation of these communities, as well as the articulation of their political identities and interests, were in turn shaped by two wider and overlapping global and historical contexts: *postcoloniality* and *the Cold War*.

Divided on many issues, especially in relation to Cold War conflicts, the African states declared unity on advocating racial equality and de-colonization when the OAU was formed in 1963. The OAU was thus founded on the construction of a postcolonial Pan-African identity and became an important inter-state actor in the anti-apartheid struggle, which it articulated in terms of de-colonization and national self-determination. When the UN General Assembly declared that it was the South African liberation movements (ANC and PAC) that were the authentic representatives of the people of South Africa, it referred to an earlier declaration made by the OAU.[38] In 1964, the OAU called for an oil embargo on South Africa. The OAU also encouraged its member states to give active support to the liberation movements and gave strong support for the call for sanctions made by the transnational anti-apartheid movement.[39]

During the period of the anti-apartheid struggle, *the Commonwealth*, an informal organization based on the historical legacy and political identity of the British Empire, was transformed into a postcolonial community. This was felt by South Africa, which in 1961 was more or less forced to withdraw its request for readmission into the Commonwealth after it had become a republic. It was also felt by Britain itself, becoming more and more constrained as the numbers of newly independent states grew, as did the commitment to issues of de-colonization and anti-racism. The issue of apartheid caused a large battle in the Commonwealth, in which Britain resisted the overwhelming majority of nations advocating sanctions. In doing this Britain confirmed that, if it was losing its grip over its old colonies, it still had status as a world power, being one of the leading members of the political community of the Western Powers and its military alliance NATO, formed in the context of the Cold War. It was only as a result of strong pressure from other European countries that Britain, under protest, in 1985 accepted the EEC policy of partial sanctions.[40]

The transnational anti-apartheid movement was allowed a space for lobbying during the Commonwealth meetings. Under the leadership of Shridath Ramphal, the Commonwealth Secretariat gave the ANC accreditation to visit the meetings together with journalists, something which upset the British, as the ANC at this time was labelled a terrorist organization by Prime Minister Margaret Thatcher.[41]

However, as accounted for in Chapter 1, in terms of providing a transnational space for mobilization, it was *the UN Special Committee*

Against Apartheid that became most important for the transnational anti-apartheid movement. In addition to organizing meetings, the committee also sent delegations to various countries to consult with national and international NGOs. The meetings did not only help the NGO-representatives to meet each other, but also to contact OAU and representatives of African governments. Thus, the case of anti-apartheid shows that the UN can be perceived as a political space where the processes of globalization from above and below sometimes intersect.[42]

However, as with any political question in the UN at the time, the apartheid issue was clearly defined by the tensions and conflicts of post-coloniality as well as of the Cold War. According to ACOA activist Jennifer Davis, the UN was regarded with suspicion in the United States during the Cold War, 'it was regarded as the creature of somebody else – either the 3rd world or the Soviet Union'.[43] In the context of the UN, the activities of the Special Committee were thus also regarded with suspicion in certain camps. None of the Western countries ever joined the committee. It consisted of representatives mainly from Asian, African and Latin American countries, as well as a few from Eastern Europe.[44]

Conclusion: anti-apartheid as globalization from below

Organizationally, the anti-apartheid movement consisted of a network of local, national and transnational groups and organizations, being simultaneously active in national, international and transnational politics. It approached, interacted, and in a few cases closely co-operated with, national governments, such as those of India, Nigeria, Tanzania and Sweden, as well as intergovernmental organizations and communities, such as the OAU, the Commonwealth, the UN and the EEC. To use Kriesi's and Della Porta's notion of an international multilevel political game, the struggle against apartheid thus included three types of international interaction – transgovernmenal interaction, transnational movement mobilization, and cross-level mobilization (between social movements in one country and a government in another country).[45] These authors specifically emphasize the anti-apartheid movement as an example of a case where transnational and cross-level mobilization put pressure on a national government (South Africa) indirectly, through influencing transgovernmental relations between Western countries and South Africa. However, I would argue that transnational anti-apartheid mobilization also *directly* put pressure on South Africa through economic (consumer) and cultural boycotts and through direct support to the internal struggle.

3
National Politics in a Global Context: Anti-Apartheid in Britain and Sweden

Introduction: national politics in a global context

Any analysis of the role of the nation state must consider the process of globalization. Although the concept of 'globalization' was quite recently established in the social sciences, it must be regarded as a historical process intrinsically connected with the history of colonialism and modernity. Contrary to many assertions, globalization does not by definition equal the erosion of the nation state. Rather, the global dissemination of the nation was a crucial aspect of a certain phase of globalization, originating in the late eighteenth century, and culminating during the decades that followed the Second World War. The era of the anti-apartheid movement was marked by the contradictions between processes of nation state building (predominantly in the South) and transnationalization.

The dominant perspective in social movement studies, focusing on political opportunity structures (POS), has tended to focus on a national level, underestimating the relevance of a global perspective on social movement interactions, networks and contexts. It is not just the issues and the networks of new movements that have become increasingly global during the post-war era. The structural processes that created the preconditions for the emergence of new forms of collective action were transnational, rather than bound to any *specific* nation state. Further, looking at the case of anti-apartheid, the different opportunities and constraints facing anti-apartheid organizations in the context of specific nation states, were to a large extent determined by the belongings of those states to different international communities and their interests, as well as by their locations in wider global and historical contexts. Thus, the analysis of the national contexts in this chapter will not stop at the national level, taking the opportunity structures of the two nation states as the ultimate reference point, but rather shift emphasis, relating the analysis to the different positions of the two states in a *historically instituted global context*.

As with the transnational movement, the national anti-apartheid movement's internal relations were marked by internal struggles as well as consensus building. The 'common ground' of the solidarity anti-apartheid movements in Britain and Sweden was largely national identity. This might contradict the fact that a crucial element of anti-apartheid identity was internationalism, as movement spokespersons claimed universal values and spoke in terms of human rights. It might even be argued that in relation to certain discourses of British and Swedish nationalism, the anti-apartheid movement was explicitly anti-nationalist. Nevertheless, inherent in the construction of national solidarity movements is an appeal for the solidarity of one nation with another. This is for example recognized by Christabel Gurney, key movement AAM activist from the 1970s and onwards, as she in an article on the emergence of British AAM states that the South Africans that initiated AAM in Britain 'had the vision to see that, if it was to grow, the Movement must put down British roots'.[1] Another way to put it is that international solidarity in Britain at the time would come easier if the persons appealing for it had a white face – and spoke with a British accent. The same goes for Sweden. Anyone seeking as broad support as possible in order to build and sustain a movement in the context of a national civil society must find strategies that in one way or another appeals to 'the nation'. This could however be done in various ways, and the identities of the movements in the two countries were shaped through articulating relations to allies and enemies in different ways, under the influence of differing national historical and cultural contexts.

In this chapter, I will investigate these processes through discussing and analysing the practices and the relevant contexts of two key anti-apartheid organizations in Britain and Sweden, British AAM and the Africa Groups in Sweden (AGIS) – focusing on four themes: (1) the (changing) relations of the two states to South Africa in connection with their positions in relation to the global contexts of postcoloniality and the Cold War (2) the relations between the movements and the states in the respective countries (3) the relations between the dominant national political culture and the movement culture of which anti-apartheid action was part (4) the relations and tensions between the two organizations and other national and international anti-apartheid SMOs.

The legacy of the Empire

In his chapter on British government policies in relation to apartheid South Africa, Roger Fieldhouse argues that all British administrations, Conservative as well as Labour, based its actions on two principles. The first was a moral principle of rejection of apartheid, based on the Human Rights doctrine of the UN. The second was a principle of prioritizing British economic interest when deciding on government policies.[2] If the second, *economic* factor, that is, the protection of major British corporations in South Africa, was dominant, it might be argued the instrumentality of British politics in relation to apartheid South Africa was also based on British *political* interests in the context of an increasingly globalized post-war world – most important its membership in NATO. But also other links – political as well as cultural, going back to the Imperial era, did have an influence. If the principles of morality and instrumentality could be seen as contradictory, and the anti-apartheid movement always publicly emphasized this, they were combined in the commitment to 'constructive engagement'.

If it is true that both Labour and Conservative governments shared the same basic approach, there were also differences. The British labour movement was an important actor when the anti-apartheid movement was initiated in the early 1960s, and anti-apartheid was often a rallying issue when the Labour party was in opposition. Its repeated decline to deliver when in power did however quickly alienate AAM. This was clearly visible in relation to the issue of the British arms embargo on South Africa – especially after Harold Wilson's famous speech in Trafalgar Square at a rally organized by AAM in March 1963 in which he strongly condemned the Conservative policy on the issue. When Wilson announced Labour's arms embargo in parliament in the House of Commons in 1964, it was a great disappointment as it excluded existing contracts.[3] The arms embargo, and the loopholes making it highly ineffcient, would continue to be a crucial issue of contest between different British governments and the anti-apartheid movement. Except for the arms embargo, the most significant signs of response to anti-apartheid pressure by a British government occurred between 1985 and 1987, when the Thatcher government accepted restrictive sanctions against South Africa. In 1990, Britain was however also the first country to lift its sanctions.[4]

While Britain's colonial history certainly influenced Britain's policy on apartheid South Africa, it could also be argued that the same historical legacy contributed in making London, and British AAM, a crucial node in the transnational anti-apartheid network. The very same history also included a political tradition of civic anti-colonialism, of which the anti-apartheid movement clearly was a descendant. Important precursors of AAM in this respect were the anti-colonial movement, including the Movement for Colonial Freedom (MCF), the Africa Bureau and the Union of Democratic Control (UDC, formed by E. D. Morel, who initiated the Congo Reform Society), which provided links with an earlier anti-colonial tradition going back to mobilization against Leopold's Congo and the Abolitionist Movement.[5]

Another dimension of Britain's colonial legacy in relation to South Africa that was of some significance for the anti-apartheid movement on the level of civil society, was the discourse of 'kith and kin'. It was expressed by English-speaking persons living in South Africa that simultaneously claimed a British identity and 'authentic experience of everyday life in South Africa', while criticizing anti-apartheid advocates for lack of deeper understanding of apartheid society. A number of anti-apartheid activists that I have interviewed have accounted for their constant encounters with the 'kith and kin' position – at demonstrations, public meetings or in private conversations. One of them is Sobizana Mngqikana, who worked as an exile anti-apartheid activist in both London and Stockholm (see Chapter 1). According to Mngqikana, the presence of 'kith and kin' was a significant difference between the national political contexts of the two countries. Another example is the account of Brian Brown, South African born Anglican priest, active in the anti-apartheid Christian Institute. In 1978, after being prosecuted for preaching anti-apartheid in church, he left South Africa for Britain, where he became the African secretary of the British Council of Churches:

> For 15 years I wandered around Britain speaking at meetings ... and in those meetings, at the end, like clockwork: 'Reverend Brown I don't want to call you a liar, but I have got my aunt Matilda who lives in Johannesburg, and she would contradict everything you said'. And I would say, yes I am sure she would, she would see things from a different perspective ... the question of kith and kin was determinative.[6]

Nationalism as internationalism

Compared to Britain, the Swedish state had a completely different agenda in relation to international politics in general, and to apartheid South Africa in particular. After the Second World War, Sweden profiled itself as a defender of international law on the global arena. As the object of constant criticism, South Africa was an important Other of the Swedish State as it constructed an internationalist national identity on the global political arena.[7] The internationalist discourse of the Swedish State also played an important role in domestic politics, as different international commitments were high on the agendas of the established political parties. There was a broad consensus in parliament when sanctions on South Africa were passed in 1979 and 1987. The only exception was Moderaterna (the Conservatives), who always opposed sanctions in its programmes and in public debates, and also voted against the law banning new investment in 1979 and the boycott legislation in 1987.

There was also a broad consensus on the Swedish aid to the liberation movements in South Africa. Southern Africa was the most important region receiving Swedish aid during the period of the anti-apartheid struggle. Of the liberation movements, the ANC was the most important recipient. The extensive support to the ANC from the Swedish state, under the government of the Social Democrats (relying on the support of the Swedish Communist Party in Parliament) as well as right-wing coalitions, could partly be understood in relation to the contacts between ANC leaders and young Social Democrats and Liberals (see Chapter 2). It might also be seen as the result of pressure from the Swedish anti-apartheid movement that emerged in the early 1960s.

Sweden's identity as an 'international critic' should partly be seen in relation to the fact that small states, particularly during the Cold War, had a common interest in a strong international law, which provided a defence from intervention of stronger states. As the wave of anti-colonialism marked global politics during the 1960s, adding a stronger North/South dimension to the Cold War Conflict, the emphasis on anti-colonialist arguments grew stronger.[8] At this time, Sweden started to give 'unofficial' aid to liberation movements in Southern Africa and Latin America. If this support expressed a moral and ideological position, based on anti-colonialism, it also represented a new agenda of self-interest. Sweden's aid to the liberation struggle in Southern Africa could partly be seen as a strategy of promoting the growth of an international community of alliance-free states, whose 'parallellity of interests' eventually would be of benefit for Sweden. In a Government Bill from 1962, written by a working group led by Olof Palme, it was argued that a 'mutual interest' could develop between Sweden and 'peoples in Asia and Africa who have recently won, or shortly will gain, full independence', as these countries had a 'policy of neutrality' in common.[9]

If the policy of the Swedish state in relation to apartheid South Africa thus was part of an attempt to initiate a non-aligned coalition in the context of the Cold War, it also represented a certain degree of continuity in relation to the construction of a modern Swedish nation state during the era of imperialism. In fact, while the support to the South African anti-apartheid movement was the major Swedish solidarity project during the twentieth century, a previous wave of Swedish international solidarity was also related to South Africa in connection with the Anglo-Boer war. As Swedish solidarity at this time was mainly directed to the Boer side, the support included a contingent of volunteers who went to South Africa to participate on the Boer side, these two solidarity movements might seem contradictory.[10] There is however a certain logic in the historical process leading from the one to the other, and Sweden's role in the history of colonialism and imperialism might shed some light on this process, and consequently, on the policy of the Swedish governments in relation to South Africa during the post-war era.

While it might be argued that Sweden played an extremely marginal role in the history of European colonialism, Sweden's economy was an integral part of the centre of the world system during the period when it rested on slavery, colonialism and imperialism.[11] South Africa was also a part of the colonized world with which Sweden at an early stage developed relatively frequent contacts. From the Dutch East India Company's establishment in 1652, a Swedish, economical as well as cultural (through the Mission), presence played an important role in the Cape colonial settlement.[12]

During the wave of Swedish nationalism at the turn of the nineteenth century, Sweden's links to South Africa also became significant in the domestic political struggle to define the modern Swedish national identity. When Liberals, Conservatives and Socialists from different perspectives constructed their different versions of the Swedish nation, the South African Boer nation was an important point of identification.[13] This identification was based on an image of the Boer as a small nation of farmers fighting a heroic struggle against a mighty empire. The silence, with a few exceptions (see later), in the public debate on the role of the Africans in a future South Africa, implicated that this Swedish nationalism shared the hegemonic Eurocentric and racist world view of European political thinking at the time – the African population simply did not count as historical subjects.

Thus, as was also the case later in the twentieth century, the different established political parties' constructions of a Swedish national identity shared an internationalist orientation with a strong emphasis on anti-imperialism in the sense of the right of a small state to defend its autonomy against the intervention of imperial powers. If this meant support to the Boer in the Anglo-Boer war, relations to the British were nevertheless ambivalent. In the conservative daily *Svenska Dagbladet*, Harald Hjärne articulated a position which most explicitly dealt with the issue of the relations of the Africans to the Boer and the British. Criticizing the race doctrine of the pro-Germanists (implicating absolute and eternal differences between races), also associating it with the Boer, Hjärne advocated an evolutionist (racist) discourse, arguing that the British, as a leading world power in the process of human progress, had a historical civilizing mission in relation to the African population.

The Liberals and the Social Democrats on the other hand voiced strong criticism against the imperial ambitions of the British, while at the same time looking to anti-imperialist and pro-Boer feminist and socialist circles in Britain for support and inspiration, arguing that the British opposition to the war, as a bearer of the tradition of progress, enlightenment and human rights, represented 'the real Britain'.[14]

During the period of the anti-apartheid struggle there was at certain moments tension between British and Swedish goverments on the issue of policy towards South Africa. This tension was recorded by the *Daily Telegraph* during Olof Palme's journey to Southern Africa in 1971, occurring just before the Swedish support to the liberation struggles took off. Standing at the river of Zambesi, on the border between Zambia and Rhodesia, Palme stated that he was 'on the border of human decency', at the same time announcing that Sweden would substantially increase its humanitarian aid to the African liberation movements. This resulted in a sharp response in an editorial on the 28 September in the *Daily Telegraph*. The *Daily Telegraph* was close to the Conservative British government, and the text was most likely representative for the British administration's view on Sweden's foreign policy under Olof Palme and the Social Democrats:

> Mr. Palme claims that the aid is tied to humanitarian purposes, and says that Sweden would not supply the liberation movements with arms or the money to buy them. This is not really a respectable argument, especially as he goes on in the next breath to avow for violent struggle for liberation. Any aid to violent movements assists those movements in their violence. Such criticisms also apply to British organisations which channel aid to the same quarters, through the World Council of Churches or directly. Sweden's attitude is particularly ambivalent, like many things Swedish. In July, Uganda seized

four helicopters in transit to Tanzania. They were built in Sweden for Tanzania's special police squad responsible for 'poachers and cattle-rustlers'. Sweden claims to be 'with the West' but to have an 'alliance-free' foreign policy. The two things do not square up.[15]

The state and other enemies

For most social movements acting in a national context, the state is a major opponent. Relations between states and movements can however be shaped in numerous ways. In democratic societies it is often ambivalent, at least when the primary aim of a social movement in relation to the state is to influence its policies through political pressure rather than engage in a revolutionary overthrow. On the one hand public criticism of the government is not only important in trying to change its policy on certain issues. It is also a crucial discursive strategy in order to mobilize support for the movement through constructing an oppositional collective identity. Any effective social movement mobilization needs a clear definition of an enemy (or several enemies) in order to be successful. On the other hand, movements may avoid being too confrontational in relation to the state as it may damage its possibilities of influencing state policy. This contradiction may also result in a discrepancy between the rhetoric of a movement in relation to the state, and on the other hand the actual practice of key movements organizations – in terms of developing contacts with government officials. Such a contradiction was definitely present both in the British and the Swedish anti-apartheid movement. This being said, it must also be emphasized that there were important differences. While the difference between the two movements' critique of the state was a matter of emphasis, there was a qualitative difference regarding the actual relations of the two movements to their respective states.

The different pamphlets published by the movements in the two countries give the impression that while both movements engaged in sharp criticism of their respective governments and publicized the involvement of British and Swedish industry in South Africa, AGIS put more emphasis on the latter. It thus seems that in the public discourse of British AAM, the state was the major enemy, while in the discourse of AGIS and ISAK, Swedish companies with subsidiaries in South Africa was the main opponent. This is also confirmed by key activists in both Britain and Sweden.[16] Mike Terry argues that this was related to different approaches regarding the role of (leftist) ideology in public campaigning. Although he states that AAM all along clearly was perceived to stand to the left in the political field, and some of its key activists were, or like Terry, had been, members of communist parties, they never saw anti-apartheid as means of mobilizing around the broader issues of anti-imperialism and anti-capitalism:

> What I think may be different from the Africa Groups, was that AAM didn't see itself as a kind of ideological movement, it didn't see its role to educate people in Britain about imperialism, capitalism and the rest of it. You can't escape from some of these issues ... there was a sense to which we saw ourselves as being in a kind of combat with big business, but not because we were against big business, but because that was the logic of the facts that we had.[17]

Considering the policies of the British governments, Labour or Conservative, it was not surprising that the anti-apartheid movement in Britain voiced a strong opposition to the state. For different reasons, criticism was particularly sharp during two administrations: the Labour government 1964–68 and the Conservative government between 1979 and 1990. While opposition in the latter case was fuelled by Margaret Thatcher's firm refusal to give way for the increasing global pressure to impose effective sanctions against South Africa, and her labelling of the ANC as a terrorist organization, the criticism against Labour grew out of a disillusion of its failed promises of a strong anti-apartheid British policy once it came to power. The disappointment was especially strong as Wilson's speech against apartheid in Trafalgar Square was made from the platform of an AAM rally, something that might have earned him some votes. All AAM activists of the 1960s that I have interviewed spoke at great length, and with a strong emotional emphasis, of the feeling of the betrayal of the Wilson government after it came to power in 1964.[18]

Anger was directed at AAM's own president, Barbara Castle, Labour MP. As Castle now became a minister in Wilson's government, she had to resign. A few key activists also demanded that she should be expelled from AAM.[19] Castle had written the foreword to a pamphlet published by AAM in 1963, titled *The Collaborators*. The 31 pages long text supplied detailed information about British economic links with South Africa, and Castle wrote that she 'welcome this pamphlet because it is a mine of information which compels us to face the truth that British firms and British people are profiting from apartheid', and stated that 'In the economic field there can be no such thing as a non-intervention policy towards South Africa'.[20] In relation to this text, the next important pamphlet published by AAM four years later represented a shift of focus regarding the target of critique. In the 27 pages long *Labour's Record on Southern Africa: An Examination of Attitudes Before October 1964 and Actions Since*, the fury against the Labour government felt by many activists was effectively translated into sharp criticism. After reviewing the actual policy of the Wilson government in relation to Southern Africa, it concluded:

> While the Government has continued to declare its dislike of apartheid in South Africa … its actual practice has been to support South Africa economically, politically and morally.[21]

When Castle left the position as President of AAM, David Ennals, Labour MP, who had played an important part in founding the organization, succeeded her. Four years later however, Ennals, who had now become under-secretary of Home Affairs, was addressed in an open letter on the first page of *AA News*, signed by the editorial board, who stated that the Executive Committee of AAM were considering expulsion of Ennals. The reason for this was a controversial Immigrant Act passed by the Labour government. Acknowledging Ennal's importance for the movement, the editorial board stated that, while AAM already 'felt betrayed' by the Wilson government, the Act 'moves us more' than Wilson's policy towards South Africa, because it introduced the 'repugnant doctrine of apartheid' (using Ennal's own words about South Africa) 'into the law of this country'. Being responsible for immigration, and the person who 'having piloted this obnoxious measure through the commons', Ennals was responsible for the fact that Labour once again had 'disabused' AAM.

The letter was an unusual move, since AAM, following its strategy of political minimalism, was always reluctant about taking up issues that was not directly related to the struggle against apartheid. In its Annual Report the following statement was made:

> The Anti-Apartheid Movement is primarily concerned with apartheid and race oppression in South Africa … But the movement cannot ignore racialism in this country. When the Commonwealth Immigrants Act wrote into the statute book the sort of racialist discrimination that is prominent in South African laws, the Movement spoke out.[22]

Moving to the Thatcher era, a crucial AAM text criticizing the government was *A Tiny Little Bit: an Assessment of Britain's Record Against*

South Africa. It was published in July 1986 and was prepared for presentation during the meeting of the Commonwealth's Heads of State and Government in August. It began by pointing to contradictory statements by Margaret Thatcher regarding the importance of the measures against South Africa that the Conservative government had finally agreed on, and the report carefully reviewed the implementations of these measures. The main title, *A Tiny Little Bit*, was a quote from a speech by Thatcher, playing down the significance of the sanctions. This was put against another quote from a speech made by Thatcher in the House of Commons, in which she stated that 'no other (major Western industrialized country) has done more than Britain'.[23] Further, the report argued, Thatcher's contradictory rhetoric was possible because of the conflict on the role of the measures between the parties that had agreed on them. While Thatcher had stated that she regarded them as 'a gesture, a signal to South Africa', the Nassau Accord of the Commonwealth Conference in 1985, during which the measures were agreed on, stated that their purpose was to bring about concrete change through hurting the South African economy. The conclusion of AAM's report was that the British government had failed to implement 'both the letter and the spirit of most of the package agreed by the Commonwealth in Nassau'.[24]

In between these attacks on the British government's policies on South Africa in the 1960s and 1980s, was a sharper focus on the other major British opponent of AAM, the British industry. This is something that, in spite of Mike Terry's statement earlier, should be seen against the background of a stronger turn to the left of AAM in the 1970s – related to the influence of the student movement.[25] The most important document in this regard is a pamphlet titled *The South African Connection*, written by three key activists of AAM, Ruth First, Jonathan Steele and Christabel Gurney. Presenting the first systematic investigation into the role played by British investment in South Africa, it became a central movement text, and was an important source of information and inspiration for investigative journalists like Denis Herbstein and Adam Raphael.[26]

Beyond its public criticism, AAM frequently sought to establish contact with the British governments, something which Mike Terry willingly admits, stating that in spite of 'our rhetoric … we always sought a relationship'. From the 1960s to the 1980s, a number of memoranda was produced, and were supported by correspondence, delegations and meetings. According to Roger Fieldhouse, the organization 'did enjoy considerable access to Government, particularly in the period after 1974'.[27]

There was however an important limit to the interactions with the state. With the only exception of the Labour government's funding of a co-ordinating committee that AAM set up in connection with the UN 'International Year Against Apartheid', AAM never received any government funding.[28] According to several activists that I have interviewed, this was a matter of principle. For example, Bob Hughes, Labour MP and chair of AAM 1976–95, argues that 'we did not actually want state funding, because we wanted to be independent, to be able to criticize whichever government was in power', and Ethel de Keyser states that 'we were reluctant to take funding from any government, because that would have impugned our integrity'. Mike Terry on the other hand, argues that this principle was not about being against governmental funding as such, but about not taking money from a government who was perceived to support apartheid actively. 'It would have been a different matter if the British government policy could clearly have been described as being anti-apartheid ... then I think there would have been a debate in AAM'.[29] In any case, the approach, and actual practice, of AAM regarding state funding was in sharp contrast to that of AGIS.

Ambivalent relations: the state as friend and foe

Relations between the anti-apartheid movement and the state in Sweden were close from the beginning to the end. The Swedish government set up the CCHA in 1964, which became instrumental for the channelling of financial support to the Southern African liberation movements, as well as to Swedish solidarity organizations. Representatives of movement organizations and opinion leaders were invited to the committee.[30] Even though individuals from the two central solidarity organizations in the 1970s and 1980s, AGIS and ISAK, were never invited to the committee, they received funding from SIDA. SIDA also recruited activists, who became civil servants, in some cases actually preparing meetings where the decisions on the support to the liberation movements in Southern Africa were made. The most likely reason as to why AGIS and ISAK did not have representatives in the CCHA is that they were being perceived as standing too close to the communist left.[31] As part of a Cold War policy of the Swedish government, whether Social Democratic or non-socialist, the Swedish Communist Party was excluded from all-parties parliamentary committees that dealt with Swedish foreign policy issues, including the CCHA, whose minutes were protected from public insight by the Official Secrets Act.

An example clearly displaying the closeness between AGIS and the government, is the communication between AGIS and Maj-Lis Lööw, Social Democratic Minister of Trade in 1985, when the latter was preparing a boycott legislation regarding trade with South Africa. First, it seemed as such a boycott would be against the rules of the GATT Agreement. However, AGIS found out about an exception in GATT, contacted Lööw and informed her that Article XX allowed for boycotts against countries using products of prison labour. This piece of information influenced and probably speeded up the legislative process.[32]

The close contacts and the government funding did not prevent AGIS and ISAK from a harsh and persistent criticism of the government through the years, also after the legislation against new investments by Swedish companies in South Africa in 1979, and the boycott legislation in 1987. In my interviews with key activists in AGIS, there is however a certain degree of ambivalence in the reflections on the relations to the Swedish government. As AGIS had anti-imperialism on its agenda and the main opponents thus, at least programmatically, were the imperial powers, the criticism of the Swedish government was framed in this context. According to key activist Mai Palmberg (see Chapter 1), this analysis created a bit of a problem when AGIS put an effort to be a driving force in the context of the broader Swedish anti-apartheid movement:

It was pretty obvious that the (Swedish) government was part of Swedish imperialism, that it was not just the corporations. But of course we could try to see it that way, that it was just the Swedish companies, particularly those in South Africa, and we didn't really have any big problems there, to argue for ourselves and for our members that we were against the Swedish companies presence in South Africa.

Magnus Walan, anti-apartheid journalist and key activist both in AGIS and ISAK from the late 1970s onwards, admits that there where moments when he had doubts about the government funding:

I remember that I saw a table displaying the increasing Swedish trade with South Africa, the figures actually paralleling those of the support of the Swedish government to the victims of apartheid. Then I started to think, is it a coincidence, or ...? So, indeed the government support was also an attempt to tone down the criticism, that is something that I don't think has been made clear in the historical records so far.

The 'image of respectability' versus
the 'consensus culture' of the People's Home

According to centrally placed AAM activists of the early 1960s, a fundamental element in the construction of AAM's identity was the image of
respectability.[33] This was what the recruitment of MPs, actors, playwrights
and academics entirely was about.[34] This strategy was also evident in its
election of presidents. While the first presidents in the 1960s were
Labour MPs, later on they were churchmen, such as Ambrose Reeves,
Bishop of Johannesburg (1970–80) and then Trevor Huddleston,
according to journalist Victoria Brittain 'an incredibly respectable
reverend ... a really difficult character to deflect'.[35] Dorothy Robinson,
AAM activist of the 1960s, states that creating an image of respectability
was a strategy related to media attention:

> It's the way that politics works here, that you try to rope in people to
> your cause. You also need grass roots of course, but it's just this thing
> that the press have, of wanting names, they are not interested in a
> resolution from a trade union branch.

Thus, recruiting 'respectable' celebrities was a well-established strategy
in the context of British political culture, going far back in movement
politics. For example the MCF was largely associated with Fenner
Brockway, a well-known Labour MP. Other anti-colonial campaigns,
such as the campaign against King Leopold II's colonial project in the
Congo, or the Abolitionist Campaign, did use the recruitment of
respectable personalities as a strategy to mobilize.

When the student generation entered the movement during the late
1960s, demanding that AAM engage in more radical, extra-parliamentary
action, it clashed with the cultivation of the image of respectability. While
many centrally placed AAM activists unofficially approved of direct
action during the Stop the 70s tour, officially AAM put a lot of effort to
draw a sharp demarcation line in relation to the practice of direct action.
As Ethel de Keyser puts it, in relation to the militant activists 'we were
respectable, we were the sober face ... we wanted to keep our MPs with
us'.[36] It is also important to emphasize that there was also an economical
aspect to the image of respectability, since it was crucial for AAM to
engage in fundraising, which to a large extent supported its activities.[37]

This is in sharp contrast to a dominant tradition of Swedish movement
culture, characterized by both anti-elitist and puritan values. Twentieth-
century Swedish political culture was to a large extent defined by the

broad wave of popular movements that started to emerge in the late nineteenth century and was integral to the process of Swedish industrialization. Three partly intersecting movements, the free church movement, the temperance movement and the worker's movement managed to mobilize a significant part of the Swedish population, a process that culminated politically in 1932, when the Social Democrats began their long reign. Staying in power for 44 years, its construction of the Swedish welfare state was firmly rooted in the political culture of the major popular movements. The concept of the 'People's Home', as articulated by SDP leader Per-Albin Hansson in the 1930s, was the crucial node in the political discourse through which Social Democracy gained its legitimacy as a people's (rather than just a worker's) party. Through the practice of creating procedures for consulting movement representatives, as well as organized talks with major Swedish business leaders, it facilitated the emergence of a political culture of consensus. The strong position of the old movements during the post-war era, including its close ties with the government, did not leave much space for the emergence of new political initiatives – this is an important reason for the relative weakness of new social movements in Sweden in terms of popular participation. As new movements did emerge, the inclusive strategy of the government undermined the possibilities of constructing a sharp border between movements and the state. The other side of the coin is however that while public participation in new social movements in Sweden – in comparison to other West European countries – has been weak, new movements have nevertheless had a relatively strong influence on government policy.[38]

Thus, although they were making a strong effort to put distance to the old movements, the new social movements in Sweden were heavily imprinted by the consensus culture of the People's Home. Many key anti-apartheid activists came from families rooted in the old movement culture. Church activists often had links to missionaries of their parent generation. While many young activists were students, they were often class travellers. While a family background in the worker's movement was regarded as 'high status' in the leftist movement culture, those with links to the free church movement did however feel that they better be silent about this background.[39] AGIS activist Mai Palmberg states that 'many years after I started to be active in AGIS, I was almost shocked when I realized how many of my comrades that came into solidarity work via the church or the mission'.[40]

In spite of the fact that the emergence of the new social movements was part of the youth revolt celebrating 'sex, drugs and rock "n" roll', the puritan values of the old movement culture had a strong influence on Swedish youth activism in the 1970s. In a study of the movement culture of the Swedish anti-Vietnam movement, which shared the same activist base as the anti-apartheid movement at the time (see Chapter 6), historian Kim Salomon shows that there was a strong emphasis on a certain form of 'moral education', which is clearly a heritage of the old social movement culture.[41] The influence of the temperance movement was particularly evident in the strong rule of sobriety. This was true also for AGIS, in which some of the leading activists were abstainers.

The 'old movement' rule of temperance became one of the aspects composing a commitment to a radical form of 'life politics' characteristic of new social movement culture. Its major code was the moral obligation to be active in as many aspects of your life as possible. Thus the fundamental code of this form of life politics implied that you showed your degree of commitment to the solidarity cause through spending as much of your time as possible in the context of the movement, engaging in a *activism as a form of life*.

In AGIS of the 1970s, the educational approach to activism was manifested through the rule that before you could become a member of the organization, you must participate in a study circle where you read and discussed texts presenting AGIS' view on the history and present situation in Southern Africa.

Although it might be argued that the norm of activism as a form of life implied a certain form of elitism (relatively few people could be active to the extent that was expected), AGIS nevertheless strongly emphasized anti-elitism. This norm, which was also a heritage from the old movement culture, meant that during a period in the 1970s, AGIS did not select a chairperson.[42] Further, articles written by members in the movement magazine, *Afrikabulletinen*, were not undersigned, a practice that was not just related to anti-elitism, but was motivated in terms of a socialist anti-individualism.

In the interaction with the British AAM, Swedish activists schooled in the Swedish movement culture sometimes felt estranged when they were invited to meetings with the British AAM in which the celebrities of the movement were present. AGIS activist Kerstin Bjurman remembers being astonished by the high society at AAM meetings she was invited to:

> They had so many lords and countesses, people of high society, as cocks of the walk in the organization you know, and they had a lot of grey haired ladies at the meetings who were having their hanky-panky

with the Archbishop. But I think because Trevor Huddleston initiated it, they were based at another level from the start. Here it rather emerged from grass roots and Social Democracy ... But I don't know what their grass roots work looked like.

When juxtaposing AAM's image of respectability with the popular consensus culture of the Swedish anti-apartheid movement, it is important to emphasize that we are talking about a difference in the context of key organizations and their public image. In spite of an emphasis of the public display of celebrities, and although AAM might have been perceived as hierarchical and centralist in its organization, it also developed into a broad grass roots movement, with local branches all over Britain. It peaked in the late 1980s, reaching 184 local groups and 14,000 members in 1990 (to be compared with AGIS, who at the same time had 33 local groups and ISAK, who had 10).[43] Regarding membership however, neither AAM, nor AGIS could be considered to be a 'mass movement'. It was only in the late 1980s that AAM's membership rose above 7,000–8,000, peaking in 1987–88 with 18,000. As mentioned, although membership of AGIS also rose steadily, it never reached far above 2,000. As Paul Blomfield, who co-ordinated local government action in Britain on behalf of AAM explains, rather than putting a strong effort on recruiting members, the strategy of AAM was rather to construct 'invisible networks of every-day-life' typical for the new social movements:

> What was important was to develop an infrastructure, a network that was able to respond quickly when South Africa grabbed the headlines.[44]

Beyond these intensified moments, this network also had an element of every-day activism to it, as it consisted of people who supported anti-apartheid through mainly expressive acts such as boycotting South African goods and spreading the message through wearing AA badges and T-shirts. This movement strategy, which was also embraced by AGIS and ISAK, is built on a relation between two forms of life politics, representing different degrees of commitment. The core activists engaging in activism as a form of life, organizing campaigns, boycotts and demonstrations, facilitates the life style politics of the people who could not be regarded as activists, but nevertheless are part of the movement through various forms of expressive every-day action.

Bearing the popular base of AAM in mind it is still highly relevant to contrast the image of respectability to the (anti-elitist) political culture of consensus because these two differences in movement culture did also have economic and political implications. Just as the image of respectability was important for AAM's fundraising, AGIS' embeddedness in the Swedish political culture of consensus meant possibilities to receive government funding (which was an important economic source for both AGIS and ISAK), as well as a close relation to government officials. For AGIS, being part of the political culture embracing anti-elitism thus paradoxically meant being close to the Swedish political elite.

During the 1970s, AAM became more oriented towards anti-elitism, as it under the influence of the values of the student left tended to play down the image of respectability. In connection with the Stop the 70s Tour, which marked the break-through of the influence of the student movement in AAM, an issue of tension arose between a number of key activists of AAM and Peter Hain, member of AAM and leader of the campaign against the tour of the South African cricket team (see Chapter 6). The shared feeling in the inner circles of AAM was that as Hain emerged as a public personality through the campaign, the role of AAM was not sufficiently recognized, neither by the media nor by Hain himself.[45]

As the influence of the New Left on the new social movement culture in Europe ebbed out during the 1980s, AAM reinforced its image of respectability through a number of media strategies (see Chapter 4). When AGIS initiated the forming of ISAK in 1979, it was part of the same process of change.

Conflicting agendas

While engaging in the relations of the transnational anti-apartheid movement also meant getting involved in its tensions and conflicts, there were also relations and tensions that were specific to the national contexts. In the following, I will briefly bring up a number of particularly relevant relations and conflicts that AAM and AGIS were engaged in, in relation to (1) each other (2) the liberation movements in South Africa (3) the labour movements (4) the domestic anti-racist movements and (5) groups of the New Left.

International networking was a strategy high on the agenda of the anti-apartheid movements in both Britain and Sweden. According to centrally placed activists in the international network, the British, the Dutch and the Scandinavian anti-apartheid organizations were the most active in Europe.[46] Relations between the British and the Swedish anti-apartheid movements were also established at an early stage. A key person facilitating contacts betwen Britain and Scandinavia was Abdul Minty, founder member of AAM and for long periods based in Oslo as the director of the World Campaign Against Nuclear Collaboration with South Africa. The leading role of AAM internationally was however at times a source of tension. AAM Executive secretary Mike Terry states that 'I think that the British movement ... would be put sociologically in a kind of hegemonistic role over the solidarity movement, it's not true, but it was perceived as playing that kind of role'. AAM did however sometimes contribute to this image. For example, in the foreword to AAM's widely distributed pamphlet *Labour's Record on Southern Africa*, its President David Steel, Labour MP, wrote that 'the Anti-Apartheid Movement in Britain and throughout the world remains the only effective rallying point for men and women of all political parties and of more, who believe in the essential equality of man and the creation of multi-racial societies'. Swedish activists who went to the international meetings no doubt perceived AAM's role as 'hegemonistic', or even, as one AGIS activist put it, 'imperialistic'.[47]

For example, when AGIS and ISAK put forth criticism of the Swedish government on the transnational arena, it became an issue of tension with AAM. According to the Swedish activists, this was because the Swedish criticism contradicted the strategy of AAM to refer to the Scandinavian governments as examples of Western governments with a strong anti-apartheid policy. Mike Terry's perception of the tension between AAM and the Swedes is however a bit different:

> I think the tension was a slightly different one, I don't remember it being a major issue, but we would tend to hold up the Swedish example as something to say, look, Sweden is doing this, why can't you do this and then, the Swedish groups, with their press on their government, then their government would turn around and say, but look we are being praised by Trevor Huddleston or Abdul Minty or Bob Hughes or Mike Terry.

It might be argued that tensions between AAM and AGIS/ISAK partly were related to the fact that the Swedish anti-apartheid movement had aspirations similar to the British in the transnational network. The influence of the latter at international meetings was however rather marginal. AGIS activist Sören Lindh argues that during the international meetings in London, there was an informal hierarchy between the solidarity organizations:

> There was very clearly an A-team and a B-team ... and we most often belonged to the B-team, although we, in terms of knowledge and resources ... felt that we belonged to the A-team.[48]

Regarding relations and tension in relation to the liberation movements, AAM formally recognized both the ANC and the PAC. In practice however,

AAM's relations with the two organizations were fundamentally different. The ANC was instrumental in forming AAM, and the two organizations continued to work closely for the whole period of the anti-apartheid struggle. Tension between AAM and the PAC became public as early as 1965, when the PAC published a memorandum in which it criticized AAM for engaging in an ineffective boycott, claiming that AAM did not recognize the armed struggle and did not protest effectively against the Labour Government's continued export of arms to South Africa. In its response AAM emphasized that it 'deeply regrets' that the PAC had decided to criticize AAM in public, something which 'play into the hands of the opponents of the Anti-Apartheid Movement', nevertheless ending its statement that it hoped for 'a new period of cordiality and co-operation'.[49] A distance between the PAC and AAM however continued, and when the BCM emerged in the 1970s, AAM failed to establish contacts, mainly because it perceived BCM to represent the same kind of Africanism as the PAC.

The core anti-apartheid activism in London was however performed through a division of labour between the ANC, AAM and IDAF, particularly regarding media work (see Chapter 4). Most tensions between the two organizations were related to their interdependency, defined by the ANC's need for a British organization to mediate their message to a British public through providing a national platform, and by AAM's need of good relations with the liberation movements for its legitimacy as a solidarity organization. According to AAM activist Margaret Ling, representatives of AAM felt that the ANC sometimes did not respect its autonomy, while representatives of the ANC sometimes felt that they were being patronized in a way much too familiar. Ling still thinks it was 'a healthy kind of tension' – it did mean that both organizations had to learn to how to deal with actual social and cultural conflicts.

An important difference between AAM and AGIS regarding the relationship to the South African organizations was that AGIS, and the whole anti-apartheid coalition that united under the umbrella of ISAK, gave sole recognition to the ANC (just as the Swedish government did). The decision was taken without much controversy by AGIS – only a few maoists and trotskyists argued that the PAC should also be supported.[50] The lack of serious conflicts around this issue was related to an informal 'division of solidarity work' between the different leftist factions in the Swedish new social movement culture – while the maoists focused on Asia, the trotskyists were strong on Latin America, while Southern Africa was the area mainly taken care of by groups standing close to the Swedish Communist Party.

Swedish political activists' international contacts with liberation movements in Southern Africa were initiated in the 1950s in the context of the different political youth internationals. Here Social Democrats, including Olof Palme, and also Liberals, made contacts and established long lasting friendships with African youth leaders (that later became leaders of the liberation movements). The fact that these contacts had been established early made it easy for the ANC to communicate with the political elite in Sweden.[51] This network, and the support of the Swedish government to the ANC from the 1970s, was a reason for the ANC to show a strong interest in Sweden, manifested in the opening of a mission in Stockholm in 1974.

After the initial controversy between AGIS and the ANC, a working relationship similar to that of AAM/ANC was established.[52] The relationship included similar tensions as in Britain, but a particular tension between AGIS and the ANC was related to the latter's close relations to the Swedish government. For example, AGIS felt that while they at a certain moment were encouraged by the ANC to criticize the Swedish government for the inefficacy of its ban on investment, at a later stage they found out that the ANC had had informal talks with the Swedish government, in which the Swedish policy was approved of.[53]

The worker's movement and the legacies of socialism/communism

As we saw in Chapter 1, there were tensions between the Africa Groups and the wider labour movement in the early 1970s. In the late 1970s however, as part of the new strategy of initiating the broad ISAK umbrella, a strong effort was made to 'make peace' with the labour movement.[54] Following this, co-operation with LO on a campaign did happen and relations were stabilized between AGIS and the unions. Unions affiliated to LO did however never join ISAK, and the conflict on isolation would continue to be a hotly debated issue, particularly as the Metal Union would continue to be strongly opposed to the call for isolation of South Africa.[55]

Just as in Sweden, there were tensions between AAM and the British labour union movement, because of the latter's reluctance to support sanctions, partly because of its membership in the ICFTU, and partly because of the potential conflict between sanctions and national jobs. Adding to this were differences in political culture; according to Christabel Gurney the TUC largely saw 'apolitical, economistic British-style trade unionism as the only legitimate model'.[56] Relations were particularly difficult in the 1970s, especially after the TUC in 1973 sent a delegation to South Africa, producing a report which acquiesced in investment in South Africa by companies which could show that they were encouraging the growth of trade unions. According to Mike Terry, AAM perceived the report as the beginning of 'the code of conduct approach'.[57]

AAM did however from the start make strong efforts to get the large labour unions on board, forming a trade union committee in 1968. And in comparison they were much more successful than their Swedish counterparts. As early as in 1964 AAM had 25 trade union affiliations at local or national level and in 1990, 665 trade union branches/regions were affiliated.[58] The 1980s marked a breakthrough, especially after the main labour organization, the TUC, changed its policy to support economic sanctions in 1981.[59] This process was facilitated by the fact that there now was a common and well-defined enemy; when AAM became a platform of anti-Thatcherism, the labour unions seemed to become more interested in getting involved in AAM's campaigns.[60] While AAM because of its alignment with the ANC had close relations to SACTU (which was affiliated to WFTU), the forming of the UDF and COSATU in the 1980s also helped, because it meant that there were now possible partnerships in South Africa beyond Cold War tensions of communism/anti-communism.

While AAM and AGIS both had links to communist parties, they chose different ways to deal with marxism as an ideological influence, at least until the early 1980s. After its initial skirmishes with the ANC, AGIS managed to avoid the serious factional conflicts that characterized leftist movement culture. Though AAM largely avoided such tension during the 1970s, it got involved in a conflict that created a serious division in the context of the broader anti-apartheid movement during the early 1980s. The conflict centred on the City of London Anti-Apartheid Group (CLAAG), dominated by the Trotskyist Revolutionary Communist Group (RCG). Supported by the ANC, AAM's national committee withdrew its recognition of CLAAG in February 1985.[61] This 'banning' of CLAAG from AAM has a touch of irony to it, as a number of people living in Britain that I have spoken to have stated that what most people think about when AAM is mentioned, is the non-stop picket outside the South Africa House in Trafalgar Square during the 1980s. The picket, which was organized by CLAAG, started on the 25 August 1982. If it was not completely non-stop for the next years, it was upheld regularly, and a non-stop vigil did finally take place between April 1986 and February 1990. CLAAG was formed in March 1982 and immediately took the role as a force of internal opposition within AAM, challenging its strategy of political minimalism. CLAAG activists argued that the anti-apartheid struggle could not be separated from wider issues of anti-imperialism, anti-racism and anti-capitalism (a perspective manifested in the title of the RCG newspaper *Fight Racism, Fight Imperialism*), and that the anti-apartheid struggle, contrary to the belief underlying AAM's one-issue strategy, would benefit from a broadening of the issue. Further it criticized AAM's image of respectability and its commitment to legal protest methods, advocating a turn to direct action and civil disobedience.

If the conflict had an important element of a factional leftist ideological battle typical of the 1970s (in this respect it came surprisingly late), it also emerged at the border between on the one hand respectable and legal methods for gaining political influence in the context of national politics and on the other hand the extra-parliamentary activism of direct action and civil disobedience that was a significant aspect of new social movement action.

Dealing with diversity

A tension that British AAM was facing to a much larger extent than the Swedish anti-apartheid movement was related to the issue of domestic racism/anti-racism, and the lack of a significant involvement of the black British community in AAM. For example Jack Jones, former General Secretary of the Transport and General Worker's Union (TGWU), argues that part of the reason for the unions' reluctance to fully support the anti-apartheid struggle was that there was a deep seated racism in the British labour movement.[62] AAM did however, after its public criticism of the Immigration Act in 1969, chose not to get involved in the broader British anti-racist movement that started to emerge in the late 1970s. As suggested by a working party set up by AAM's Annual General Meeting, this strategy was an important reason as to why there was a low degree of involvement of black and Asian people at grassroots level in AAM.[63] This view was confirmed in 1989 in an internal ANC paper, which stated that black communities would not support AAM because they perceived the organization as 'run by white people for white people'.[64] Roger Fieldhouse suggests that the problem partly was related to AAM's hesitation to engage in direct action, as black and Asian activists seemed more attracted to the more militant movement culture committed to direct action.[65] This argument is supported by the fact that one of the most important occasions when a significant and highly visible participation of black people in the anti-apartheid struggle occurred, was the direct action campaign against the Springbok rugby and cricket tours in 1969 and 1970.

In Sweden, domestic racism as a political issue, and anti-racism as a significant movement, came much later, during the early 1990s. This anti-racist movement definitely brought changes to the Swedish new social movement culture, as one of its most visible elements was a new, young and militant anarchist faction, combining anti-apartheid direct actions in which Shell petrol stations were bombed, with a militant anti-fascist struggle, sometimes violently played out in the streets of the big cities. This new anti-racist movement was part of the first political generation in Sweden during the post-war era that completely dissociated itself from the political culture of consensus of the People's Home. The militant attacks against the Shell petrol stations caused the youth wing of Folkpartiet (the Liberal Party) to leave ISAK in 1989 because it claimed that ISAK was not being firm enough in condemning these attacks in their campaign against the company's involvement in South Africa.[66] Mainly due to the generation gap, and ISAK's strategy of political minimalism, no significant links were however established between the anti-apartheid movement and the anti-racist movement.

Another tension related to the organization of the national anti-apartheid movements. According to Roger Fieldhouse AAM's tendency of organizational centralism restricted the autonomy of the special committees that were formed to deal with the representation of particular groups in the movement, such as the Women's Committee, the Multi-Faith Committee and the Black and Ethnic Minorities Committee.[67] The effects of efforts of constructing a de-centralized organization in both AGIS and ISAK were also limited, as many local activists felt that they did not really know what was going on at the central level of the organization.[68] Thus, although it is important to emphasize that in both countries there was a significant, and for the impact of the movement very important, degree of activity at local levels, local activists felt a low degree of influence concerning the decisions and policies at a central level. According Margaret Ling, one of the activists that initiated AAM's Women's Committee, the tension central/local was also a gender issue:

> If you looked at the top leadership of the movement, it was rather male, whereas if you looked at the local groups, you found that who was actually doing the work, who were the secretaries of local groups, they were often women, so that committee was concerned about that.[69]

When the gender issue was in focus of the solidarity organizations, it was more an issue of focusing on the South African women, including their social situation and their participation in the struggle, than of focusing on internal gender relations.

Conclusion: radical or respectable?

How should one account for the differences between the anti-apartheid movements in Britain and Sweden? The explanation of social movement action in a national context offered by the theory of political opportunity structures (POS) emphasize (1) the relative openness or closure of a political system (2) the role of elite alignments and (3) elite allies.[70] First, the Swedish political system was clearly more open to influence on this issue. Second, alignments between economic and political elites were tighter in Britain, particularly during periods of Conservative rule. Third, while movements in both countries had elite allies, the allies of the Swedish anti-apartheid movement were closer to state power. All of these factors thus indicate that the political climate in Sweden made it easier for the Swedish anti-apartheid movement to have an influence on state policy. It might be argued that the anti-apartheid policy of the Swedish State was a result of pressure from the anti-apartheid movement. However, an anti-apartheid policy was already emerging when the Swedish anti-apartheid movement got on its feet.

Another assumption made by POS theory is that transnational networks primarily emerge when national political institutions are closed to social movement activists.[71] However, Swedish anti-apartheid organizations were involved in frequent transnational networking in *spite* of the oppenness of Swedish political institutions. While I have argued that national identity implicitly played an important role in the context of solidarity mobilization in Britain and Sweden, this example shows that the political structure of the nation state cannot be taken as a self-evident point of departure for the analysis of anti-apartheid action. As *national political structures* do not provide a sufficient explanation for the character of the anti-apartheid movements in Sweden and Britain, I have emphasized the role influence of both historically instituted *national political cultures* and the influence of *transnational processes*.

A significant difference between the two movements is the role of civil disobedience/direct action. While this was an important, although far from uncontroversial, element of the broader British anti-apartheid movement it was not the case in Sweden (with the exception of the protests against the tennis game between Sweden and Rhodesia in 1968, see Chapter 6). In Britain, there was a relatively strong tradition of civil disobedience of the 'old social movement culture' – also with significant transnational links – going back to the anti-colonial and suffragette struggle. It might be argued that the low degree of use of direct action after 1968 in Sweden might be explained by the fact that it was not needed considering the anti-apartheid policy of the Swedish government from the 1970s onwards. However, the influence of the old Swedish social movement culture also played an important role, as it sharply dissociated itself from such action during the post-war era, something that partly could be explained by its close relations to the Social Democratic government.

Two previous studies on British AAM have put forth different opinions regarding the importance of its extra-parliamentary actions – one emphasizing AAM's new social movement tactic of extra-parliamentary action, the other arguing that AAM was basically engaged in 'legitimate, conventional, normal political pressure within the framework of the political establishment'. I would argue that the British anti-apartheid movement was defined by *the use of a double strategy of acting both on the outside and on the inside of the established political system* – a highly significant characteristic of new social movement politics. If there was tension and conflict between the two approaches, they could nevertheless be seen as complementary. While AAM as a key SMO indeed was hesitant regarding direct action, it was an important dimension in the context of the broader British anti-apartheid movement in which AAM was the key organization. While any social movement could be composed of a number of internally different SMOs, the existence of more militant SMOs often strengthen the possibilities of negotiation and influence of SMOs considered to be more 'moderate'.[72] Further, as I have showed, in the case of British AAM, activists consciously calculated on this as they informally supported direct action while officially denying this.

In the introductory chapter, I argued that new social movements in Western Europe partly emerged under the influence of the anti-colonial struggle. While it is reasonable to conclude that the anti-apartheid movements in both Britain and Sweden were located at the intersection between the old and the new, British AAM was clearly more imprinted by the new social movement culture, something which partly can be explained by the fact that from the beginning to the end it had closer connections to the anti-colonial movements.

The two movements did however share an emphasis on another defining aspect of new social movement politics – media orientation. This crucial dimension of anti-apartheid action will be the subject of Chapter 4.

4
The Struggle over Information and Interpretation

It is my personal belief that there has been no other liberation movement in modern history that has coincided with the media revolution in such a way and exploited it, and used it, sometimes accidental, certainly initially accidental, but waking up alongside that.

Tariq Mellet (Patric de Goede), ANC

Every political movement, it's success or failure, is dependent on what sort of coverage it gets in the media. It's different from a repressive society, but you are dependent to get your message across.

Bob Hughes, AAM, Labour Party

So your question is really, what did we do, what was our strategy? I think that certainly to cultivate particular journalists, which we did, quite effectively.

Ethel de Keyser, AAM

Introduction: the importance of media and information

During the period of the international anti-apartheid struggle, anti-apartheid activists all over the world came to realize the increasing importance of media work in order to mobilize national public opinion and influence governments. British AAM developed contacts with journalists working for large established newspapers, such as *The Sunday Times*, in the early 1960s.[1] If many other organizations came later, it is fair to say that in the 1980s, media work dominated the activities of most anti-apartheid organizations outside of South Africa.

Media work was not just important in relation to *national* public opinion and *national* politics. As shown in Chapter 1, it was a key factor in facilitating transnational anti-apartheid communication and mobilization.

In 1965, AAM started to produce *AA News*, which was distributed internationally. The ANC started to develop a conscious media politics in the early 1970s, when the Department of Information and Publicity, headed by Thabo Mbeki, was set up in London. I would even argue that the emerging global success of the ANC in the late 1980s, which was extraordinary in relation to other liberation movements in Southern Africa, was partly due to the fact that they – and the organizations that were working closely with them – came to understand the importance of media work.

One extremely important media strategy of the ANC was to broadcast anti-apartheid radio programmes that reached people living in South Africa. In the late 1970s, the ANC was given time by radio stations in Tanzania and Zambia. Later, the organization received facilities at a powerful station in Ethiopia and the broadcasts were then named Radio Freedom. In the late 1980s, Radio Freedom had five different radio stations broadcasting short-wave programmes to South Africa – except for the one in Addis Abeba also Luanda, Dar Es Salaam and Lusaka.[2] Radio Freedom was an important part of the underground media that gave the ANC a presence inside the country in spite of the fact that the organization was banned, and that its leadership was either in prison or in exile. Several activists that I have interviewed testifies that Radio Freedom was an extremely important factor in keeping the ANC alive in the minds of the black population during the long period of its exile. Nceba Faku was one of the activists in the mid-1970s who was politicized through the Black Consciousness Movement:

> I was not a member of the ANC, but the underground media of the ANC, mainly the Radio Freedom, was the kind of media that we would listen to. It was even banned to listen to Radio Freedom, but that was our source of information.[3]

For the PAC, the lack of a radio station like Radio Freedom was a great disadvantage to the organization when trying to recruit new members in South Africa, particularly during waves of mobilization like the Soweto uprising.[4]

In the context of the anti-apartheid movement inside South Africa, media was not just crucial as a channel for receiving messages and information from the outside world. Just as important was to let the outside world know about what happened inside the country through international media. Reports on the oppression of the apartheid state, and the resistance against the system, be it 'underground' or from the within prison walls, formed an important part of transnational anti-apartheid communication and mobilization. Mandela biographer and anti-apartheid journalist Anthony Sampson emphasizes that in South Africa, getting a message across the borders to the outside world was perceived as extremely important, particularly by those activists that were most isolated:

> For the leaders in Robben Island, as they have explained it to me, that was almost the most important part of the struggle, to keep their situation, their problems known in the outside world.[5]

It was only in 1976 that television came to South Africa, the broadcasts of course strictly controlled by the government. However, a few programmes broadcast live on South African Broadcasting Corporation (SABC) learned the apartheid government that the content, and the interpretation, of a visualized media like television might be more difficult to control than newspapers and radio broadcasts. This was for example the case when anti-apartheid protesters in New Zealand stopped the live broadcast rugby match against South Africa (see Chapter 1).

Thus, television was no doubt one of the factors that made it increasingly difficult for the South African government to fence itself off from the outside world. Further, the 1970s was a period when the South African government realized that the anti-apartheid movement was an increasingly *transnational* phenomenon and that its agenda was becoming alarmingly influential in the global media. For example, in 1977 the annual report of the Department of Information stated:

> When the General Assembly of the UN proclaimed on December 14 last that 1978 was going to be the International Anti-apartheid Year, it brought to a climax the worst period of anti-South African publicity and hostility in the country's history.[6]

Apartheid media strategies

As a response to what was perceived as 'a propaganda war against South Africa' led by the anti-apartheid movement, the South African government took action to attempt to control the image of South Africa in international media. Thus they engaged in what James Sanders has called 'a war of representation', referring to 'a struggle for influence between South Africa and the global anti-apartheid movement'.[7] At stake were not only the symbolic representations of 'apartheid' and 'South Africa' and its global political implications. These representations were nodes in a network of contested political concepts, including 'national sovereignty', 'human rights' and a number of other concepts closely associated with the Cold War conflict, such as 'communism/ anti-communism', 'democracy' and 'Western civilization'. The transnational struggle for the representation of apartheid was thus part of the Cold War propaganda battle that ultimately was a contest for global cultural hegemony. In this struggle South Africa was part of the Western bloc.

In the 1970s, under the Minister of Information Cornelius Mulder, the Department of Information undertook a secret information campaign, which shows that the South African government was willing to put in considerable resources to counteract negative images of South Africa in international media. Between 1973 and 1978, it secretly financed 32 large advertisements in major newspapers in Europe and the United States.[8] They were signed by 'front-organizations' called the Committee for Fairness in Sport (CFS), who protested against the Sports boycott, and the Club of Ten, who argued against anti-apartheid messages put forth by organizations like the UN and the World Council of Churches as well as by newspapers like the *Guardian* (see Chapter 7). Further, the Department of Information did not only try to buy the South African publishing group SAAN and secretly launch an English-speaking newspaper, *The Citizen*; in 1974 an attempt was made to purchase the *Washington Star*. However, the American publisher that was supposed to carry out the operation swindled the Department of Information. Subsequently, when several operations had failed and corruption was revealed by the South African press, the information campaign turned into the public 'Muldergate' or 'Information scandal' and in 1978 the Department of Information was subsumed within the Department of Foreign Affairs.

More successful in influencing international media was the private organization The South Africa Foundation (SAF). The organization was set up as early as in 1959, as a direct response to the founding of the Boycott Movement in Britain. The SAF is frequently mentioned by activists that I have interviewed as a key actor in national and international public spheres where the anti-apartheid information struggle took place.[9] The Foundation set up offices in both London and Washington.

Its strategy was to attract journalists, through defining itself as scholarly, only indirectly defending apartheid, for example through financing advertisements appealing against economic sanctions.

Perhaps more important than these more spectacular attempts to influence international public opinion were the restrictions and regulations that faced any journalist – local or foreign – working in South Africa. There were particular restrictions on foreign journalists. However, since international journalists writing about South Africa, whether they were reporting from inside or outside the country, in most cases had to rely on either the South African press (legal or illegal) or on local journalists, in order to get access to vital information, the apartheid regime's national media strategies were also aimed at the international press.

While the SABC, running the main TV and radio stations, was directly controlled by the government and functioned as the regime's propaganda instrument, Pretoria relied on the more indirect control of imposed 'self-censorship' on South Africa's commercial media, which was largely under white monopoly ownership.[10] The instruments that secured that the commercial media in most cases were delivering the expected 'responsible reporting' were comprehensive and sometimes confusing regulations, banning threats and actual bannings. For example in the wake of the reporting from the Soweto uprising *The World* and *The Weekend World* were banned in 1977. This is not to say that the commercial press never challenged the government. In spite of the fact that South Africa was ruled through dictatorship and that it was imprinted by a 'culture of censorship'[11] it might still be possible to say that there existed a fragile civil society. Michael Lapsley reflects on the issue against the background of his deep involvement with the TRC:

> Even at the height of apartheid what was amazing was that considering the myriad of laws to contain the press, the amount that was published. There was never a major trial that took place and in which allegations about torture were not made and were published ... There were successive bannings of media, but there were always other things that then came up and replaced them, above ground as well as below ground.

During periods of the 1980s 'black' newspapers as *City Press* and *The Sowetan* had a mandate to be fairly critical of certain aspects of apartheid and could even call for the release of Nelson Mandela.[12] Allowing particular press voices to be critical *within certain limits* could of course in itself be seen as a part of Pretoria's media strategy, since it could be used as an attempt to dethrone international criticism of press censorship. Foreign journalists were closely scrutinized before a permission to work in South Africa was issued. Work permits had to be renewed after a certain period. Visits to townships were restricted. Many journalists were banned after writing articles that were critical against the regime. The regime even listed a number of 'Subversive Statements' that foreign journalists were forbidden to transmit or publish.

As the South African regime realized the devastating impact of the televized images of naked police brutality that was broadcast both in and outside of South Africa in connection with the Soweto uprising, it took further measures to cut the flow of images through restricting photographers and journalists reporting protest events. During the uprising the government quickly put out a restriction that forbade journalists to go to the townships in their own cars – approved journalists were offered to travel with police buses in a South African version of 'embedded journalism'.[13]

Influential correspondents of internationally important American and British media, particularly the large news agencies, were definitely obeying the rules and restrictions. Freelance journalist and author Denis Herbstein remembers sitting in a taxi during the summer of the Soweto uprising together with the chief representative of one of the major news agencies, who told him that he had been to South Africa for several years but that he had never been to Soweto.[14] During the 1970s, none of the three major international news agencies, Reuters, Associated Press (AP) or United Press International (UPI) employed any African journalists. Further, major international broadcasters did not open bureaus in South Africa until the SABC launched its broadcasting service in 1976 and provided footage to the international broadcasters.[15] Considering this, it is not an understatement to say that international news to a large extent, and for long periods, were in the hands of Pretoria.

Journalists did of course break the regulations in various ways, but it was a high-risk project; except for official charges for breaking the regulations, harassment of journalists were common. A way for international journalists to avoid being banned was to travel on a tourist visa and write articles 'under cover'. For example AGIS/ISAK activist Magnus Walan also worked as a freelance journalist. During the 1980s, he frequently visited South Africa on a tourist visa, publishing articles in Sweden under the name of 'Herman Andersson'. However, as Walan was aware of, this strategy had its risks and therefore its limits, as he might be used as a tracker by the South African Intelligence. Thus, he avoided visiting key individuals in the underground structures.[16]

The apartheid regime did not only attempt to win the struggle for information through restrictions and regulations. Its various forms of media strategies included attempts to glorify the apartheid system, to frame the reporting of events and to distort the information and the public image of its opponents.[17] In terms of *glorifying the apartheid system*, the regime put a heavy emphasis on portraying the bantustans as territories of 'black self-rule' and 'separate development' as the alternative 'African way' to the threat of communism and tribal conflict.

In terms of *reporting protest events* and violence, an important strategy was the framing of the events in terms of 'black and white', as well as 'black on black'. The strategy of 'black and white' framed protest drama in simplistic polarized scenarios. On the one hand, protesters were presented as extremely violent, as criminals and looters who were not refraining from cruel violence, not only against their 'white enemies', but also against suspected 'black traitors'. On the other side were the SAP (South African Police) and the SADF (South African Defence Force) as the defenders of the civil order using violence to defend themselves and 'innocent citizens' only when no other option was at hand.[18] The frame of 'black on black' constructed political conflicts, violent clashes and (government-supported) massacres occurring between black groups and organizations in tribal terms.

These frames were also intended to influence international media. This was particularly successful in the case with the 'black on black' frame, especially the late 1980s and early 1990s, at the height of the violent conflict between supporters of the ANC and the Buthelezi-led IFP.

In the long run however, the South African government and the supporters of apartheid lost the global struggle for information and representation. The Wembley concerts in 1988 and 1990, broadcast to millions of people all over the world, could be said to symbolize moments when the anti-apartheid movement stood victorious in the global media space (if not yet in South African politics). In the following sections, we will take a closer look at the emergence of the different forms of media activism that made this happen.

Media activism and information networks

Media activism in the context of the anti-apartheid movement involved two main and interrelated *strategies*: (1) Approaching media industries in order to influence their reports and views, or attracting their attention in order to achieve media visibility and thus getting an anti-apartheid message across to the public (2) developing alternative media through producing and distributing information through self-controlled channels. News bulletins, magazines as well as films and videos were produced and distributed to members and sold publicly. The materials of bulletins like *AA News* in Britain (that was also read by activists in other countries) or *Afrikabulletinen* in Sweden, often relied on sources within the movement's transnational information networks. Here, contacts in South Africa established by activists played an important role.

The ultimate aim of the second main strategy was to create an independent platform, an alternative public sphere that would make it possible to address the public directly, thus freeing the movement from any dependence on media industries. However, it nevertheless became closely interrelated to the first strategy; as anti-apartheid activists early in the process of the struggle realized, building up archives of well-researched information material and photographs created an important base for attracting established media.

It is fair to say that the transnational anti-apartheid movement during its final phase had constructed an alternative 'anti-apartheid public sphere', which was part of a larger transnational movement culture. In the late 1980s and early 1990s, anti-apartheid media could even be considered a minor industry in itself, as books, records, videos, films, photographs, posters, leaflets and T-shirts were produced and distributed – and a number of cultural events, including concerts broadcast on television, were organized. By this time, after decades of difficulties to reach out to a wider audience through the established media, there is no doubt that the anti-apartheid movement had, through its informational and media activism, a considerable impact on the ways that apartheid/anti-apartheid was represented by the established international media.

However, rather than being the product of a master plan, this development had been slowly emerging for several decades as the result of the information and media work of thousands of interacting activists and groups in different countries. This activism started on a very small scale and was mainly based on voluntary work and informal networks. In the beginning, information was collected from whatever sources available. For example, when Dorothy Robinson, member of British AAM, gathered information for a pamphlet on British firms with subsidiaries in South Africa in the early 1960s, she went to the Westminster Library in London and copied by hand from a book called *Who owns whom*.[19] At this time, activists in Britain even used material from the South African press that was written up for a British audience, particularly the *Rand Daily Mail*.[20] One of the most important sources of information for the transnational anti-apartheid movement from the early 1960s was the UN Special Committee Against Apartheid. Informal networks from early on could also sometimes include individuals working for governments, who, being sympathetic to the cause, anonymously would provide anti-apartheid media with inside information. For example, according to Bruce Page, *Sunday Times* journalist who volunteered for *AA News*, there was in the early 1960s in Britain an anonymous correspondent, who used to give *AA News* inside information from the government, informally, 'and we used to run if it sounded likely'.[21]

An extremely important component of early anti-apartheid informational activism emerged out of contacts between on the one hand solidarity activists and on the other hand South African activists that either communicated from inside South Africa or were coming into exile.[22] Since the majority of anti-apartheid activists that left South Africa came to Britain, the British anti-apartheid movement became a key node in the transnational information network. In the early 1960s British activists started to interview South African activists on their arrival, some of them movement leaders, like Oliver Tambo and Nelson Mandela, others grass-roots activists with personal stories to tell. Some movement travellers would also bring prisoner's letters from South Africa, a lot of them designed by the prisoner to be published.[23]

The transnational information networks were also crucial for the construction and reproduction of an 'underground public sphere' inside South Africa. In the 1970s a lot of the material made for distribution in South Africa was printed in East Germany. Some material was also produced and printed in London. A dramatic change occurred after 1984, when a bomb blew the ANC headquarters apart, including its printing press. In terms of the ANC's media production, the incident paradoxically became a favour to the organization. New equipment and bigger printing presses were bought with money that to a large extent came from the Swedish government. Compared to the previous facility, the new press made a huge difference; while the small facility did a few thousand sheets at the time, the new facility produced between four and five million sheets in a year. The press in London operated as the main underground printing press for the ANC, producing material that was sent to the frontline states and smuggled into the country.[24]

Information and printed material were also sent with couriers as well as through the mail, and since activists knew that the South African intelligence knew, the materials were seldom sent from the British capital. Barry Feinberg, an exile South African living in London, worked for the 'the internal propaganda committee' of the ANC:

> In some cases we were involving sectors of the anti-apartheid organi-
> zations in illegal work in South Africa. We were producing internal
> propaganda ... and we had to find ways of getting it into South
> Africa, evading the very organized South African postal and police
> response to this .... So we set up groups in Holland, Germany, Italy,
> and so on, and we would travel to them, taking the stuff that we had
> produced and they would parcel it, and it was much easier.[25]

I would argue that this practice of *systematically developing activist networks into informational networks* formed the base and the strength of the
media activism of the anti-apartheid movement. A crucial organization
in these networks was IDAF. As it had stated as a mission to 'keep the
conscience of the world alive to the issues at stake in Southern Africa', a
central aspect of its activities was to collect and produce information
material and making it easily accessible for other anti-apartheid organizations as well as for journalists and the public.[26] In relation to the
media work of other movement groups and organizations, IDAF defined
its own role by emphasizing that its research and information department was tasked to produce material that was clearly distinguished from
'propaganda material'. Its material was also widely distributed and used
not just by British AAM, but also by a number of other organizations
worldwide. The IDAF research, information and publication department
also built up a large archive with films and photographs related to South
Africa and the anti-apartheid struggle. The way that the photographs
were collected underlines the importance of the anti-apartheid activist
network for the informational work; an appeal to the South African
expatriate community was sent out, asking for photos and films.
Further, the ANC photo collection was brought to London from South
Africa. As the material was organized and curated, and the rumour
spread of the growing archive, people around the world spontaneously
started sending material. Eventually around 100,000 photographs were
collected, including historical material of the ANC.[27]

From the beginning, information was collected in connection with
the production of movement print media – pamphlets, brochures, information sheets, newsletters, books and magazines. An early and internationally important initiative was British AAM's production of *AA News*.
According to Ann Darnborough, the AAM of the early 1960s considered
establishing a journal a top priority. Except for the internationally

circulated media, produced by AAM, the UN Special Committee, IDAF, the ANC and a few other organizations, magazines and newsletters were produced and distributed nationally in a number of countries by local anti-apartheid movements. This production was also connected to a kind of *'everyday informational activism'*, which beyond the quickly forgotten news headlines of massacres and riots in South Africa represented a long-term perspective on media and informational work. Activists travelled around the country, giving public lectures and talking to school children, and brought movement media to hand out or for purchase. According to Mike Terry, in a long-term perspective, what was more important than to reach out through established media, was to address a broader social movement based alternative public sphere:

> There was a longer term perspective of building up a consensus among the larger group of people in this country, that apartheid was wrong, that it had to be put down, isolated, you had to support those resisting. And that meant in a way, it was more important to have a good article in say the *Methodist Recorder* than showing on the front page of the *Guardian*, because it would be there today gone tomorrow ... So that kind of long term media strategy I think in the end achieved an awful lot. It wasn't headlines, it wasn't something you reported about, but what it did was that it built up this constituency of support.[28]

This is a view that is also expressed by a number of other activists that I have interviewed: it is the slow and everyday informational work and 'consciousness raising' that is considered as making a difference. However, as Terry adds to the quote, 'it is not to say it was not important to get front-page news', he actually points to a fundamental tension or ambivalence that is present in the media activism of new social movements – that the established media are regarded both as friends and foes. On the one hand, partly because of the fact that the established media are considered as producers of a dominant ideology that is challenged by the movements, and consequently are regarded as biased in their reports on the movements and their issues, movement activists often argue that addressing established media is not particularly important. This approach is, however, often contradicted by the actual practice of highly media oriented action strategies, in fact one of the most important characteristics of new social movement politics.[29]

This tension sometimes gave rise to debates and conflicts within the anti-apartheid movement.[30] However, to argue that this tension is often present in social movement media activism is not to say that there is a necessary and irresolvable contradiction between on the one hand the practices building up alternative media and on the other hand addressing established media.

In the transnational anti-apartheid movement, established media were approached with two major purposes: (a) to influence the reports and views of the established media on what happened in South Africa, and (b) to achieve media visibility for the movement and its issues in the established media, and thus getting an anti-apartheid message across to a wide audience. This was carried out through a number of strategies. There were the institutionalized practices of organizing press conferences, writing letters to the editor – often signed by prominent members – and producing information material designed for journalists. Anti-apartheid activists often publicly critiqued news agencies, questioning the way that they uncritically relied on certain sources in South Africa – with special reference to the above mentioned strategies used by the South African government to plant the 'official version' of events in South Africa. Anti-apartheid organizations also invited journalists, academics and activists to conferences in which the themes focused the structure of the international media and how power relations embedded in these structures influenced the reporting in 'invisible' ways.[31]

Looking at how the anti-apartheid movement achieved influence on the established media, the two most important media strategies were the least conventional, at least at the time when anti-apartheid activism began. First, the most successful strategy in order to influence reports and views in the established media was to develop contacts with professional journalists that were perceived as standing close to the movement. Second, the most effective strategy in order to get visibility in the established media was the construction of political drama, performed through the staging of 'events' in public space, such as 'political happenings', demonstrations or concerts. In the following, we will take a closer look at these two main strategies.[32]

Approaching established media

One of the keys for understanding the relations between the informational activism of the anti-apartheid movement and the established media, is to look into the interaction between the movement and certain individual journalists that were influential in reporting on South Africa. In Britain, AAM established contacts with professional journalists in its early days. Through their contact networks, ANC representative

Raymond Kunene and AAM information officer Anne Darnborough (now Anne Page) managed to pull together a handful of professional journalists to join a meeting at the Pen Club in Fleet Street. The latter explains how AAM at the time looked at the contacts with the professional journalists and on the relation between *AA News* and the established media:

> Occasionally, people wrote something in the established media, and we wanted that, we wanted a spin-off effect. We wanted a collection of information, for the purpose of the members journal to provide a source for ideas and stories for the main stream media, because the point of the exercise was not to produce a newspaper for its own sake, but to get the news on the struggle for a much wider audience.[33]

It is possible to distinguish between different kind of relations between movement organizations and particular individual journalists, but also between the role of the activist and the journalist, as some individuals were performing both at the same time. According to the professional norm of 'objectivity' a journalist should not be representing the interest of any organization in her professional activity. For some journalists standing close to the movement this sometimes posed a dilemma. Others never perceived any such dilemma, feeling that anti-apartheid activism and the journalist profession on a fundamental level shared a commitment to the values of democracy and free speech and an obligation to oppose any force that worked against these values. Still, whatever the personal considerations regarding this issue, there were structural tensions that the anti-apartheid journalist had to face in his/her professional activity. And if s/he wanted to reach out beyond the movement media, these tensions had to be dealt with. How the individual journalist actually dealt with the issue was related to the degree of identification with the role of activism and/or the role of professional journalist, and consequently, in which cultural sphere (the culture of the movement or the one of the professionals) one chose to move most frequently. Four different roles – or positions – of anti-apartheid journalism emerged during the anti-apartheid struggle; *the media activist, the activist journalist, the committed professional journalist and the committed public intellectual.*

Commitment and journalism: in between movement and media

The role of *the media activist* is rather unambiguous; the mission is to serve the cause and to produce what in previous political language was called propaganda. The aim is to get across the movements' message to as many people as possible, either through communicating directly through material produced by the movement, or indirectly, through attracting attention from large media. One example is Danny Schechter, a well-known name to all of those who are familiar with alternative media in the United States. In the 1960s he was one of the founders of the so-called 'yippie movement', which staged spectacular and media oriented actions that became an important part of the public image of the student protests against the Vietnam War.[34] In 1968 he went to South Africa, partly on behalf of *Ramparts Magazine*. Since that journey most of his political activities have been related to South Africa, first and foremost being involved in media work, producing articles, radio and television programmes. Together with Steven van Zandt, guitarist in Bruce Springsteen's E Street Band, he produced the record and video *Sun City*, managing to get 54 well-known artists to participate. *Sun City* was the name of a holiday resort in South Africa, where a number of internationally well-known artists had played for an exclusively white audience, in spite of the cultural boycott. Together with 'Free Nelson Mandela', performed by the British Special AKA, the song became a signature for the transnational anti-apartheid movement's intensified campaign on sanctions against South Africa at the end of the 1980s.

If Schechter started out being a voice mainly speaking from a position *outside* of the established media in the United States, he subsequently tried to establish an alternative voice *within* the world of established media. After forming the media company Globalvision, he produced South Africa Now, which was shown in the United States every week between 1988 and 1991 and was also sold to a number of other countries. This was the reason that Schechter was asked to bring a film team and follow the newly released Nelson Mandela on his world tour in 1990.

Looking at differences between *the activist journalist and the committed professional journalist*, as well as the ambivalences of anti-apartheid journalism, Anders Johansson provides an interesting case. Johansson, born in 1942 in Tidaholm, a small town in the southwest part of Sweden, became active in a local Sydafrikakommitté, one of the first anti-apartheid grassroots organizations in Sweden in 1963. Johansson belonged to the committed activists, writing letters to AAM in London as well as to the UN Special Committee. At the time, he was employed by the local daily *Jönköpingsposten*. Johansson says that at that time he used his 'double role':

It could mean that you wrote a protest appeal, or initiated a campaign, for example getting county councils to boycott South African goods. Then you made sure that there was an article about it in *Jönköpingposten*, and I was also a stringer for TT, Tidnignarnas Telegrambyrå (the largest Swedish news agency, author's remark), so I could write a short paragraph for them, quoting from the article in *Jönköpingsposten*. And not everyone would consider that ethically professional, what you would do as an 'impartial, objective journalist', but I could nevertheless do it for some time.

At a certain point however, he was called to the chief editor, Yngve Hamrin, who was also a Liberal MP and a prominent member of the Alliance Mission, which had activities in South Africa, something that was heavily criticized by the South Africa Committees. Hamrin asked Johansson to keep his roles as activist and journalist separate and finally prevented an article by Johansson to be published. At that time Johansson left *Jönköpingsposten* and a few years later, in 1965, he got a job at the foreign news desk at DN, Sweden's largest daily. If it was possible to manage the 'double role' in a small town context, working at this level meant that Johansson had to quit being an activist. According to Johansson, by this time, he also looked at the 'double role' of being an activist and a journalist a bit different:

I thought it was principally wrong, I had to draw a line, I reckoned I could continue my commitment to Africa in my role as a professional instead.

In the 1970s he began as the paper's Africa correspondent, based in Zambia, in fact the only permanent Swedish news correspondent in Southern Africa. The network that Johansson had built during his activist period became crucial for his work as a professional journalist. Persons in the international anti-apartheid movement that he used to contact as an activist continued to provide him with vital information on South Africa and the liberation movements. Johansson also helped several ANC activists, such as Joe Slovo and Ronnie Kasrils, to publish debate articles in DN and *Aftonbladet*, often written under pseudonyms.

Looking at their articles, or for that matter their views on what they were doing, the perspective of the committed professional journalists need not necessarily be qualitatively different from the activist journalist's. But as professionals they were to a larger extent pressured to deal with the rules, norms and demands that follows with the 'professional code' of journalism. This is evident in the case of Denis Herbstein, born in Cape Town in 1936. Herbstein started his journalistic career at the *Cape Times* in the early 1960s, moving to London in 1968 where he started to work at *The Times*, quickly moving to *Sunday Times* in the same year. Herbstein was never an activist, but a committed anti-apartheid journalist. According to Herbstein, he has never on a personal level felt any conflict between his commitment to the anti-apartheid struggle and his role as a journalist:

> Well I mean there is no such thing as objectivity, you can't be a decent journalist unless you are committed to a cause, there is no doubt about that, and my cause ... what I did hate was racial discrimination, and particularly the vicious form in South Africa, and the fact that I was a Jew also, and as a very young child hearing the verdicts of the Nürnberg trials, I mean these things, you know were obviously influential.[35]

If Herbstein felt that his commitment to anti-apartheid perfectly corresponded to the professional commitment of a journalist in a liberal society, as he perceived it, he nevertheless experienced that his freedom as journalist was not unlimited. At the end of 1975, he went to South Africa to see his family and to do journalistic work. During 1976, Herbstein wrote a number of articles on the Soweto uprising for the British press, until he was finally expelled from South Africa. As he came back to Britain and saw his editor Harold Evans, he did not receive the warm welcome back that he had expected:

> When I came back from South Africa after being expelled, I had spent a year there, in which I had done excellent things for the *Sunday Times*, and for the *Guardian* as well, when I came back to see my editor, Harold Evans, expecting that he would say, Denis you did a great job there, he said you know maybe it's time for you to leave, maybe you should go to the *Observer*. That was a great blow to me, but anyway I didn't, I just went off, took a year off, got paid by the *Sunday Times* and wrote a book (*White Man We Want to Speak to You*, author's remark).[36]

The space of freedom for journalists working in the established media also of course depended on whether they were free-lancers or had a position at an established newspaper – and further, by the political views of the editorial board of the paper. Victoria Brittain is an example of a journalist that was given the opportunity for a kind of activist journalism while working on a large newspaper. Brittain was born in India in 1942 and started to focus her writing on Southern Africa in 1981, as she came to London after six years as a journalist in Northern and Eastern Africa. Brittain became the editor of a page in the *Guardian* called The Third World Review. In the early 1980s she was invited by Mike Terry of AAM to interview the first South African UDF activists who had been allowed to visit Britain after being invited by AAM. This was the starting point of a close relationship between Brittain and the leading anti-apartheid organizations that lasted during the whole of the 1980s:

> I was doing something that I think was quite unusual, and I rather doubt that I would get away with it today, because I wasn't a very prominent journalist, I could be writing all that stuff in the *Guardian*, which I pretty much got away with, and at the same time, speaking on a lot of platforms. And I think that it was generally known that I was very close to a lot of people in the ANC and AAM, SACP and so on, and that I had a lot of information. I think now, when the whole kind of question of journalists' impartiality is quite fashionable, the kind of American model, some idea of journalists being neutral which has begun to catch on also in Britain, I think I might have got a warning, but in fact I never did.[37]

If Victoria Brittain is an example of a professional journalist that was increasingly attracted to the movement to the point where her position is hard to distinguish from that of an activist journalist, and was allowed the space for that, other committed journalists wanted to avoid to stand too close to the movement. The ambivalence regarding the relation between the journalist profession and a commitment to anti-apartheid expressed by certain journalists that I have interviewed was not about restricting themselves in critiquing the apartheid regime. It concerned their relations to the anti-apartheid movement, as many wanted to avoid being seen as mouthpieces for particular anti-apartheid organizations. Several journalists that I have interviewed have argued that a decisive moment for the committed and activist journalists came when acts of ill-treatment, torture and executions in refugee and military camps run by the ANC were revealed.

In between movements and established media, there were also a few individuals that played the role of public opinion-makers, or what I would call *committed public intellectuals*. They were often standing close to the movement, sometimes being part of it, but still saw themselves (and were seen) as independent voices. Although journalism might be their formal profession, and although they were often not active members of anti-apartheid organizations, the position of the committed public intellectual was different from the committed professional journalist, because they first and foremost appeared in public space as spokespersons for the anti-apartheid cause. Even though they were often appearing publicly in a national context, their 'professional activism' was largely transnational, as their books were translated to different languages, and as they travelled extensively. Examples in Britain are British educated authors such as Basil Davidson or Anthony Sampson, or South African exiles such as Nadime Gordimer, or Ronald Segal. The position taken by these individuals in relation to the movement, and the experience of a certain ambivalence, is clearly articulated by the leading committed public intellectual in Sweden, Per Wästberg:

> I first and foremost see my self as a writer, an author and an individualist that has done my own opinion campaign against apartheid, for this purpose trying as much as possible to use newspapers, radio, television, my own books, lectures, speeches all over Scandinavia and in some other countries as well. So I think that the work I have done for organizations has been secondary, especially if you consider the effect. ... It is a feeling of both-and; it is a feeling that moves, from one side to the other. Most often I thought that I, as an individual and a writer, could give support to the movement ... In general, I thought that I could stand up for ANC's politics, although there were elements of that DDR-propaganda machinery.[38]

As we saw in Chapter 1, his support for the ANC did not prevent Wästberg from critiquing the ANC in public when he felt that they were moving too far East. Wästberg got involved with anti-apartheid when he went Rhodesia on a Rotary scholarship in 1959, studying for Terence Ranger in Salisbury. After writing articles in the Swedish press, he was expelled from South Africa in 1959. Wästberg's political commitment to the liberation struggle in Southern Africa led to a number of books and hundreds of articles. Being involved in IDAF, Wästberg also became friends with leading British anti-apartheid public intellectuals. One of them was Anthony Sampson, who was born in England in 1936 and after a period at Oxford University travelled to South Africa in 1951, invited by a friend to help him to run a new 'black' magazine called *Drum*. Reflecting an extremely creative period in South Africa, artistically as well as politically, *Drum* became a leading anti-apartheid voice. For Sampson, it was a period of

> mixing with people of all kinds, black Johannesburg, musicians, artists ... politics was only a part of that, but of course it was a part of

the same movement, the discovery of a black identity, and a hope for a future that was going to bring them a wider world.[39]

He met the people who became the core leadership of the ANC, and made friendships that lasted for decades; eventually trusted to be Mandela's biographer after his release from Robben Island.

The movement as a stage – protest simulacra and the turn to cultural politics

A strategy of political communication very much different from the one of making contacts with the media on a personal level, was a 'dramaturgical approach', a defining aspect of the action repertoire of the new social movements, including the construction of 'protest simulacra'.[40] This strategy implies a visualization and an aesthetizaiton of political action and as a historical phenomenon it is intimately connected to the global media revolution during the post-war era.

In constructing this kind of direct action, the movement in more than any other activity had to mobilize its creative energies, embarking on public performances that would move beyond the boundaries between art and politics. As art and politics fused in the expanding youth culture of the 1960s, many political activists were influenced by performance art, street theatre and the public happenings designed by the Situationists. One of them was Ethel de Keyser, a South African exile and executive secretary of AAM during the 1960s:

> I think our main thrust was to try, if we demonstrated, to do it imag-inatively, to think about the visual impact, which was quite new for us, very very anti this rigid puritanical sort of approach ... We thought of *how* do to things, not just of *what* to do, and that became quite important during my time. So it was a question of *how* you looked, whether you stood outside South Africa house, you stood in a particular way.[41]

The height of the staging of political dramas during Keysers' period as secretary of AAM was the public happening in London on the tenth anniversary of Sharpeville in 1970. On 21 March, which was a Saturday, the shootings at Sharpeville were 'recreated' in Trafalgar Square. The spectator would first see a gathering of South Africans (many of them exiles). Then, a number of men dressed in South African police uniforms appeared, aiming at the protesters with guns; and to the sound of recorded gunshots the protesters fell to the ground. After that, the president of AAM, Bishop Ambrose Reeves, made a speech in which he talked about the acts of the apartheid regime during the past ten years, ending with a call for opposition to the 1970s South African cricket tour and with a demand that Britain break trade and investment links with South Africa. The drama at Trafalgar Square made the first page with large images in three Sunday newspapers in Britain. Further, it was shown on television throughout America and featured by newspapers in Africa, including South Africa.[42]

This event might also be seen as a culmination of the era of the 1960s, a period in which the anti-apartheid movement had made itself attractive to the established media, both through personal contacts and through its expressive movement culture. With the 1970s came a more chilly relationship between the movement and the media. James Sanders characterizes the movement's relationship to the media during the 1970s as contradictory. On the one hand it realized it had to continue to make friends with the media in order to get its message across, on the other it constructed the media as a foe; in a report, the ANC talked about 'imperialist news-media'.[43]

Regarding the relative absence of apartheid/anti-apartheid in the media during the early 1970s Abdul Minty, founder member of AAM, has stated that 'there wasn't publicity because there weren't continuos events' (in South Africa).[44] However, this might not be a sufficient explanation, considering that, during 1969–70 AAM had, in the absence of events in South Africa, managed to create their own events through the campaigns against the tours of South African rugby and cricket teams and the event on Sharpeville day.

There are several reasons for the fact that there was lack of media attention to the apartheid issue and the anti-apartheid solidarity organizations during the first half of the 1970s. First, there is no doubt that events in South Africa, particularly the visibility of the liberation movements, were crucial for the possibilities for the solidarity organizations to get attention. According to Sanders, AAM 'had to attempt to influence a media which between 1972 and 1975 denied that a resistance movement existed, because there was little evidence of ANC activity within the Republic'.[45] The ANC's visibility during the early 1960s culminated in 1964, when news about the Rivonia trial was cabled throughout the world. After Mandela and other leading activists went into jail, the organization disappeared from the headlines. Adding to this, there was the internal crises both in the ANC and the PAC in the late 1960s and early 1970s.

Further, the chilly relations between the movement and the media at this time was also related to the increasing importance of the Cold War frame. If the established media were increasingly inclined to buy in to this frame in the 1970s, it was further strengthened to do so when faced by the anti-apartheid movement's strong turn to the left, and to a rather orthodox marxist analysis of the media, which came in the aftermath of the student movement.

However, things changed dramatically during the 1980s, as the apartheid issue, and the anti-apartheid movement, started to get continuous media attention. This change was related to mobilization and protests in South Africa (the rise of the UDF). But it was also a result of a renewed pro-active media orientation in the context of the anti-apartheid movement.

What on the surface appeared as a higher degree of visibility of the anti-apartheid movement, not just in the media but in public space at large, through the production of imaginative and colourful posters, stickers, badges as well as public demonstrations and actions, was not just the impact of a kind of PR thinking, a product of the 1980s that even had an impact on movement cultures. More important, it was a result of a deeper ideological shift in the context of the anti-apartheid movement. And it was crucial that this process was rooted in the leading liberation movement itself. Leading anti-apartheid activists argued for the re-evaluation of the role of culture in the anti-apartheid struggle. In a situation characterized by a huge gap between the theories that guided the leading core of the movement and the 'mass inaction' that threatened to disillusion the whole movement, an emphasis on cultural struggle brought theory closer to action – and indeed offered a solution on the difficult issue of how to bring back broad public action in support for the anti-apartheid cause. For such action to occur, not just an increased awareness of the brutal oppression of apartheid was needed, but also an imagination of an alternative. Barry Feinberg, who was at the centre of this discussion in the ANC exile circles, gives the following account for the background of the formation of the two cultural groups Mayibuye and Amandla, and a process that might be seen as a 'cultural turn' in the struggle against apartheid:

It started in 1975, a few of us got together and talked about the need for our culture, the culture of the struggle as well as the culture of the South African people, to be projected abroad. ... And we also felt that everybody has a contribution to make, cultural workers above all, because they actually often grabbed the limelight and grabbed public attention. We set up with a small manifesto along these lines, which was published in *AA News*, and we then set up what was called the Mayibuye group. We started collecting freedom songs, many of them were being generated in MK camps, and more and more people were coming to London who were well versed in singing them, so gradually we put together a singing group, and collected poetry. We tried to put theatrical elements to it, but most of the audiences that came were most moved by the songs.[46]

Invited by solidarity groups, the group toured around the world, as did the Amandla group, which was formed in ANC military camps in Angola. Feinberg also started to work with visual material, drawing on his experience as an artist. According to Feinberg the ANC had, up to this point (around 1975), produced mainly bland, textual materials. The work that was initiated with the cultural turn aimed at increasing the amount of visual material produced by the movement, particularly the making of films about South Africa. But just as important it was done in a different way than previously; 'it had to be done in an artistic way, in order to compete with so many options that people had in book shops, and in movie houses'.[47]

If Feinberg was right at the centre of the process in which the turn to cultural politics emerged, Tariq Mellet (then Patric de Goede) came into exile precisely at the moment when the shift was taking place at large scale. In the context of the broader transnational anti-apartheid movement, this also meant a more independent role in relation to AAM, on which the ANC to a large extent had relied for media work directed at a larger public both nationally (in Britain) and internationally. In fact the three London based organizations IDAF, the ANC and AAM developed a dynamic relationship around media work during the 1980s, playing different roles of 'bringing information to the world at large', as Mellet puts it. While IDAF was the resource type of organization that produced in-depth research and addressed journalists as well as a broader public in different forms of packages; books, poster packages, recordings, videos, popular media, the ANC produced material in which it constructed itself as the 'authentic voice' of the oppressed South African people; and AAM was the organization that produced material addressing people outside of South Africa to act in solidarity.

At this time, the ANC even started to think in terms of 'logo' and 'branding', concepts very much in the spirit of the 1980s commercial culture:

When one looks at the ANC up until 1984, you see very little branding. The most well known brand was the picture of Nelson Mandela, otherwise the ANC did not have a logo, its colours were not well known. We began to work on popularizing the colours consciously, popularizing as a means of branding, so people began to associate black, green and gold with the ANC. We wrestled with the idea of a logo, it did not come easy. ... We realised that if we came up with a logo it also has to be owned by its membership, because then it is more powerful.[48]

So a competition was organized in the ANC military camps, where people were asked to draw logos. From that a small group of people including Mellet and a professional designer, picked a handful of the suggestions which stood out as best, took elements from them and constructed what today is the ANC logo in black, green and gold. 'So we had a logo, we had corporate colors, we then began to use it ... it then became an institution.'[49] And as the ANC towards the end of the 1980s moved upwards the diplomatic scale of international politics, business cards and letterheads were also printed for the representatives.

The cultural turn in movement politics during the 1980s was not specific for the anti-apartheid movement. It must be seen as the articulate response to structural changes of a transnational movement culture that included feminist, green and solidarity movements. However, seen in a broader context, the most important influence came from the expressive youth culture of rock and pop. An important event in this context was the Live Aid Concert in 1985. Mellet summarizes the effect of the cultural turn in terms of how it changed activism on a broad base and the identification with the movement, its cause, and the culture it set out to represent:

All of this made people feel more inclusive, their body, their emotion, and their mind was being asked to get involved in this ... You found that for instance when people abroad learned the South African freedom songs, it did something different to the nature of solidarity than before, when they learnt this toi-toi, it did something qualitatively different. It began to make them feel there is a cultural dimension to solidarity. The colours, the logo, the badges, the caps, all of this began to make people feel a bit South African, the power of culture was being realised, and it was the pop medium that we learned from, rock n roll and pop music, that injected this.[50]

Considering the role of rock and pop music it was thus significant that the culmination of the cultural turn in the anti-apartheid movement, and the two most important events in terms of its media work, were the two Mandela concerts in 1988 and 1990, that filled the Wembley stadium and were watched on television all over the world.

Conclusion: technology and solidarity

There is no doubt that the struggle over representation and information is crucial for any movement acting in a media society. The anti-apartheid movement was no exception. On the contrary, it was at certain moments one of the most globally visible movements during the period between 1960 and 1990.

In the discussion on contemporary global civil society, there is often a heavy emphasis on the role of technological change. In the era of the Internet, many social scientists seem to be committed to a kind of technological determinism. The anti-apartheid movement happened mainly before the arrival of the Internet. However, if we analyse the process of building and expanding transnational anti-apartheid information networks from the late 1950s to the early 1990s, there is no doubt that technological change played a vital role for the development of these networks. It is a long way from the reading room of the British Library in 1960, where Dorothy Robinson sat and copied texts by hand, to the Wembley concerts, organized by AAM activists, who managed to use a globalized media system in order to get their anti-apartheid message across. While the first AAM Annual Reports consisted of a few typed sheets, which were copied by a stencil machine, the last ones were small booklets with images, printed in thousands of copies.

An important step on the way was of course the photocopier, which meant that the tiring work with the stencil machine could be abandoned. Further, a lot of the activists that I have interviewed have testified to the groundbreaking impact of the fax machine for the media work of the movement, both internally and externally. For example, in the context of the European anti-apartheid network, draft documents were sent out by fax, so that it in a short interval of time it could be commented and discussed before being fixed. Further, certain documents that previously had to be smuggled in and out of South Africa could now be sent by fax machines, which could not easily be controlled by the South African government. In Sweden the fax machine was used by ISAK in order to mobilize demonstrations on a short notice. As for printing, *AA News* was started at the time when the small London printers started to use photo offset, which made things a lot easier than previously for small journals. In the late 1980s, as the computer arrived, the change was even greater, when the practice of cut and paste, of making photographs in the darkroom and of making plates, was replaced by making layout and design on a data screen and having a laser printer printing it out. For most activists, personal computers came too late to influence everyday activism the way that has happened in the past decade. However, American students used e-mail in order to mobilize for anti-apartheid demonstrations, and the staff of AGIS' journal *Södra Afrika* started to search information on the Internet during the 1990s – instead of taking the train to Uppsala to read and copy the international magazines in the library of the NAI. As one of those Swedish activists who used to do these trips, and who were active in the struggle for 25 years stated, 'every new thing was a wonder'.

As many contemporary social analyses in the wake of the IT-revolution does come close to technological determinism, it is perhaps necessary to underline what a sociological perspective on technological development implicates; it is the social use, or construction, of technology, particularly its embeddedness in economic, political and cultural institutions, that defines the social meaning of technology during a particular historical period. Although a specific technology is always produced for a specific use, a new technology might nevertheless open up a certain space for social creativity in order to invent and establish practices for its use that might not originally have been intended. Social movements have historically been an important context for such innovations.[51] I would argue that the story of this chapter shows that the new social movement culture, emerging during the post-war era, and in which the anti-apartheid movement played an important role, was an important context for establishing certain uses of new media technologies.

Part II:

Public Debates on Apartheid/Anti-Apartheid in Britain and Sweden 1960–90

5
Beginnings: Sharpeville and the Boycott Debates

Introduction: the role of Sharpeville as a media event

In a small town called Vereeniging, in Transvaal (now Gauteng), not far from Johannesburg, the treaty that ended the Boer War was signed in 1902. Fifty-eight years later, on the 21 March 1960, in a township on the outskirts of Vereeniging called Sharpeville, a demonstration against the pass laws was held in the morning. The demonstration was organized by the PAC. After the ANC had declared the 31 March as a nation-wide protest day against the pass laws, which restricted the movements of the black population of South Africa, the PAC answered by declaring the 21 of the same month as a day of mass action against the pass laws. PAC activists paid the area around Vereeniging special attention.[1]

Without warning, several policemen opened fire at the demonstrators. One of the journalists present, Humphrey Tyler, a white South African writing for *Drum* magazine, reported that 'when the shooting started it did not stop until there was no living thing on the huge compound in front of the police station'.[2] Sixty-nine people were killed, and 186 others, including 8 children, were seriously injured. Many of them were shot in the back. The police claimed that demonstrators had shot at the police first, but no evidence were presented and none of the photographs that were taken from the scene shows a demonstrator holding a gun.

The next day, Sharpeville was on the front page of newspapers all around the world. And in many papers, South Africa stayed on the first pages during the following month as tension increased and the apartheid regime declared a state of emergency and banned the ANC, the PAC and other anti-apartheid organizations.

Sharpeville has often been recorded as a watershed in the history of South Africa, as well as a starting point for the international anti-apartheid movement. For example, in *The Making of the Modern South Africa*, Nigel Worden states that the shootings in Sharpeville 'marked a dramatic turning-point in South Africa's history. ... And internationally the shootings had a major effect'.[3] There is no doubt that the shootings in Sharpeville had effects, and that they gained an immensely important symbolic significance in the context of the anti-apartheid movement. During the coming decades 'Sharpeville day' became an event commemorated all over the world through demonstrations or public actions, and – often as a result of this – the day would be an occasion when newspapers focused on the oppression of the apartheid system in South Africa.

However, as discussed in the introductory chapter, mobilization against apartheid in South Africa was interwoven with transnational networks before Sharpeville. It is true that the first large wave of international mobilization took place around 1960. It is also true that the reporting of the events in Sharpeville fuelled it, but it was not initiated by it. Rather, it was initiated as a result of the common efforts of a network of the South African Congress movement to intensify the national struggle as well as to internationalize it through making a call for an international boycott of South African goods. In December 1959, the ICFTU, which at the time had 56 million members in 96 countries, held a meeting in Brussels. Here, it responded to the call for an international boycott by urging its member organizations to contact its respective governments regarding launching some kind of boycott.[4] In Britain, the call from South Africa resulted in the forming of the Boycott Movement (later AAM), which through its release of *Boycott News* was a part of the anti-apartheid mobilization in 1960 that preceded Sharpeville. Further, the world of international politics, including international media, already had its eyes on the situation in South Africa.[5] The decolonization process going on in Africa had put the light on the continent. 1960 was declared 'The Year of Africa' by the UN. Anti-colonial movements and uprisings were taking place all over Africa. A month before Sharpeville the British Prime Minister Harold MacMillan had visited the South African parliament, where he made a speech that attracted much attention around the world and provoked the South African leaders; 'The wind of change is blowing through this continent', he declared.

Boycott News

In February 1960, the first issue of *Boycott News* was released in Britain. Here, many of the defining characteristics of what subsequently became the British anti-apartheid movement, as well as of the whole transnational struggle, were clearly visible. The headline of the first page read: 'A Direct Appeal From South Africa', and the text below cited leaders of the Congress Alliance as they appealed to the people of Britain for support for a boycott of South African goods.

In order to display a broad support base, the paper further stated that 'In Britain, support for the boycott snowballed in the last weeks of 1959', and listed a number of organizations that supported the boycott, among them The Labour Party, The Liberal Party, The TUC, The Women's Liberal Federation and Christian Action. Links to the peace movement were also present through a large ad for *Peace News*. Attention to the reaction of established media was paid in an article titled 'Enthusiasm for the Campaign in British Press'. It recorded that editorials published in late 1959 in both the *Observer* and the *Guardian* had supported the boycott. And although an editorial in *The Times* had been profoundly critical to the idea of a boycott, *Boycott News* asserted that the *The Times* had also published answers from Trevor Huddleston and leading South African liberals such as Alan Paton and Patrick van Rensburg, defending the boycott. The importance of being able to recruit the support of 'Eminent People' that became significant for British AAM was also evident in the first issue of *Boycott News*. It listed signatories from more than forty British citizens, 'prominent in various walks of life', including Lords, MP's, university professors and church leaders.

The article with the largest headline, which stated 'What you can do to help the Boycott', made clear that although the Boycott Movement in a sense was a 'single issue movement', it nevertheless had a multifaceted action repertoire, suggesting participation in solidarity action in the form of 'life politics'. Following the seven points of the programme meant integrating political action in your everyday life in various ways – including getting together with your neighbours to persuade local shopkeepers not to stock South African goods, raising the issue in any organization of which you are a member, and sending copies of any resolutions or decisions to the Boycott Movement. Further, sympathizers could distribute campaign leaflets and sell *Boycott News*, protest to their union or local Chamber of Commerce; or participate in a rally on Trafalgar Square. Finally, those who wanted to do even more could write to the Boycott Movement office for help with further suggestions, literature and speakers. The second issue of *Boycott News*, which arrived in March, once again emphasized a politics of everyday life, particularly addressing women, as the first page headline stated 'You can Fight

Apartheid With Your Shopping Bag', and included a list on 'What not
to buy'.

Boycott debates

In this initial phase, one of the major forces in the mobilization of
public opinion against apartheid was the labour movement. During the
months before Sharpeville the labour union magazines published
articles related to the boycott. In its February issue the TUC magazine
Labour ran an article on the boycott called 'Thirty-one days of protest',
which accounted for TUC's previous protests against apartheid, going
back to 1952.

There was however also deep tension around the boycott within the
labour movement. In the January issue of *Metallarbetaren* (no. 1–2),
the largest Swedish union magazine, there was an article reporting from
the ICFTU meeting that declared its support of the boycott of South
African goods in December 1959. According to the author, Gösta A.
Svensson, three people dominated the congress; the chairman Arne
Geijer, Swedish Social Democrat, the 'expansive' American Walther P.
Reuther and the Kenyan Tom Mboya, representing 'an Africa on march'.
The conference was sketched in terms of a Cold War drama. Mboya
pleaded for support for the union movement in the African countries, in
order that it should be able to become an independent force for change.
Reuther emphasized a Cold War frame, defending the use of nuclear
weapons in 'the service of mankind'. In between them was Geijer, who
had been elected as president not just on personal merits but because he
represented an unaligned country in the North. The article expressed
particular criticism toward the speech by the president of the US union
AFL-CIO, George Meany, who argued that anti-communism was the most
urgent issue for ICFTU. The response to this speech by Harry Douglass
from Britain was also cited: 'It is meaningless, he cried out, to preach
anti-communism to empty stomachs'.

In the second issue of *Boycott News*, there was an article written by
John Stonehouse, Labour MP, on an emerging conflict on the boycott
issue in the context of the British Labour movement. According to
Stonehouse, the boycott had put the Co-ops in a dilemma. Even though
Co-op had declared that it strongly objected to the racist policies in
South Africa, the Management Committees were cautious about participation in the boycott because they were afraid it would threaten their
trade. A circular by the Co-operative Union in Manchester responded to
the call for a boycott made by the Labour Party and TUC by advising

co-operative societies to 'have nothing to do with the campaign'. Following a meeting in the National Council of Labour, the Co-operative Union and the Co-operative Party had issued circulars emphasizing that the boycott was of *individual nature*. Stonehouse was strongly critical to the Co-operative societies for failing to make a collective decision with regard to what he argued was the 'great moral issue of our time', referring to the historical legacy of the labour movement:

> There would have been no Co-operative movement, and certainly no Co-operative Party, if this pusillanimous attitude had been adopted in the past.

In Sweden, a heated debate broke out in the Swedish press as soon as the main Swedish labour union LO announced the boycott.[6] With one exception – the extremist *Nordvästra Skånes Tidningar*, supporter of Verwoerd as well as of Franco – there was no defence for the apartheid regime in the debate. In fact, this debate shows that all of the arguments for and against boycotts – as well as sanctions – that were put forth in debates up until the 1990s were already formulated in 1960. In the beginning much of the focus of the debate was on the fact that there was a split in the labour movement regarding the boycott. However, it then slowly turned into a left/right debate – with the Liberals in this case siding with the left.

The debate started in January when it was announced that LO would propose a consumer boycott. An editorial on 2 February in the major labour morning paper *Arbetet* stated that there certainly were good reasons for union action against South Africa, but that it was doubtful whether the consumers would care about where their fruit came from. Further, since every nationalist dictatorship needs external enemies to frighten its subjects into obedience, a boycott is 'a double edged sword'; it could actually be used by internal propaganda to strengthen the support for the Nationalist government in South Africa.

A strong conservative reaction to the boycott also came immediately; on the 28 January an editorial in *Svenska Dagbladet* (SvD), titled 'Emotions and Blockades', put forth a number of arguments that would later be repeated several times in other papers. The article started by referring to a Norwegian attempt of a boycott against Franco's Spain just after the Second World War. As the workers in the harbour refused to unload fruit from Spain, the result was that 'agitated housemothers, who rather wanted the fruit to be eaten than to rot, took matters in their own hands and started to unload, and that was the end of the blockade'.

This example was, according to the editorial, a 'reminder of the difficulties with attempting to co-ordinate trade with ideologies or emotional modes, justified or not'. Further, SvD cited and supported the arguments against the boycott made in the labour movement's own papers (*Arbetarbladet* and *Aftonbladet*); that a boycott is pointless because the government of South Africa was already aware of the views of the Swedish public on apartheid; the proper forum in which to put forth the Swedish standpoint on apartheid was the UN, and this had actually been done several times. Finally an economic argument were brought in, as it argued that a boycott would contradict Sweden's national self-interest.

On 2 February, editorials in both *Arbetarbladet* and *Aftonbladet* (AB) referred to the British debate, arguing that if there was hesitation within the labour movement in Britain, there must have been reasons for the Swedish LO to reconsider its decision. It is significant that, although a number of arguments were put forth, the hesitation that both of these labour papers expressed against a boycott to a large extent seemed to be based on a *scepticism toward – or even a fear of – the boycott as political action*. *Arbetarbladet* asked, 'as an important matter of principle', 'if it is suitable that unions participate in these kind of actions of trade politics, thereby introducing a private foreign policy'.

The debate rarely referred to the anti-apartheid movement in South Africa. However, in an editorial on 22 February in *Dagens Nyheter* (DN) it was pointed out that those who argue that a boycott would make the situation worse for the oppressed people in South Africa, ignored the fact that the call for a boycott initially came from South African organizations representing the oppressed. On 23 February, an African leader was for the first time present in the debate as *Nyheterna* in an editorial quoted a letter from the ANC President Albert Luthuli published in the British journal *The Spectator*, in which he urged the British people to participate in the boycott.

The day before the final decision on a boycott was taken by LO, on 6 March, the formerly sceptical *Arbetet* published an editorial titled 'Why Boycott?', expressing strong support for the boycott. It now recognized that, since the unions in the United States, Britain and Scandinavia stood behind the boycott, the effect could be greater than what one initially could have expected. The main argument for the support was consideration for the African unions, who, according to the article, 'has put all its prestige on this boycott'. If the European and American unions 'had not put itself in solidarity with this action, it would no doubt had felt as a betrayal', which might have caused further split in the context of the African unions, the editorial argued. This statement did not only refer to the split between the African unions who had chosen different sides in the Cold War Union struggle and the risk of strengthening the Soviet side. In the article, the growth of Pan-Africanism even appeared as a larger threat to the further development of the African union movement. Should more African unions, as for example LO in Ghana, 'isolate itself from the international union community, it would evidently weaken itself'. The editorial concluded this reasoning by stating that the most important impact of a boycott thus would be to strengthen the African union movements' confidence for 'the union movement in the white world'. Because without help from the latter, the editorial continued in a paternalist mode, it 'can hardly ever build efficient and reliable organizations in the new states'.

The Cold War logic was also invoked on 14 March in the editorial in *Eskilstunakuriren*. LO's call for a boycott was not particularly impressing, the editorial argued, since the organization did not make any protest regarding the atrocities committed by the Soviets in Hungary. This was according to the editorial because LO did not dare to obstruct the recently renewed invitation to Nikita Chrustjev by Swedish Social Democratic Prime Minister Tage Erlander. This editorial provoked a response from several of the largest Swedish newspapers. In an editorial on 16 March, the labour AB strongly objected to the 'irresponsible analogy' of *Eskilstunakuriren*. According to AB, the race policy of South Africa risked the 'the white worlds' future relations with the black continent'. 'The white world' was however here another name for Europe and the United States; the article thus turned the table around, using the Cold War logic when arguing that supporting the boycott served the self-interest of the Western World.

In Britain the media also paid attention to the response of the South African government to the boycott. On 9 February, an article titled 'Natives "happy" in South Africa' in the *Observer* reported that the South African High Commissioner, A. J. Van Rhijn, had stated that 'the situation developing over the boycott of South African goods was ironical', because it contradicted the message of the 'Commonwealth Weeks' that were being held all over Britain and which encouraged trade between the different parts of the Commonwealth. Rhijn also cited Harold Macmillan's Cape Town speech, in which the prime minister had declared that he was against the boycott.

On 28 February, the day before the boycott was going to be launched at a mass meeting on Trafalgar Square, a correspondent of the *Observer* in South Africa reported that an anti-boycott legislation was going to be introduced in South Africa. According to the correspondent, this legislation was the start of a South African 'Let's get tough' policy, typifying the 'South Africa after Macmillan era'. A large part of the article accounted for the reactions of Macmillan's' speech, which 'is still exploding in Nationalist minds like a series of time-bombs'. It also quoted Albert Luthuli, who welcomed the speech 'with only one reservation: the Prime Minister's condemnation of the boycott of goods'. The correspondent concluded:

> For the first time in 11 years the Nationalist Government faces serious trouble internationally which in return is producing cracks in the internal facade.

Sharpeville in the news: 'learning the lesson the hard way'

Turning to the news reports from Sharpeville in *The Times*, the *Guardian*, DN and SvD during the week after the shootings, the media presented a highly polarized 'black and white' drama. This drama was not without its ambivalences, and it did not look identically the same when comparing the different front pages studied, but reports nevertheless shared a narrative depicting a basic sequence of action, implying causes and effects and a bipolar structure of relations between a set of actors, whose roles were defined through ascribing them certain actions as well as different degrees of activity/passivity in the chain of events.

The news reports reproduced two dominant and contradictory stereotypes of 'Africans', deeply anchored in European colonial discourse and well established in the media at the time.[7] First, there was the stereotype of the African as a passive victim, an object of brutal police violence, particularly in the front page images of dead people lying on the ground. Second, frequently using the word 'mob', the reports depicted the demonstrators as an anonymous collective, beyond control of their emotions and therefore inclined to violent disruption – implicitly 'explaining' the shootings as a reaction of white fear of black violence. For example, on 22 March, headlines stated: 'Whites opened fire at besieged police station' (the *Guardian*), '56 killed in riot near Johannesburg' (*The Times*), 'Fire against the coloured by police in panic/Race riot ended in tragedy' (DN). This picture, indicating that the police had been acting in a tight spot was further confirmed in the front page articles, as for example in SvD, which stated that 'it was the police station in Sharpeville, … that was attacked'.

To what extent the actors appeared as active subjects, and which roles they were ascribed, also depended on if they were allowed space to comment on the events, and *how* they were quoted. On 22 March, a front page article in the *Guardian* quoted the police commander at Sharpeville, Colonel J. Piernaar:

> I don't know how many we shot ... It all started when hordes of natives surrounded the police station. My car was struck by a stone. If they do these things they must learn the lesson the hard way.

It further quoted a speech made 'before it was known how many died in today's riots' in the South African House of Assembly by Carel de Wet, Nationalist Party MP, saying:

> It is very disturbing to me that when there are riots of this kind, whether it is rioting by whites or non-whites, that only one should be shot ... I say this because whites in this country also have the right to protection.

It is obvious that to the average liberal minded reader of the *Guardian*, the white Boer South Africans being quoted appeared as extremists. Thus, the drama was narrated as *a battle between extremists*: ideologically misguided African (PAC) and Afrikaaner (NP) leaders and their troops in a battle on the ground; the use of words like 'riot' and 'under siege' strengthening the image of uncontrollable, irrational action in a war-like situation.

The organizations of the South African anti-apartheid movement were rarely mentioned in the news reports – and only in a few cases were representatives allowed space to comment on the events during the week that followed. When both the *Guardian* and *The Times* published a picture of Luthuli burning his pass on 28 March, it was the first time since the shootings that a South African leader/organization was present in any of the papers in the capacity of an acting subject. Both newspapers also cited a statement issued by Luthuli after he had burned his pass, saying that the ban on the ANC had put the obligation on the organization to 'take a last stand against the pass system'.

Sharp criticism was put forth against the apartheid regime in the editorials of all the papers. For example, after South Africa's banning of the ANC and the PAC, an editorial in *The Times*, who just a few days before had argued that the call for a strong criticism of the apartheid regime made by the Labour and Liberal opposition in the British parliament was 'irresponsible' ('Unreal Gestures', 23 March), sharpened its tone against the South African government. In its editorial on 26 March, it argued that apartheid represented 'a bankrupt policy' and 'that its appetite for repressive action seems to be growing'.

While there were often striking differences between the views implicated by the framing of the news reports and the opinions expressed on the editorial pages, *it is important to emphasize that there were also correspondences between the explicitly expressed views and values in the editorial articles and the frames of the news reports*. Editorials put the PAC and the ANC into *a frame of moderates versus extremists*, which was linked to the frame of battle between extremists, as it contrasted the PAC, the organizers of the demonstration, as extremist, against 'the moderate ANC'. For example, in its editorial on 22 March, DN commented the new mass action which was not organized by the ANC but by 'the new, more aggressive and bitter Pan-African Congress', that 'sees all whites as guilty'. In its editorial on 28 March, the *Guardian* expressed scepticism against Luthuli's burning of his pass, arguing that 'that would be a desperate step for an African to take ... He would be burning his boats with his pass'. However, if this judgement risked portraying Luthuli as a radical, the editorial in the next paragraph contrasted Luthuli's ANC with the militant PAC, stating 'that these two bodies are in fact strongly opposed to each other'.

The frame of moderates versus extremists was however also contested by the South African Prime Minister Verwoerd. In a front page article on 23 March in the *Guardian*, he was cited commenting on the fact that the Opposition had urged him to make contact with Luthuli,

> on the basis that the African National Congress was a decent group, while the Pan-Africanists were extremists. It was true that the Pan-Africanists broke with the ANC, but it was not less culpable than the PAC for what was happening at present. The ANC had created a background of and an atmosphere in which the Pan-Africanists had been able to act.

Both the *Guardian* and *The Times* did several times quote comments on the events made by the apartheid regime and particularly Verwoerd, appearing more moderate than 'the men on the ground'. For example, on 26 March, both papers published a full statement issued by the South African Department of Foreign Affairs. It was titled 'S. African crowds not unarmed' in *The Times* and 'Africans "shot first" ' in the *Guardian*, and it claimed that demonstrators in Sharpeville attacked the police with 'assorted weapons, including firearms'.

Looking at the reports on the British anti-apartheid movement demonstrations, there was a clear difference between the *Guardian* and *The Times*. While the demonstrators in the *Guardian* appeared as large gatherings of peaceful individuals, representing a wide spectrum of British civil society, the number of people always appeared fewer in *The Times*, whose reports also tended to focus on disturbances. For example, on 24 March, *The Times* headline read 'Demonstration at S. Africa House/600 in Scuffle with police', the text reporting that a Nigerian was arrested 'after demonstrators clashed with the police'. Inside the paper, there was an image of police and demonstrators in London with the text: 'Police trying to control the crowds outside the South Africa House, London, yesterday, when demonstrators protested against the Sharpeville shootings'. The headline of an article in the *Guardian* on the same day stated 'Silent protesters at South Africa House'. The article painted a picture of a protesting civil society, consisting of both individuals and organizations, as it stated that the demonstration began as a completely unorganized response to the news reports: 'men and women who had read the news felt they must at once make their own individual protest'. The police was described as 'as helpful and sympathetic as they could be'. It further mentioned a number of organizations flooding South Africa House with protests and making appeals. Swedish DN (but not SvD) also reported on the demonstrations in London on 23 March, stating that 'a large crowd demonstrated outside of the South African embassy to express its disgust over the massacre on the coloured'.

'To civilize the African'

If strong condemnation of apartheid was the most obvious tendency in opinion articles in the major media after Sharpeville, it is also important to observe that there were certain silences, implying tacit assumptions on the limits of change in South Africa. There is not a single opinion article explicitly suggesting that full democracy is the immediate political answer to South Africa's problems. In fact, when the issue of democracy was brought into the debate, it was rather related to doubts as to whether South Africa – and particularly its black population – was 'ripe' for full democracy. This is the case in Dame Rebecca West's report in the *Sunday Times* on 27 March, titled 'The Nemesis of Apartheid'. On the one hand, there was no hesitation in West's condemnation of apartheid, in which 'there is not a grain of humanity'. However, regardless of apartheid, to West, South Africa seemed to offer an impossible political situation, because a majority of the Africans were illiterate:

> Only a racketeer in left-wing optimism could regard this as anything but an unsmiling political landscape, because an illiterate voter, no matter of what colour, is a mischief, and an illiterate African voter, soured by apartheid, would be a very powerful public mischief to the literate African voter who wants to get on with the real business of government.

This evolutionist paternalism was put in a more blunt, explicitly racist way by the voice of kith and kin in the conservative *Daily Telegraph* on 6 May. A distinguishing quality of this voice in the British press was that it often transcended certain limits of what appeared as morally acceptable to say in defence of the South African apartheid regime in public at the time. This was made possible by referring to 'direct experience', a discursive strategy creating a privileged position in the debate, making it possible for the speaker to claim that s/he better knew 'how the Africans really were' than people who had actually never been to South Africa (especially those supporting anti-apartheid). The article was titled 'South Africa's White Outcasts' and the author was presented as follows: 'an English-speaking South African, whose name cannot be disclosed for obvious reasons, points to the dilemma of those caught between African and Afrikaner'. There are two important dimensions of the 'in-between' position that the article constructed. On the one hand, the author of the article argued that the identification as a 'British South African' equalled an experience of isolation:

> I speak as a South African of British descent living in a political no-man's land in the most bitterly hated country in the world. Mine is the utter desolation of a child isolated from the love of both its parents; England identifies me with a government I have never supported and, because of my allegiance to Britain, I am condemned as a traitor in the country of my birth.

On the other hand, while taking a distance from the Nationalists' 'inborn prejudice' against 'the African', the author identified with their basic idea of racial separation. The basic problem with the Nationalists' apartheid policy was not that it kept the races separate, but that they refused to take on 'the white man's burden' to civilize the Africans:

> Generally speaking, the African is still primitive. His personal habits, manners and background are such that he would be as ill at ease in

our society as we should be in his. While the rest of the world cannot accept this truth, Nationalist South Africa cannot accept its responsibility to civilize the African, nor can it realise that it is not for the white man to oppress the black but that it is his duty to lead him.

Thus, against the apartheid ideology's racist notion of absolute difference between the races, the article expressed the idea of separation in terms an evolutionist racism that had been an integral part of European colonial discourse since the late nineteenth century.

In the liberal press, a number of in-depth reports with a clear anti-apartheid stand were published by already established anti-apartheid journalists like Anthony Sampson and Colin Legum (both writing for the *Observer*). Further, new writers who would become well-known committed anti-apartheid journalists during the coming decades were introduced to the reading public. For example Mary Benson, Executive of the Africa Bureau, published an article in the *Observer* titled 'Pass of Slavery' (27 March). Ronald Segal, anti-apartheid activist and editor of the magazine *Africa South*, who had fled from South Africa to Bechuanaland together with Oliver Tambo, at the time acting president of the ANC, published his story in the *Daily Herald* in April (11–13 April).

In Sweden the climate of the boycott debate was definitely changed by the shootings in Sharpeville; at least for a couple of weeks the temperature was heightened. A quote from an article titled 'The Wrath Goes Deep', in the labour *Stockholmstidningen* on 3 April catches the mood of many articles:

> The great importance of the boycott is related to the fact that hundreds of thousands of Swedes daily, for two months, in every contact with a grocery store, can not refrain from reflecting on the barbarism of race oppression; they are forced daily to think about the deepest meaning of democracy, of the demand for human rights. Making the trivial choice of dried or fresh fruit, of grapes, it is today impossible to refrain from reflecting on where the fruit has come from. A South African Brand consciously or unconsciously associate to images in newspapers and TV of coloured people who are rushing forward and are met by murderous bullets from the weapons of white men of power.

The days after Sharpeville, several editorials turned against the outright defenders of apartheid that operated in the margins of the Swedish public sphere. Several editorials brought up the right wing *Nordvästra Skånes Tidningar*'s (NST) comments to the massacre, as it argued that the financial support from the labour unions, through its subscriptions for South African organizations, was the cause to the bloodbath. For example, in an editorial titled 'A disgrace' on 24 March, labour *Arbetet* included the following quote from NST:

> to get arms for the Negroes, money is needed, arms with which they can tear down and spoil the culture and social order that the white man has built. Now, one has apparently succeeded.

The editorial in *Nyheterna* feared that the unions would use the strategy of completely ignoring the statements by NST, as they had done when previously attacked. In this case, however, the editorial argued, it would not be suitable to remain silent, because the NST editorial was so provocative, so far from decency, that it needed to be publicly refuted by the unions.

Conclusion: framing the struggle

Just as the collective identity and action strategies that would define the British anti-apartheid movement until the 1990s were already visible in the first issues of *Boycott News*, many of the frames, positions, arguments and representations that would define the debate on apartheid/anti-apartheid in the established media during the coming three decades were present in the press reports and editorials that were published during the first half of 1960.

As I argued in the Introduction, the apartheid issue, when debated by the anti-apartheid movement and its antagonists, as well as within the movement itself – was often a debate about anti-apartheid and its action strategies. When the transnational anti-apartheid movement for the first time became clearly visible in major media in Western countries in early 1960, the news was the boycott, and the conflict within the worker's the movement that it caused. This debate existed in both Britain and Sweden, but it was more intense in Sweden, something that must be seen in relation to the fact that the main labour union, LO, was closely linked to the Social Democratic government, making the boycott a political issue of high national relevance. The arguments in this debate were centred around morals, efficiency and self-interest, and would be repeated again and again in the context of boycott and sanctions debates for the next 30 years.

The criticism put forth in the Swedish *Arbetarbladet*, discussing the boycott 'as an important matter of principle', deserves specific attention, as it argued that such an initiative taken in the context of civil society 'cannot be tolerated', because it meant performing foreign policy, a domain of action that belonged to the government. It thus expressed a defence of the established political procedures of parliamentary democracy that would often be put in response to the different forms of extra-parliamentary action – such as boycotts or civil disobedience – that would increasingly be used by the new social movements during the 1960s and onwards. While the critics of extra-parliamentary action thus would argue that this form of action was problematic from a democratic point of view, because it meant that people were illegitimately taking politics into their own hands, its proponents argued that it was legitimate, and even deepened democracy, when it brought forth issues that had a broad support base but were nevertheless neglected by the political establishment.

Turning to the news reports from Sharpeville, the frame of moderates versus extremists provided a possibility to express support for one section of the anti-apartheid movement, while at the same time repudiating those activists perceived as too militant, thus threatening to disrupt the social order. The main message embedded in this frame was that the government should talk to the moderates – the non-violent, multiracial ANC. It is also worth noting that the news frame reproducing a colonial stereotype presenting Africans as a violent mob also corresponds to a post-war, pre-1968, dominant discourse on social movements, in which collective action, particularly in its public manifestations, were conceptualized as 'crowd behaviour', a basically irrational form of action in which the individual loose self-control and becomes inclined to participate in collective violence.[8]

6
Sports as Politics: The Battle of Båstad and 'Stop the 70s Tour'

Introduction: student activism and sports as politics

In the late 1960s, a new generation of activists entered the anti-apartheid movement, extending its action repertoire. In this phase, the solidarity movement moved from opinion making by conventional means to extra-parliamentary actions of civil disobedience as the new generation introduced themselves through campaigns against sports events in which South Africa was involved.[1] When the South African cricket team toured in Britain in 1965, AAM organized demonstrations outside every ground where a game was being played. Action against sports in Britain did however enter a new level after the cancellation of the British cricket tour in 1968, which was caused by the South African government's refusal to accept that the British team included the coloured Basil D'Oliveira. It culminated with the Stop the 70s Tour, which caused a huge debate on the anti-apartheid movement and about the relations between apartheid politics and sport in the British press.

Before we go into this debate we will take a look at the protests that stopped the tennis game between Sweden and Rhodesia in Båstad in May 1968. At the time, it was the largest and definitely most successful social movement direct action in Sweden during the post-war era. Regarded as sensational by the Swedish media, this was as close as the Swedish student movement would get to what happened in Paris the same month or in Chicago during autumn in the turbulent protest year of 1968. If the protest was not related directly to South Africa, it is still relevant here for two reasons. First, the organizers were the same people that formed the core of solidarity activism related to South Africa, and second, because the fact that the attention that the events gained meant that new activists were recruited to the struggle against apartheid in South Africa.[2]

May 1968: the battle in Båstad

Båstad is a small town on the West Coast of Sweden, south of Göteborg. In addition to it being a spot for summer tourism, it is known for its tennis tournament, sometimes called 'the Wimbledon of the Nordic countries'. When Sweden was to meet Rhodesia in Davis Cup in 1968, between 3 and 5 of May, Båstad was not the obvious choice as the place for the game because the summer season had not begun. But since protests against the game were expected, the Swedish National Tennis Association (NTA) decided to go for Båstad after advice from the Swedish National Police Commissioner.[3] A matter of relevance is that the non-socialist coalition was supported by an overwhelming majority of the Båstad constituency and that the city is known as a place of gathering for the uppermost Swedish economic elite. Further, of those who had a daily morning paper in Båstad, 73 per cent subscribed to the extremist right wing *Nordvästra Skånes tidningar* (mentioned in Chapter 5 for its defence of the apartheid regime after the Sharpeville shootings).[4]

However, Båstad is also close to the university town of Lund, at the time known for its radical student activism. Among the many left wing groups that had its base in Lund at the time was one of the most active of the Swedish South Africa Committees, who published the nationally distributed information bulletin *Syd- och Sydväst-Afrika*. Of those who participated in a survey made after the demonstrations in Båstad, nearly 50 per cent were active in the South Africa Committees (while two thirds were active in FNL, the leading Vietnam solidarity organization).[5]

The month before the game, a debate broke out in the Swedish media about whether the NTA was right in participating in a game against Rhodesia, a country that oppressed its black population, just like South Africa, who because of this was no longer allowed to participate in the Olympic Games. NTA defended its position to invite Rhodesia by making a distinction between Rhodesia and South Africa. The coach of the team Mats Hasselquist argued in *Kvällsposten* that 'when people speak about apartheid policy in Rhodesia, it is wrong. Such policy is prohibited in Rhodesia!'.[6]

The press had their eyes on the actors that played the key roles in the build up of the protest drama that was expected to occur in Båstad. On 25 April, in a first page article in *Aftonbladet* (AB) titled 'Students Stop the Rhodesia-Game', it was reported that a coalition of left students in a meeting in Lund had decided to go for action against the game. The article quoted representatives from the group stating that 'we will use all means except hand grenades'. Further, it was reported in several papers that a team of vigilantes had been formed in Båstad to protect the city from the demonstrators. On 3 May, *Kvällsposten*'s headline reported: 'Voluntary "Tennis Police" in Båstad: "We Will Strip Them Naked"'. Thus, as the press was depicting the build up of a situation of violent conflict – headlines talked about 'the Tennis War' – the Swedish public had been made aware by the press that the stage was set for a battle in Båstad on the day of the game.

The demonstration on the first day of the game, that after some hesitation by the authorities got a formal permission, was organized by the youth section of the Social Democrats, Folkpartiet (the Liberal Party) and the Centre Party. Participating in the demonstration was also a coalition called the Action Group, which broke with the conditions of the demonstration permit as they performed a sit-in action outside the gates of the tennis court in order to stop the game from taking place. According to reports, in the tumult that followed as the police tried to remove the demonstrators, the police used batons, tear gas and water canons in order to remove the demonstrators, while the activists threw eggs, sand and gravel at the police. Oil bags were thrown into the court in order to make it impossible to play on. As the police retreated the team of vigilantes attacked the demonstrators. Finally, the NTA took a decision to stop the game.[7]

What makes the debate that followed on the demonstrations particularly relevant here, is that the main focus shifted from the issue of whether to engage in sports with Rhodesia to the legitimacy of the demonstrators and the use of civil disobedience/direct action. Thus, it became a debate on the legitimacy of the action strategies of the emerging new social movement culture of which the second wave of anti-apartheid movement mobilization was part.

On 4 May 1968, the big headlines of the first page of the liberal *Dagens Nyheter* stated 'Acid and Clubs Against Teargas and Water'. 'Acid' meant hydrochloric acid; the headline as well as the large image of the demonstrators did not refer to a peaceful hippie generation, but rather indicated the arrival of a Swedish wing of the militant international student generation.

The editorial did however put an emphasis on criticizing the police and the Tennis association. Among the demonstrators were a 'tough minority ... who had made no secret of their purpose to stop the game by all means'. If there was any chance to lead the demonstrators into more peaceful ways the local police spoiled that opportunity through its too restrictive measures, the leader argued, concluding that NTA 'has challenged the politically conscious opinion in Sweden by welcoming representatives of the oppressive regime in Rhodesia, boycotted by almost the whole world'. Although the editorial found the methods of struggle used by the demonstrators indefensible, it also argued that it was difficult to make any other conclusion than that 'the tennis organizers only have themselves to blame'.

In contrast, the first page article in conservative *Svenska Dagbladet* on the same day, titled 'New Place for the Game Top Secret', paid more attention to the discussions on where the game would be played than to the demonstration, thus emphasizing that the game was postponed, not stopped (the game finally started on 5 May on a private court in the village of Bandol at the French Riviera, surrounded by secrecy). On its editorial page, on the other hand, it used strong language as it condemned the demonstrators. According to the article the game was stopped by

> paving stones, iron poles and oil bags, used by reckless demonstrators. Mob manners have once again turned out to be successful ... The society and its constitutional order are the losers.

The demonstrators' arguments and actions were also according to the editorial completely illogical, since a soccer game between Sweden and Franco's Spain was played in Malmö the day before the tennis game, just 150 kilometres away from Båstad. The editorials' conclusion was however not that more sports games should be boycotted. Rather, sports and politics must be kept apart, because if Sweden would cancel all sports exchange with countries in which oppression or dictatorship occurred, 'we could simply not participate in the international life of sports'.

Of the newspapers having nation-wide coverage, it was the labour AB that paid most attention to the demonstration during the weeks that followed, its news reports and editorial comments clearly more in favour of the demonstrators than was the case with any other major newspaper. It also allowed space for a debate on the events in Båstad.

In the editorial on 5 May, AB contextualized the protest in Båstad by putting it into the context of the international student revolt, 'a truly universal revolt, in which the importance of national borders is reduced'. Here, it referred to one of the social philosophers celebrated by the contemporary student movement, Herbert Marcuse of the Frankfurt School, and his book *Protest, Demonstration, Revolt*, recently translated to Swedish. Citing the philosopher, the editorial argued that the contemporary global opposition, based in the underprivileged classes and in groups of politically conscious among the privileged classes, were met by stronger repression, more policemen and a stronger army. It was in the light of such an analysis the events in Båstad should be seen, the editorial argued. It further referred to a speech on Labour Day (1 May) by Olof Palme, then minister of Education, that the youth were protesting against the democratic institutions not because they are democratic, but because these institutions were passive in relation to 'the crucial social problems of our time'.

On 12 May, in a debate article in AB titled 'The Båstad Game and a Forgotten Act of Law', the priest and anti-apartheid activist Gunnar Helander (see Chapter 1) asked if the demonstration could not be regarded as a legal action in order to prevent a game that would violate of the Swedish law against 'racial agitation'. On the same page, in an article titled 'Testimony about Racism and Police Protection', five students from Uppsala University accounted for their experience of the demonstrations, 'in carefully considerate terms', as AB stated in its intro-duction to the article. This introduction particularly emphasized the student's account for the sequel to the demonstration, arguing that it led the thoughts to the atmosphere in the American South. According to the students, there was 'an atmosphere of lynching' after the game had been stopped. During a meeting in which two black Rhodesian students made speeches, a group of locals that attended had shouted 'Hang them! Throw them into the lake! Nigger bastards!'. The main point of the article was that while the majority of the media in its reports, 'has over-estimated the limited violence on the demonstrators side', painting images of a war and that the democracy was under threat by the student's action, little attention was paid to the violence from the vigilantes – and to the fact that the police failed to protect the demonstrators from this violence.

The protests were also front-page news in Britain, mainly being framed in terms of a 'riot'. In *The Times*, a headline on the first page on 4 May stated 'Rioting over Davis Cup Match', and it reported that 'More than 1000 demonstrators stormed the tennis stadium here today and stopped Sweden's Davis Cup match against Rhodesia, after bombarding the court with bags of oil, stones, eggs and bottles'. The *Guardian* ran an article inside the paper with the headline 'Eggs Thrown by Rioters Stop Tennis'. The short article quoted the Swedish Federation Secretary Sten Heiman, saying 'I feel ashamed of my country – and I regret that the police were unable to control the demonstrators as they had promised'.

Although 'the battle in Båstad' was not a protest action directly related to apartheid in South Africa, it is clear from the interviews that I have made with Swedish activists that Båstad was an important event for those that began their commitment to the struggle against apartheid in South Africa in the late 1960s and early 1970s. 'Båstad' has a mythical status in the narratives of Swedish anti-apartheid activists of the student generation. Its symbolic significance is related to a sense of 'victory', and of the possibility of making a change through collective action. To anti-apartheid activists 'Båstad' showed that a local fight against racial discrimination in an area as distant as Southern Africa was meaningful, and there was also a feeling of pride as attention to the protest was paid internationally, both in the old colonial empire of Britain and in African countries.

It is also clear from activist narratives about 'Båstad' that if the major part of the media reports did not represent the demonstrators in a positive manner, it was through the media reports on the protests, nationally and internationally, that 'Båstad' gained this symbolic signif-icance. For example, AGIS activist Ingvar Flink states that although he had been 'emotionally committed since Sharpeville' it was the news about Båstad that was the immediate reason for him to make contact with the Swedish anti-apartheid movement, in which he was active for more than 20 years. Ann Schlyter, another AGIS activist that was a stu-dent in Lund at the time and participated in the Action Group in Båstad, told me that she shortly after the demonstrations, in her capacity of a student of architecture, went to Zambia for a semester of work together with her husband. As she went to a meeting in Lusaka in support of the ANC, there were reports on international events and solidarity action and when Båstad was mentioned, they were called to the stage to receive applauds for their participation in the protests.[8]

Stop the 70s Tour

In 1968, the English cricket team was going to tour South Africa. One of the stars of the team at the time was the South Africa born Basil D' Oliveira, a 'Cape Town coloured' in the book of apartheid classification. When the team was announced, Oliveira was not in it. Because Oliveira was the only non-white player, and considering that South Africa had declared that it would refuse to receive a New Zealand Rugby team if it included Maoris in 1967, it was perfectly clear to everyone why Oliveira was not on the team. After a wave of protest, including statements by AAM as well as a number of critical editorials in the liberal press, Oliveira was allowed to replace an injured player. This led the South African government to refuse to accept the English team. As an editorial in the *Observer* on 19 September, titled 'Mr Vorster vs. MCC', quoted the

South African Prime Minister John Vorster stating that Oliveira 'had been chosen by the anti-apartheid league', the cancelling of the tour was actually being framed as a victory for the British anti-apartheid movement. Further, on 8 September, an editorial in the the *Sunday Times* reported that Vorster at a Nationalist meeting had said that 'relations between Britain and South Africa had been "bedevilled" by the "Communist-controlled" Anti-Apartheid movement'. The editorial discussed this statement with mild irony, emphasizing that the South African Prime Minister was over-estimating the importance of AAM, as it claimed that 'Anti-Apartheid are very flattered by Mr. Vorster's generous estimation of their importance', and further ended the article underlining the respectability of AAM:

> And what exactly does Mr. Vorster want our Harold to do, anyway? Have no more dealings with such well-known Communists as Jeremy Thorpe and Dingle Foot, two of Anti-Apartheid's vice presidents?

From the perspective of British AAM, the 'Oliveira affair' was the starting point for a massive campaign against South African sports, which not only resulted in the definite isolation of South African sport internationally, but also caused one of the major public debates on apartheid and anti-apartheid in the British press during the whole period of 1960–94.

In the beginning of 1969 the English cricket authorities, despite the 'Oliveira affair', announced that the white South African team would still be invited for the planned 1970 tour. In May the same year SAN-ROC held a public meeting in London, in which it was argued that the anti-apartheid movement should move from merely symbolic protests to direct action, trying to stop the 1970 tour by physical, although non-violent, means. During the following months SAN-ROC played an important role in forming a network and in September the Stop the Seventy Tour Committee (STST) was launched at a press conference. Peter Hain, a young South African exile, member of the Young Liberals and AAM, was elected Press Officer and declared that STST would not only pledge mass demonstrations and disruptions during the 1970 cricket tour, but would also organize demonstrations against the tour of the South African rugby team that would start in November 1969.[9]

Eager not to damage its image of respectability, the AAM National Committee never sanctioned direct action during the sports campaign of 1969–70. However, there are reasons to doubt whether the general public took notice of AAM's fine distinction between the campaign to stop the tour, which it supported, and the protest methods advocated by the leaders of the campaign, which it rejected. This was perhaps especially so as the conservative press made an effort to undermine this strategy. In an article published on 23 January, titled 'I Did Not Agree to Cricket Violence – Lord Collision', the *Daily Express* said that it had evidence that 'clearly indicates that the people who lead the movement and the Stop the 70 Tour Committee – gave a nod and a wink to its militants while at the same time saying: "Don't associate us publicly with this" '. Further, it cited Lord Collision, a '60-year-old sponsor of the Anti-Apartheid Movement', dissociating himself from the demonstrations inside the cricket grounds.

Just as in the case of Båstad, the student movement's entrance into the anti-apartheid movement, bringing more militant methods into the struggle, caused debate in the media on the action strategies introduced by the students, particularly the legitimacy of the use of civil disobedience and direct action in a democratic society. In an article titled 'The Writing on the Wall' in the *Guardian* on 25 January 1970, Mary Holland reported about 'the aims and dilemmas of the various groups of anti-apartheid protesters'. Holland had talked to a number of anti-apartheid activists, and it turned out that they had also been involved in a number of other protest activities, such as squatting, tenant's associations 'and other kinds of extra-parliamentary protest'. Discussing their methods, Holland asked a number of questions:

> Where does civil disobedience end and violence begin? Is it civilly disobedient to shine a mirror in a batsman's eyes or to chant slogans at a bowler? Is it violent to daub a cricket ground, or to dig up a carefully nurtured pitch, or does violence begin with burning down the pavilion at Lord's? Is it civil disobedience to kidnap a player, as was tried in London recently, or to practise the kind of harassment used against the Springboks when the fire alarm was set off in their hotel in the early hours of the morning before a match?

These questions should be understood as rhetorical, but as Holland interviewed Peter Hain in his capacity as chairman of STST, he assured that as a sportsman, he thought that 'digging up a pitch ... just to stop one match is morally indefensible'.

Many local AA groups participated actively in organizing the demonstrations and direct actions during the rugby tour – and STST informally got all support they needed from the AAM office. According to the AAM Annual Report 1969/70, the AAM London office alone distributed 200,000 leaflets, thousands of posters, stickers and background sheets (not including the material distributed by the STST).[10] *AA News* also frequently reported and campaigned on the protests against the tour during 1969–70 – and so did the established media. According to Peter Hain, this media attention was of great benefit to the protest organizers: 'Local organizers suddenly realised they were part of a mass movement'.[11] According to *AA News*, there were demonstrations at every game. Direct action included demonstrators running into the pitch and interrupting the play, throwing orange smoke pellets among the players, and activists chaining themselves to the driver's seat of the South African team's bus. In order to delay the players to one of the games, an activist at one occasion gummed up the door locks of the South African players hotel rooms with solidifying agent. All of this, according to campaign leader Hain, produced 'dramatic television and newspaper pictures'.[12]

There were also violent clashes between police, demonstrators and sometimes also vigilantes. In the December issue of *AA News*, an article titled 'Kicks, Punches at Swansea Demo', reported that between 40 and 60 demonstrators were so badly hurt by violence performed by police and vigilantes ('stewards') that they had to go to hospital.

The tour was not stopped, but several times it was seriously disrupted and apartheid sports, and the anti-apartheid movement, stayed on the headlines for several months in the British press. There is hardly any doubt that the protests were a success in relation to convinced supporters, mobilizing them and making them prepared to stage further action against the cricket tour. However, looking at the reports and the editorials in the major British press, it is not self-evident that the campaign strengthened AAM in relation to a wider public. In an editorial in the *Observer* on 30 January 1970, titled 'The Extremists Help Each Other', it was argued that

The signs grow that the Springboks' reception in Britain is providing positive political advantage to the South African government by increasingly white solidarity, bringing English-speaking opinion to the Afrikaner viewpoint, and providing opportunities for propaganda against 'Liberalist' decadence and racial hypocrisy in Britain ... To this degree, the anti-apartheid demonstrations have achieved the opposite of their objects. Their violence has in the event tended to strengthen their opponents' case for keeping links open, apart from its being an attack on British liberties.

The quest for order

On 3 March, *The Times* published a letter to the editor in which Maurice J. C. Allom, chairman of the British Cricket Council (MCC), explained the view of the Council. Allom began by quoting a radio statement by the British Prime Minister Harold Wilson regarding the 'Oliveira affair', which according to Wilson put the South Africans 'beyond the pale of civilized cricket'. According to Allom, Wilson did not mention that the decision not to accept D'Oliveira was not taken by the South African Cricket authorities, but by the government. Allom claimed that South African cricketers had always 'been keen to play with and against cricketers of any race wherever and whenever they can' – and continued sending a message to Wilson:

> The South African Cricket Association does not represent the policy of the South African government any more than the Cricket Council necessarily represents the policy of Her Majesty's Government.

Thus, Allom's basic argument was that sports only become politics when politicians make the mistake to intervene. Allom also sent a message to the anti-apartheid movement when he stated that 'threats of disruption, and demonstrations that encourage violence' would damage their own cause. Rather, those against apartheid would be more likely to influence the South African government 'by welcoming and encouraging South African sportsmen who share their views on multi-racial sport'.

Ten days later, on 13 March, in an editorial titled 'The Intimidators', the *Daily Express* made a more blunt statement regarding the campaign of what it called 'the enemies of freedom in sport': 'The right of law-abiding people to enjoy their sport in peace must be vigorously defended'.

In the debate that raged during the spring of 1970, there was a clear division in the British press. Of the major newspapers, *The Times*, the *Daily Telegraph* and the *Daily Express* defended the MCC, the tour, and sometimes also the South African government, while the *Observer* and the *Guardian* criticized the Council and, in the case of the latter, sometimes defended the protesters.

The debate had similarities to the one related to the Båstad game in Sweden, as it centred on two main issues; first, whether the MCC was right in inviting the South African cricket team, an issue involving differences as to whether sports should be separated from politics, and second, the legitimacy of direct action in a democratic society. There were however also important differences. First, Britain's old colonial links with South Africa and its position in the Commonwealth community, in which sports had an important ideological function, automatically gave the issue a higher degree of political importance than in Sweden. Further, 1970 was a year of national election in Britain. This meant that the issue became intrinsically connected to the up-coming election campaigns of both Labour and the Conservatives. In this context, the most important dimension was that the conservative press, following the Conservative Party, used the frame of 'law and order', thus making the anti-apartheid demonstrators a symptom of a society out of control, threatened by anarchy and decay. This was indeed a global sign of the times from the Conservative viewpoint, but in a British context nevertheless something that Labour rule ultimately must be held responsible for.

For example, an editorial in the *Sunday Telegraph* on 26 April, argued that 'any society that succumbs to unruly pressure groups is doomed'. On 2 May, an editorial in *The Times* titled 'Why not to Cancel' argued that to stop the tour was to 'substitute mob rule for the rule of law'. Defenders of the tour most often emphasized that this did not mean defending apartheid racism, but argued that sports were, and must be kept, separated from politics. However, the frame of law and order also brought out a guarded defence of the South African regime in the conservative press, as it was argued that British and South African society had common enemies and common merits. In an editorial on 2 May, titled 'A Man of Discrimination', the *Daily Telegraph* criticized Harold Wilson for taking a distance from the Springboks in the following terms:

> These young men come from a country governed in a manner open to harsh and legitimate criticism. Yet it is also fair to point out that some Africans, judging by the number entering every year, seem to think better of South Africa than we do, and that the rule of law is better observed there than in Russia or in most other African countries.

The *Guardian* on the other hand provided a kind of guarded defence of the protesters' direct action through relating the protests to the issue that they were focusing on – the violence of apartheid. An editorial in the *Guardian* on 13 May, titled 'In the Springboks Homeland' began as follows:

> Swoop on to the pitch at Lord's, lock up the Springbok team plus the English eleven, keep them in gaol for a year, and you will have no more human suffering, no more denial of basic human liberty than the South African Government is guilty of in the current Terrorism Act case.

The *Guardian* also made the law and order frame into an issue of debate. An article in the *Guardian* on 10 February by Peter Jenkins, titled 'Padding up Vorster', put the protests, as well as its critics, in a broader ideological and historical perspective. Jenkins argued that 'the slogan "law and order" ' was an 'umbrella under which to shelter miscellaneous fears aroused by unconnected or only very tenuously connected phenomena – organized crime, urban unrest, racial tensions, industrial disputes, student protests, sex and pot'. According to Jenkins, the frame of 'law and order' was in a contemporary Conservative context introduced by Ronald Reagan in California and then used by Richard Nixon in his presidential campaign. Putting both the use of violence and the quest for order in a historical perspective, Jenkins quoted the US sociologist Charles Tilly, arguing that if we look at the history of political processes in Europe, collective violence has been regularly used as part of political struggles:

> The oppressed have struck in the name of justice, the privileged in the name of order ... Great shifts in the arrangements of power have ordinarily produced – and have often depended on – exceptional movement of collective violence.

Although Jenkins stated that it was hard to say if the present was a historical moment in which great shifts were taking place, he nevertheless concluded by saying that 'It is not very surprising therefore that the movements for student rights and racial equality have been accompanied by some violence; what is remarkable is how little violence so far'.

In April, the President of the Supreme Council of Sport in Africa declared that 13 African countries would boycott the Commonwealth games if the cricket tour in Britain went ahead, thus giving the protesters, as well as the Wilson government, yet another argument. Further, as the debate went on and the tour, as well as the national elections, came closer, the debate crystallized around one specific argument, linking the issue of racism to domestic British race relations, arguing that the tour would be an offence to the British immigrant population. This could be seen as a Labour move that was designed to meet the Conservative quest for order; it was an argument that – in terms of a liberal rather than Conservative discourse on social order – emphasized 'social cohesion' and 'social harmony'. Further, it was a move that made the argument for stopping the tour appear not as succumbing to the protesters, but being sensitive to the feelings of migrant groups that identified with the oppressed population in South Africa. This was a line of argument that the *Observer* had put forth quite early in the debate, as it had stated on 1 February in an editorial that 'The casualty in all this will be racial harmony in Britain'. On 14 May, an editorial in *The Times* admitted that it 'should not be denied' that race relations in Britain could be damaged by the tour.

This argument was also prominent when on 21 May, the day after an opinion poll showed that 58 per cent of the British population wanted the cricket tour to be cancelled (the *Guardian* 20 May), a press statement was sent out quoting a letter from the Home Secretary James Callaghan to Maurice J. Allom of MCC, stating that

> The Government have ... been carefully considering the implications of the tour, if it were to take place, in the light of the many representations that have been received from a wide variety of interests and persons. We have had particularly in mind the possible impact on relations with other Commonwealth countries, race relations in this country and the divisive effect of the community ... The Government have come to the conclusion ... that on grounds of broad public policy they must request the Cricket Council to withdraw their invitation to the South African Cricket Association.[13]

In the conservative press, there was an immediate outcry. As its defence of the tour, and its criticism of the protest movement, had emphasized the frame of law and order, it could now claim that the Labour government no longer performed its central function (according to Conservative discourse) as the ultimate guardian of national law and order. The editorial in *The Times* on 22 May argued that public policy had been dictated by 'mob action' with serious implications for British society. In a large article titled 'Mob Law is an Election Issue', in *The Sunday Telegraph* on 24 May, Peregrine Worsthorne compared the successful protest to the French Revolution:

> The protest industry last week won a famous victory; its most significant to date in the civilised world ... The protest industry has done what war and slump had failed to do: interrupted the Englishman at play, destroyed the team, disrupted the illusion. The fall of the Bastille marked the end of the *ancien régime* in France. The humiliation of the M.C.C is a comparable act of revolution, none the less sinister for being played out behind the scenes ... Nothing will be the same again ... Mr. Callaghan has acted like Louis XVI. He has given way to the mob.

The editorial on the same page, titled 'Hollow Victory', summed up the achievements of the Stop the 70s Tour, or as it appeared in the article, of its chairman:

> Mr. Hain, the young conqueror, surveys the stricken fields this weekend ... He has besmirched our national game, given a political tinge to delicate race relations, salved the consciences of Liberal bishops and, as Peregrine Worsthorne trenchantly points out on this page, set a precedent for mob law under our present rulers.

The *Guardian* applauded the government in an editorial on 23 May, titled 'The Right Decision at Last', and the editorial in the *Observer* on 24 May emphasized that the decision was primarily for the sake of national unity, as 'the very real prospect of violence and race hatred in Britain this summer has been removed'.

In an editorial titled 'This is How Blackmail Works' on 25 May, the *Daily Express* looked ahead on the next target of the young anti-apartheid student activists, as it reported that 'The bully-boys who succeeded in having the Springbok cricket tour banned now plan to disrupt banks and firms doing business with South Africa'.

This observation was confirmed in the editorial on the first page of the June issue of *AA News*. Summing up the campaign, the editorial declared that the tour was as 'symbol of British collaboration with racialism' and that its cancellation was 'a gesture of appeasement to the great body of opinion in this country that is opposed to apartheid'. However, it played down the importance of the stopping of the tour, as it declared that 'more than symbols and gestures are needed, if anything effective is to be done to help the people in Southern Africa who are struggling for their freedom'. The main part of the text was devoted to a discussion of how British capital was under-pinning the apartheid economy. In an article in the same issue, titled '... What We Do Now', it was declared that 'we must act against all links – especially the economic links between Britain and South Africa'.

Thus, as the Stop Seventy Tour had put focus on the apartheid issue, AAM took the opportunity to mobilize anti-apartheid protesters in a campaign against British economic links with South Africa. The most immediate result was the linking up with the student campaign against Barclays' bank that emerged at universities all over Britain at the time.[14] The emphasis on economic links also points to the third phase of the transnational anti-apartheid movement, as putting pressure on national government to impose economic sanctions on South Africa became the predominant anti-apartheid strategy.

Conclusion: direct action versus 'law and order'

The period of public student anti-apartheid activism, politicizing sports through direct action, happened in the middle of what is often described as a the long and difficult period for the anti-apartheid movement. In this context, the students entering the anti-apartheid movement for a short period managed to put apartheid back on top of the political agenda in both Sweden and Britain through using extraordinary strategies of polit-ical action. Both campaigns implied two dimensions, aiming concretely to stop the sports games, and symbolically to create a debate on – and an opinion against – apartheid. The campaigns were successful in the sense that they caused huge debates, and stopped the actual games. The debates did however not in any unambiguous way come out in favour of the anti-apartheid movement in any of the two countries.

As in 1960, it was an anti-apartheid strategy that was made the focus of the debate. However, while in 1960, it was the *effectiveness* of the boy-cott that was under debate, in 1970 it was the *legitimacy* of direct action and civil disobedience that was the focus of the debate (although, as we saw in Chapter 5, in the margins of the 1960 debate, the legitimacy of the boycott as a form of collective action was also being questioned). According to Bruce Page, working both for the *Sunday Times* and volun-teering *for AA News* in the 1960s, the apartheid regime, as well as their Conservative supporters in the West, were after Sharpeville looking for 'defensible positions' in a situation in which it had become difficult to explicitly defend apartheid in public.[15] Because of the popularity of sports, the anti-apartheid movements' strategy of politicizing sports provided an opportunity to create such a defensible position in the apartheid/anti-apartheid debate. Further, the use of direct action by anti-apartheid protesters provided the Conservatives with an opportu-nity for a more pro-active approach against the anti-apartheid move-ment. Through the introduction of *the frame of law and order*, the British Conservatives even managed to connect the demonstrations against the Springboks tour to the up-coming national election, blaming the Labour government for the 'disorder' now ruling British society and in some cases even cautiously defending the apartheid regime, by pointing to the common basic need for law and order that the British people and the white South Africans shared, and which were now threatened by global forces of anarchy and disruption. The success of this discursive manoeu-vre was also confirmed when a liberal version of the frame of law and order was articulated as a response, emphasizing 'social harmony'. As was pointed out, and indeed prophesized in the article by Peter Jenkins, the frame of law and order would be a major discursive element in the strange hybrid of neo-liberalism and conservatism that was launched by the Reagan and Thatcher governments, and that would shape not just British, but indeed global, politics during the decades to follow.

As the tour was cancelled, implying that the strategy adopted by the campaigners had been effective, and causing a rage in the conservative press, the frame of 'the protest industry' was added to the conservative repertoire. Contrary to the frame of law and order, this concept was in general more ambivalent regarding the 'disorderliness' of the movement, as it implied a certain emphasis on organized and strategic action. Portraying the activists as professional protesters, people who had nothing better to do (implying that they were either misguided students or unemployed), alternatively actually making a protest career (which was implied for example in the case of Peter Hain), it was no less effective, as it appealed not just to Conservative voters, but to a broad range of working people.

There is no doubt that the emphasis on direct action of the Stop the 70s Tour was problematic from AAM's point of view, causing an ambivalent approach to the protest publicly. AAM's declaration that it supported the campaign but not its main method, being direct action, might have been perceived as confusing, or simply not accepted, by the general public. It may be reasonable to conclude that during the course of events during autumn 1969 and spring 1970, AAM lost the image of respectability it had so carefully built up since 1960. This contributed to making AAM more marginalized in British public space during the 1970s than during the 1960s and 1980s.

The battle in Båstad was a major event mobilizing Swedish student activists in the context of the solidarity struggle against apartheid in South Africa, mainly benefiting the Africa Groups. For the same reasons as in Britain, a similar process of marginalization in public space occurred in Sweden. This changed only in the late 1970s with the new wave of anti-apartheid solidarity mobilization following on the increased international focus on South Africa in 1976, the year of the Soweto uprising.

7

'A New Black Militancy' – Before and after the Soweto Uprising

Introduction: Tutu's 'nightmarish fear'

On 16 June 1976, the *Guardian* published an open letter from Reverend Desmond Tutu to the South African Prime Minister John Vorster. It had previously been published in the South African newspaper the *Sunday Tribune*. Vorster had declined to reply in public, instead accusing Tutu of making propaganda. In the article Tutu stated that he was writing 'as one who is a member of a race that has known what it has meant in frustrations and hurts, in agony and humiliation, to be a subject people'. After naming a number of concrete injustices that black people were suffering in South Africa, Tutu continued:

> How long can a people, do you think, bear such blatant injustice and suffering? Much of the White community by and large, with all its prosperity, its privilege, its beautiful homes, its servants, its leisure, is hagridden by a fear and a sense of insecurity. And this will continue to be the case until South Africans of all races are free ... I am writing to you sir, because I have a growing nightmarish fear that unless something drastic is done very soon bloodshed and violence is going to happen in South Africa almost inevitably.

On the same day, *The Times* was running an article by Bernard Levin, comparing the censorship of the South African government to that of the Soviet Union. It was titled 'In the State Where Criticism is a Crime' and most part of it cited a speech held at the University of Natal by Donald Woods, a white South African journalist, who had become a close friend of Steven Biko, and who had been prosecuted and imprisoned for refusing to reveal the names of his informants. Levin reported that immediately after Wood's speech, five shots were fired into his house, where his wife and his children were staying.

As the subscribers to the *Guardian* and *The Times* in Britain read these articles in the morning of the 16 June, secondary school pupils marched in the township of Soweto, protesting against a decree that half of the curriculum in black schools were to be taught in Afrikaans. The police responded by using tear gas and fired into the crowd, killing at least one youth, Hector Pieterson, who became a martyr of a new generation of anti-apartheid activists in South Africa. This was followed by an insurrection that spread from Soweto to other black townships all over the country. By the end of the year the government put out an official estimation (regarded as under-estimated by historians) that 575 people had been killed and 2389 had been wounded in conflicts taking place after Soweto all over South Africa.[1]

In the history of apartheid and anti-apartheid, 'Soweto' has gained the same kind of significance as 'Sharpeville'. The symbolic equivalence between these two names of South African townships, both signifying the forced segregation, the brutal oppression and the violent conflicts of apartheid South Africa, was established immediately after 16 June 1976, as a number of editorials referred to Soweto as 'a new Sharpeville'. Just as Sharpeville, Soweto is often said to be an important watershed in the history of apartheid, and as marking the beginning of the end of a long and difficult period for the anti-apartheid movement. For example, Dan O'Meara states that Soweto 'was one of those rare historical catalysts which irreversibly transform the political landscape, whose very name becomes a metaphor for lessons learned by the whole society'.[2]

There is no doubt that the Soweto uprising was of huge importance for the anti-apartheid struggle. Nationally, it became associated with a protest generation that grew up to lead the internal insurrection during the 1980s in South Africa. Regionally, it supplied the armed struggle, taking place in Southern Africa during the same period, with thousands of new recruits, fleeing South Africa. Internationally, Soweto is often mentioned as initiating a renewed international engagement in South Africa. A photograph of a crying young black man carrying the dying Hector Pieterson, taken by Sam Nzima, working for The South African *The World*, was published all over the world on 17 June. During the decades that followed, it would gain the status of an iconic representation of South African apartheid.[3]

However, just as in the case with Sharpeville, things had been building up before the actual event. Following the oil crisis affecting the global economy, causing a drop of the gold price, heightened inflation and a period of economic recession in South Africa, numerous strikes involving more than 200,000 black workers took place in the industrial areas around Durban in 1973. Historians have argued that this renewed worker militancy, organizationally drawing on memory from union action in the 1950s, influenced the events in 1976. The international media did however fail to acknowledge the importance of these strikes.[4]

A more immediate influence was the Black Consciousness Movement, which had a strong intellectual and cultural emphasis as it initiated the formation of a new political culture in which 'black' was the central, and highly politicized, identity concept. It got an important political expression in the Black People's Convention (BPC), an umbrella organization launched in 1972, involving church, union and – most importantly – student activists. On the universities the leading BCM organization was SASO, founded by black students who in 1968 broke out of NUSAS. Black Consciousness discourse, and particularly the writings of Steven Biko, the medical student who became its leading intellectual, was in its ideological outlook more globally oriented than the Pan-Africanism of the previous generation. For inspiration, Biko and BCM turned both to the writings of Frantz Fanon as well as to the American Black Power Movement. This global orientation also had an impact on the language issue. According to James Barber, in contrast to the Afrikaner nationalists, the new generation of young students regarded English as 'a global language which could help free them from the confines of the Apartheid State'.[5] If the initial protest in Soweto was not a result of the mobilization of university students but of secondary school students (it was organized by the school based South African Student's Movement, which had its strongest base in Orlando), Biko was eager to establish a link between the revolt and BCM; when asked if he could point to a broad support for BCM, he replied 'Yes – in one word: Soweto'.

The ANC was present as an underground structure in South Africa at the time, but did not have much to do with the organization of the Soweto uprising. However, through its underground structures and media the ANC was present and well respected among young activists.[6]

If mobilization had occurred some time before Soweto, internationally Soweto was in itself a major mobilizing factor. However, as was the case with Sharpeville, an increase of international media attention preceded the 'event', something that is evident when looking at media coverage of South Africa in British and Swedish press during the first six months of 1976. In addition to reports on 'a new black militancy', media attention was related to two issues that put South Africa high on the international political agenda during the spring of 1976. First, in March the South African government took a further step in its policy of 'separate development' as it made an announcement that Transkei would be the first 'homeland' to approach independence. The majority of the states of the international communities of the UN and the Commonwealth saw this as an attempt by South Africa to appear to make a move toward independence and democratic rights for the black population, while actually further strengthen the apartheid system.[7] Second, during a trip to Southern Africa in April, Henry Kissinger, US Secretary of State, held a widely reported speech in Lusaka, in which he admitted a US neglect of Africa, and declared that the United States now wanted to see 'a comprehensive solution to the problems of Southern Africa'.[8] The speech was part of a renewed US attempt of taking an initiative toward a new policy in Southern Africa, following the installation of socialist governments in the former Portuguese colonies of Mozambique and Angola. Kissinger believed that South Africa was the key to a change that would prevent further socialist and Soviet influence in the region; his plans included a release of Namibia, a peace agreement in Rhodesia and an alteration of apartheid in South Africa.[9] Following this, a series of talks between the South African Prime Minister John Vorster and the US Secretary of State, Henry Kissinger, were set to begin in June 1976.

'A new black militancy'

During spring 1976, a large number of articles in major British newspapers put focus on South Africa, as well as on different sections of the anti-apartheid movement. Regarding the presence of anti-apartheid actors in the press, it is notable that during this period, the churches were being presented as prominent anti-apartheid actors. AAM appeared in an article in The Times on 25 February, as it had protested at a press conference held by the new 'Ballet International', who was going to tour in South Africa.

In its first three monthly issues of 1976, AA News focused on the South African invasion of Angola announcing a 'Torchlight vigil and mass picket' outside South African House on 11 of February. In the April issue, a front page article, titled 'ANC Underground Strikes in Jo'burg', stated:

South Africa's underground freedom fighters struck again on March 18 with the explosion of a leaflet 'bomb' in Johannesburg. AA News has received an eyewitness report of the incident and of the 2000-strong demonstration outside the trial of 8 people under the Terrorism Act, which took place just before it.

This text, as well as the fact that the text of the leaflet was published in the same issue, thus defined AAM as linked with the 'underground movement'. At the same time it defined an important mission of *AA News* as a media in between the underground struggle in South Africa and the above ground struggle in Britain, bringing the messages of the former to the latter. In Sweden, the ANC was visible in AGIS' publication *Afrikabulletinen* 32/1976, as an article accounted for various ANC activities in South Africa, mentioning underground media on various African languages, and stated that 'every day the South African people can listen to the radio programme the Voice of Freedom'.

The ANC's presence as an underground structure in South Africa was made visible also in the established media on 20 April in an article titled 'Why Window Dressing will not Satisfy South Africa's Militants' by Nicholas Ashford in *The Times*. Ashford reported that:

> The recent black disturbances outside the Rand Supreme Court in Johannesburg and the distribution of pamphlets supporting the banned African National Congress are examples where the growing sense of militancy has come to the surface.

In connection with the Transkei issue, it was reported that the South African government was considering the release of Nelson Mandela and other prisoners on Robben Island. According to the *Daily Telegraph* on 5 April, The Transkei had asked the South African government for an amnesty for political prisoners from the Xhosa tribe, among them Nelson Mandela, presented by the paper as the leader of the 'militant arm of the banned African National Council' (sic!).

The weeks before Soweto there were further articles reporting that things were moving among the blacks in South Africa. In *The Times*, Andrew Faulds, Labour MP, published an article titled 'Hard Lessons from Africa the West Must Learn' on 7 June. Faulds pointed to a new black political activism as 'strikes has grown in size and determination' and 'Black Consciousness is developing'. Faulds's basic argument was put in Cold War terms, as he argued that the West must support the liberation movements if 'we want the Africans to come out on the right side' and that 'a non-communist Southern Africa is worth some considerable degree of economic inconvenience and commercial loss'.

On 12 June in the *Guardian*, Peter Niesewand published an article titled 'Hell Behind Prison Bars' in which he interviewed Jack Tarshish, who had just been released after 12 years in South African gaol for his connections to Umkonto we Sizwe. Tarshish assessed the political situation in South Africa as follows:

> It's too late now for peaceful change in South Africa, but if people in Britain really brought pressure to bear, they could cut down the amount of bloodshed that there would finally be.

Two days before the Soweto uprising began, there was an article in *The Times* contradicting reports on a growing 'black militancy' in South Africa. It was written by Jerome Caminada, who argued that 'South Africa will move, provided the world gets off her back'. Caminada saw no signs whatsoever that the black population would not patiently await reforms – assuring that 'there is no tension in South Africa today as the Middle East and Asia know it':

> The humour of the working Africans seems to me as fresh and captivating now as when I grew up among the Zulu's. Appearances can, of course deceive, but if there is a revolution brewing behind those smiles today it is remarkably well hidden.

In spite of this report, I would conclude that there had been enough focus on what was actually going on in South Africa to make the international media prepared as protest and violence exploded in Soweto and other South African townships in June.[10]

Soweto in the media: 'It's no good firing over their heads'

In his chapter on the international news coverage of the Soweto uprising, James Sanders quotes an editorial in *The New Statesman*, published on 25 June and titled 'Naught for Dr Kissinger's Comfort' in which the response to Soweto in Britain is compared to the reactions to Sharpeville:

> Sixteen years ago there was no doubting the universal sense of outrage – uniting left and right alike – that greeted the Sharpeville massacre; this week Mr. Vorster was to be heard from Germany not only actually quoting with approbation from the *Sunday Express*, but

also congratulating 'all the British newspapers' on the tone of their comments on the latest police carnage – a tone, he said, that he found 'an agreeable contrast' to the reaction of the press in his own country.[11]

On 20 June, an editorial in the *Sunday Express* had argued that the 'rioting' in Soweto was organized by forces behind the scene 'to sabotage Dr Vorster's meeting with the US Secretary of State, Dr Kissinger'. On the same day the *Sunday Telegraph* ran an article by Peregrine Worsthorne, titled 'Black Day for Black South Africa', in which it was argued that just as Sharpeville demonstrated 'the inevitability of white supremacy', the action of the South African police in Soweto should be seen as a manifestation of strength. Worsthorne further stated that 'the South African whites are not like most of the rest of Western mankind, whose will to defend itself has been softened by Liberal inhibitions, post-imperial guilt and the fear of thermonuclear destruction'.

There were indeed differences regarding the major newspapers' interpretation of the events in Sharpeville and Soweto, but as we will see, there were also many striking similarities. The images from Soweto in *The Times*, the *Guardian*, SvD and DN during the first days largely repeated the two stereotyped images of Africans that dominated the reports after Sharpeville – on the one hand the passive victims of police violence, on the other hand the faceless rioting mob, steered from behind by extremist Africanists. On 17 June 1976, all four newspapers carried Nzima's photo of the dying Hector Pieterson on its front pages. While DN did not use a frame of 'riots' and 'mobs', the front pages of *The Times*, SvD and the *Guardian* described the shootings in Soweto as a response to a black 'riot', its headlines stating 'South African Riot Evokes Shades of Sharpeville' (the *Guardian*), 'Five Die after SA Police open Fire on Rioters' (*The Times*) 'Seven Killed in Race Riots' (SvD). If the introductions to the front page articles confirmed this image, a certain ambivalence regarding the sequence of events was also expressed in the *Guardian*, in which Denis Herbstein stated that 'the exact sequence of events has not been established', and by Nicholas Ashford in *The Times*, who wrote that what happened after the police had surrounded the 10,000 school children who had marched through Soweto, singing Nkosi Sekeleli Afrika, 'is still unclear'. Ashford also quoted a South African policeman:

Asked whether the police had first fired into the air he said: 'No, we fired into the crowd. It's no good firing over their heads'.

This quote appeared in many other papers in different parts of the world. Thus – again – the figure of a stubborn, narrow-minded police officer, who is stupid enough to say what he thinks, disregarding how it will look to the rest of the world, played a significant role in the media's immediate representation of brutal apartheid violence. Again, the clashes between police and demonstrators were framed as a battle between extremists.

Looking at the editorial comments, *differences between the liberal and the conservative press were now more clear and accentuated than 16 years earlier*. While all the editorials sharply condemned the apartheid regime after the shootings, the conservative papers also put emphasis on criticizing the anti-apartheid protesters, thus implying that not only the apartheid regime was to blame for the situation in South Africa. *The Times'* editorial comment on the 17 June, titled, 'From Sharpeville to Soweto' used the frame of battle between extremists:

> An explosion has long been predicted, and the wonder has rather been that – in spite of many strikes, demonstrations and protests that have taken place with occasional casualties – the South African police have so long managed to keep the lid down.

Harsh criticism against the regime was also put forth, as it argued that the authorities 'have lost disastrously ... their political prestige and the credibility of their racial policy, at a time when they never so desperately needed to claim it was working'. However, although the killing of children could not be defended, the editorial nevertheless implied that not only the South African authorities should be blamed, since the protest was due to the work of calculating, sinister forces that could be connected with similar political forces in Northern Ireland and the Middle East:

> the row over Afrikaans as a medium of instruction put a new and terrible weapon in the hands of those who wish to raise protest loud enough to reach the outside world despite the apparatus of police security. The use of children, indeed the sacrifice of children, in political violence had already spread from Belfast to the West Bank of the Jordan. The lessons of events in such places, and the impossible predicament, in which humane security forces are placed, will not have been unobserved in black South Africa. The younger generation, suffering injustice, is eager to seek an excuse.

The editorial on the same day in the Swedish conservative SvD, titled 'Yet another Sharpeville', sharply condemned the police, but also claimed that 'also the demonstrators was, according to the reports, guilty of severe atrocities'. In contrast, the author of the editorial in liberal DN on 18 June was rather pleased to see protests, arguing that Soweto might be a sign that the opposition in South Africa 'has a strength that we are not yet aware of'. The *Guardian's* first editorial comment on 18 June, titled 'The Illusions that Lie Dead in Soweto', solely focused its criticism on the apartheid regime:

> In 1960 the White South African police killed 69 black South African adults in Sharpeville. On Thursday they started killing children. There can be no place yet for Dr Vorster's regime in the ranks of the civilized and democratic Governments.

All four newspapers put more focus on international than domestic reactions to the shootings than was the case with Sharpeville. This was related to the 'new deal' on Southern Africa presented by the United States and the up-coming meetings between Vorster and Kissinger, and also meant a stronger emphasis on the Cold War frame.

On 25 June, the US veto against Angola's application for membership in the UN made the front page in *The Times*, which reported on criticism against the United States coming from all around the world. Critics related the veto to the talks between Kissinger and Vorster, arguing that Kissinger's new deal for Southern Africa was in fact a support for South Africa and its role in the region. However, *The Times'* editorial defended the veto against a 'Marxist applicant for UN membership', arguing that the veto should not be seen as a support of South Africa. The editorial in DN on the same day argued for the opposite, as it stated that the outcome of the meeting, as well as the US veto against the acceptance of Angola as a member of the UN, was a success for the South African regime, concluding that 'Vorster can be happy about the fact that the leaders have made a promise to stay in regular contact in the future'.

Compared to reporting from Sharpeville, the presence of South African anti-apartheid activists as speaking subjects was more immediate and frequent after Soweto. A major tendency, particularly in the conservative press, was that quotes tended to emphasize activist's militancy. In the front page article in *The Times* on 17 June, Ashford's interpretation of the protests as an expression of a new militancy was confirmed by a quote from Winnie Mandela, stating that

> The language issue is merely the spark that lit the resentment that is building up amongst black people. Every car that looked like a white man's car was burned. That was nothing to do with Afrikaans.

When SvD cited anti-apartheid voices, it focused on representatives of the churches. In its front page article on the 17 June, Desmond Tutu appeared as a moderate as he was saying that 'I can only appeal to the people in Soweto to keep their temper, how hollow it may ring'. On the 21 June, an article in SvD reported that Tutu in his cathedral had said that he wanted to see a 'gesture of reconciliation' on behalf of the government. Quotes from members of the South African government also emphasized the militancy of the South African movement organizations. For example, in an article on 23 June in *The Times*, James Kruger, Minister of Justice, was cited saying that he had warned the white Progressive Reform Party that it should stop supporting 'the Black Power Movement', which he described as 'one of the most dangerous in South Africa'. Kruger was also quoted saying that 'South Africa needed the tough security laws it had to combat such organizations'.

Representatives of the domestic anti-apartheid movement were quoted in the British press the day after the shootings, but judging from the reports on protests in London, they appeared to have involved fewer people than in 1960. On 18 June, *The Times* ran an article titled 'London Protest Against Police Action at Soweto', reporting that around 50 people 'with black armbands had gathered outside of South Africa House' and that the protest was organized by AAM and 'supported by other groups'. Peter Hain, presented as the Young Liberal leader, was quoted saying that the protest was held to 'indicate that there is a feeling of outrage in this country against the sort of overkill police state operation going on in South Africa'.

When paying attention to British protests, SvD again focused on the church in an article titled 'South Africa on the Verge of a Volcano' on 21 June:

the struggle against the South African regime was on Sunday also carried out in the British national sanctuary Westminster Abbey in London. At High Mass, the bishop of Johannesburg Dr. Timothy Bavin thundered against the white regime in one of the sharpest attacks for a long time coming from the establishment.

Both DN and SvD mentioned anti-apartheid activities in Sweden on 22 June, as they quoted a protest statement made by 'Africans in Sweden from five political organizations', and reported that a demonstration outside the South African legation would be held on the same day.

'An insupportable tyranny'

During the months that followed on 16 June, it seemed to become increasingly difficult to defend South Africa in the British press. In two editorials published in August, even the *Telegraph* sharply criticized the Vorster regime, a criticism primarily grounded in the frame of 'law and order'. If this frame thus provided the basis for the conservative press' critique both of the anti-apartheid movement and the Vorster regime, the defence of white South Africa at this time increasingly emphasized 'the rights' of the white minority as reform seemed inevitable. On 14 August, an editorial in the *Daily Telegraph* argued that the South African government 'now presents the face of an insupportable tyranny', claiming that 'the rioters' had not only destroyed their own townships, but also 'destroyed the impression of South African stability and invulnerability'. As the editorial further considered what kind of reforms that could be contemplated, it refuted 'majority rule' because

> It is simply not appropriate to a State composed of several racial groups with no feeling of common loyalty and citizenship. Nor would it ever be accepted by the white electorate.

The correct approach, according to the editorial, was a federalism based on ethnic groups rather than on geographical territories. In an article titled 'The Other South Africa', in the *Sunday Telegraph* on 19 September, Peregrine Worsthorne accounted for his discussions with white – English and Boer – and black South Africans as he travelled in the country, drawing his own conclusions on the political situation. Regarding the issue of democracy, he quoted a Nationalist MP, whose 'kind of talk' on a prospective future South African democracy; he found 'immensely encouraging':

> It won't be Westminster democracy or parliamentary government, but more like some kind of white-dominated multiracial junta, reflecting the realities of power in the era.

Worsthorne also thought that Mangosuthu Buthelezi was 'immensely impressive' representing 'a new spirit of mutual respect and understanding between the races, born of a genuine change in their respective power relationships'. This points to the emergence of Buthelezi and the Inkatha movement as a new 'black moderate' force in the public discourse of apartheid/anti-apartheid in the wake of Soweto, a position that had been vacant ever since the ANC took up arms.

The ANC and the PAC were largely absent from the reports in the major British press following on the Soweto uprising. With regard to South African anti-apartheid opposition, there was further focus on 'the new black militancy'. For example, in an article on 11 July in the *Observer*, titled 'Vorster Facing Rise of "Black Consciousness"' Stanley Uys reported that 'Young militants are taking over from older, more moderate leaders in South Africa's African townships after last months bloody riots', stating that young activists supported both SASO and BPC, but that the new black leadership did not yet have a formal structure.

AA News did however focus on the ANC in its September issue, some-thing which reflected the continued links between AAM and the ANC. The headline on its front page declared that 'South Africa's Townships Erupt with Hatred of Apartheid/The People of Southern Africa are on Advance' and the text beneath it reported that the ANC underground had called for a three-day work stoppage. In Sweden, the first issue after Soweto of AGIS' *Afrikabulletinen* (no. 34/September) carried an editorial signed by the board of AGIS, declaring a change of emphasis in the organization's solidarity work, as the headline stated 'South Africa the Centre of Solidarity'. The text presented a brief analysis of the situation in Southern Africa, arguing that the liberation movement's victory over Portugal meant that 'the most important stronghold of imperialism in Africa, South Africa, is threatened'. Because of this new situation, AGIS would now focus more and more of its solidarity work on South Africa.

In Sweden, the Soweto uprising, as well as the more general situation in Southern Africa, became part of the Social Democrat's election campaign. On 6 August, a month before the election, Olof Palme held a speech in Skövde. It was an appeal for a new initiative on Southern Africa of Social Democracy in Western Europe, apparently intentioned to be an answer to Kissinger's new approach. The speech was the starting point of an intensified commitment to Southern Africa of the Swedish SDP, led by Olof Palme, who argued that efforts should be made to actively support the liberation movements as well as the independent states in Southern Africa.

In Sweden the speech was widely quoted and debated in the press, putting the issue of Sweden's policy regarding South Africa even further up on the election agenda. Strong support for the speech was provided in the labour press. On 7 August, an editorial titled 'Solidarity Against Oppression' in the labour *Arbetet*, argued that Palme's speech was well timed, because the occurrences in Soweto was an indication that South Africa could turn into a new Vietnam, 'a new devastating war between whites and coloureds, between East and West'. An editorial in DN on 7 August pointed to a contradiction in Palme's approach; on the hand he called for a solution to the conflicts in Southern Africa that avoided that the region was further turned into a battle ground of the Cold War super powers, on the other hand he made an appeal to the European Social Democrats to initiate such a solution. But the Social Democrats in Europe was not a third part in region, the editorial argued, as both the British and the West German Social Democrats were governing parties of states that were not, like Sweden, alliance-free, and which were deeply economically involved in South Africa.

Olof Palme and the Swedish Social Democrats never got the opportunity to prove that they meant business regarding imposing a law preventing Swedish companies from further investments as they lost the elections in September and Sweden got its first non-socialist government in 44 years, a coalition between Centerpartiet (The Centre Party), Folkpartiet (The Liberal Party) and Moderaterna (The Conservatives). However, as opposition leader increasingly focusing on Sweden's international commitments, Olof Palme now turned sanctions against Africa into an instrument of putting pressure on the new government.

The final result of the debate in Parliament was that the Swedish parliament passed a law on a ban of new investments in South Africa two years later, in June 1979. As it was realized that Swedish sanctions against South Africa would not have any effect if the UN was not united in the issue, the new law was defined as *a symbolic act* – as a dissociation from South Africa and as sending a message to the rest of the world.[12] This was an important turning point in Sweden's policy on South Africa that, according to political scientist Ove Nordenmark, was a direct consequence of 'the strong opinion triggered by the Soweto-occurrences' in Sweden.[13]

During the last two months of 1976, the British media also increasingly turned to British investments in South Africa – no doubt an effect of increasing campaigning on the issue by anti-apartheid actors, such as the churches and AAM, but also boroughs and Universities, who decided to take action to promote disinvestment. For example, on 11 November, *The Times* reported that 'The Anti-Apartheid Movement in London accused Barclays Bank International of "blatant complicity with apartheid" '. Thus, the year of 1976 was a breakthrough for a renewed campaign on sanctions and disinvestment against South Africa that would dominate the anti-apartheid struggle outside of South Africa for the coming decade.

Conclusion: increasing polarization

As references to Sharpeville were being made immediately after Soweto, historians have compared the symbolic significance of the two events, arguing that 'Soweto' was interpreted in a different way than 'Sharpeville', particularly regarding the representations of the demonstrators. According to James Sanders, those who died in Sharpeville were merely seen as passive victims, while the protesters in Soweto were seen as heroes in an active struggle against apartheid.[14] However, as I have shown in this chapter, the frames of the news reports from Sharpeville and Soweto did not differ that much, as the contradictory stereotypes of the Africans as either passive victims, or as a violent mob, reappeared.

Differences were more clearly visible in the different positions of the editorial comments, as they reflected changes occurring both in the context of South African society and in World politics between 1960 and 1976. First, the increasing polarization between left and right that was visible in the comments on the situation in South Africa in 1976, must be seen in relation to the fact that the region, in the wake of the US defeat in Vietnam and the victory of the socialist anti-colonial movements in the Portuguese colonies, had become an area of intensified Cold War conflict.

Second, in the case of Sharpeville, the news frame of the battle between extremists was in the debate accompanied by the frame of moderates versus extremists, which was largely absent in the immediate editorial comments on Soweto. This difference might be partly explained by the relatively weak links in 1976 between the internal South African movement, dominated by the BCM, and the European solidarity movement, who still mainly relied on its contacts with the ANC and the PAC, now exile organizations and not to a large extent involved in the events in South Africa. Further, after its turn to armed struggle, the ANC did not appear to have the same kind of support in established circles, including the media, as it had in 1960, when it was represented as the 'moderate' alternative to the 'extremist' PAC. Consequently, the role of 'moderate' alternative was vacant, a factor that also contributed in making the debate more polarized in 1976.

Doubtless, as also the Conservatives found it increasingly difficult to defend the apartheid regime without pointing to a black alternative when it sharpened its critique of the apartheid regime towards the end of the summer of 1976, all of the established political camps in Britain were looking for a new 'moderate' alternative, clearing the way for Mangosuthu Buthelezi to take on this position. As Chief Minister of the KwaZulu Homeland and the leader of the Inkatha movement, Buthelezi represented a different political interpretation of the concept of 'multiracial' than that of the ANC. However, if Buthelezi was embraced by the Conservatives because of his advocacy of 'constructive engagement', he was denounced by the major forces of the anti-apartheid movement and hence never had the kind of broad support that the ANC had when it represented 'the moderates' in early 1960. On the left and the liberal side, the role of 'moderates' was rather at this time ascribed to the anti-apartheid churches, and particularly to bishop Desmond Tutu.

An important difference between the debates of 1960 and 1976 is that the issue of democracy was more explicitly on the agenda in 1976. As violence continued, some kind of immediate reform seemed inevitable, even if it was for the sake of 'law and order'. Further, and perhaps more important, what the West had to offer the black population demanding change in the context of an intensified Cold War conflict was parliamentary democracy. But as democracy in a country with a white minority would mean the end of white supremacy, 'those sympathetic to the cause and rights of white South Africans', to borrow an expression from the *Daily Telegraph*, would have to find other discursive strategies than just defending status quo.[15] It was against this background that different alternatives to one man one vote were presented in the conservative press. Further, the increasing international pressure for reform was what made the Transkei a highly contested issue – it was an answer to the demand for change and was presented as a democratic reform, providing autonomy to the homelands – while in practice conserving the power structures of apartheid South Africa and the power balance in the region.

However, it was the ANC that gained the major long-term benefit from the Soweto uprising and the increasing attention that was paid to apartheid/anti-apartheid. When an estimated 12,000 anti-apartheid youths fled the country,[16] its long-term building of a military structure bore fruit; it was the only exile organization that had the capacity to receive many of these politically motivated refugees. Adding to this, the increased global attention to, and moral outrage concerned with, the apartheid issue that came with Soweto was also largely to the benefit of the ANC, as it was the most well-known organization in the West. As the ANC realized that it had not had the capacity to seize the moment immediately in 1976, taking full advantage of the events, it initiated discussions on a change of strategies in 1978. This resulted in a greater emphasis on connections with the internal struggle, something that laid the ground for the successful co-operation with the UDF and COSATU in the 1980s.[17] Though links between the South African BCM and the European anti-apartheid movement were weak, BCM had established contacts with a growing anti-apartheid movement in the United States. The US anti-apartheid mobilization, to a larger extent than previously involving blacks, was further triggered by the Soweto uprising and also by the death in detention of Steven Biko in 1977.[18] When Ronald Reagan wanted to continue a 'friendly' approach to South Africa, he faced a wave of domestic mobilization that during the 1980s grew to become a major force in the context of global anti-apartheid. Its influence peaked in 1985, when Reagan was pressured to introduce a package of sanctions. Thus, the last phase of the anti-apartheid movement's transnational mobilization had started. As its major opponents were the Reagan and Thatcher administrations, the tendency of increasing international polarization on the apartheid/anti-apartheid issue continued to prevail.

8
Sharpeville Revisited and the Release of Nelson Mandela

.

The 'total strategy' and the rise of the UDF

In 1985, South Africa was repeatedly on the news headlines all over the world. In both Britain and Sweden, the amount of news coverage far exceeded previous peaks in 1960 and 1976. Reports depicted a country on the brink of civil war as the apartheid government, led by P. W. Botha, in vain tried to put down an insurrection that was intended to make South Africa 'ungovernable'. If news from South Africa now more frequently than previously became global media events, there were in particular three moments of intensified media attention in 1985; on Sharpeville day, 21 March, 20 people were killed in Langa when they took part in a peaceful procession commemorating the victims of the massacre that occurred at the same place 25 years earlier; the declaration of a state of emergency in July; and P. W. Botha's 'Rubicon speech' on 15 August, turning out as a large disappointment to all of those who believed that constructive engagement would finally bring about the end of apartheid.

P.W. Botha came to power as Nationalist Party leader and Prime Minister of South Africa in 1978. In 1979, Botha presented a 12-point plan for reform, including constitutional, economic and social changes as well as a reorientation of South Africa's relations in the region. The reform programme became known as 'the total strategy'.[1] The new constitution replaced the previous Westminster model with an Executive State President and an ethnically based three-chamber parliament, organized according to the racial classification of the apartheid system, one for 'whites', one for 'coloureds' and one for 'Indians', thus excluding the vast majority of the South African population. In 1983, a referendum on the new constitution was held and in 1984 Botha was elected as South Africa's first Executive President.

174

In relation to its neighbouring countries, where yet another trustworthy ally disappeared as Rhodesia became Zimbabwe in 1980, P. W. Botha launched a policy that became known as 'destabilization'. During a meeting in 1982 the Frontline states declared that South Africa was waging 'a non-declared war against the free and independent states of the region'. Botha replied that the Frontline states were undermining South Africa through supporting 'terrorist organizations'.[2] In 1984, South Africa managed to pressure Mozambique to sign the Nkomati Peace Accord, under which the FRELIMO government closed down its ANC mission and expelled its cadres.

Only 13 per cent of the 'Indians' and only 18 per cent of the 'coloureds' participated in the elections in 1983.[3] Instead, the most important response to Botha's reform programme from South Africa's civil society was a revitalized black political activity, with the forming of UDF and NF in 1983 (see Chapter 2). Further, the Inkatha movement intensified its activity and actively opposed the new constitution, releasing a statement that it was a 'treacherous betrayal of black liberation'.[4] IFP's major support base did however continue to be in KwaZulu Natal, and Buthelezi was seen as a 'collaborator' both in the UDF and the NF camps. Buthelezi's meetings with Botha in 1980 and 1984 had tarnished his reputation among the black population. The rivalry between AZAPO and the UDF on the other hand, was communicated to a world public in January 1985 when AZAPO organized demonstrations against US Senator Edward Kennedy, who was invited to South Africa by the UDF.[5]

This new phase of political activism had its roots in the Soweto uprising and also had an important context in the rising unemployment due to economic recession in the 1980s.[6] As the uprising spread in 1985, and as the government responded by further violence and repression, the number of people dead and injured in clashes between police and activists increased. As violence rose, the South African regime increased its emphasis on the discourse of 'black on black' violence, claiming that most deaths were related to ethnic tensions. Later, Eugene Kock, instrumental in police covert operations, admitted that this discursive strategy

> was a handy propaganda tool because the outside world could be told ... that the barbaric natives ... started murdering each other at every opportunity. We contributed to this violence for a number of years both passively (by failing to take steps) and actively (by sponsoring training and protecting violent gangs).[7]

Violent clashes between black groups did occur, but were to a large extent politically rather than ethnically motivated. Particularly violent was the conflict between Inkatha and the UDF/ANC in the Midlands of Natal. However, in 1992, in what became known as the 'Inkathagate', it was also revealed that the South African government, while carrying out negotiations with the ANC, had assisted Inkatha and its extremely violent attacks on the UDF/ANC.[8]

During the summer of 1985 Botha was being put under increasing pressure both from the uprisings within the country and from the outside world, and the state of emergency declared in July did not improve neither the situation nor his position. On 31 July, Chase Manhattan Bank announced that it would not grant South Africa any further loans. Shortly after this, it was announced that Botha would give a speech on 15 August, intended as a manifesto for the future of South Africa. The message was spread that in this 'Rubicon speech', epoch-making changes would be declared. Because of the expectations that the speech would be the beginning of the end of apartheid, it was sent live in Britain, Germany and the United States. However, it turned out that all that Botha had to say to the world that was watching was that he firmly resisted demands for any major changes, concluding that the only possible alternative to his policy would be 'bloodshed, turmoil and murder'.[9] As a result of the speech, the demand for international sanctions immediately intensified, more foreign banks declared that they would not renew their loans and in a week, the Rand lost a third of its value. Inside the country, the black community's resistance was further mobilized by the speech, and Botha's white support was weakened.

In a sense, the Rubicon speech could be seen as the symbolic turning point Botha never intended it to be. During the month that followed, a group of leading South African business people went to Lusaka to meet the ANC, and thus yet another of the processes that ultimately brought apartheid down was initiated. Further, the intensified mobilization in the United States, demanding sanctions against South Africa, ultimately resulted in the passing of the Comprehensive Anti Apartheid Act in the US congress, as the House of Representative turned over Ronald Reagan's presidential veto on 29 September 1986.[10] However, it would take more than four years of internal uprisings, international pressure and informal negotiations before the South African government under F. W. De Klerk, who replaced P. W. Botha in 1989, finally agreed to engage in a serious peace process, starting with the unconditional release of Nelson Mandela.

As Mandela was released from prison on 11 February 1990, images of celebration were brought to the world by the media. However, if the release of Mandela was celebrated worldwide by the anti-apartheid movement, it did not mean that the struggle was over. Quite the opposite, a new and difficult phase of the struggle began. As Margaret Thatcher had been the last of the major political leaders of the West to be pressured to agree on sanctions against South Africa, she was the first to propose that sanctions now should be lifted.

'Take your bloody money and go'

As in other countries in which a significant anti-apartheid movement existed, the sanctions debate peaked in both Britain and Sweden in 1985. On the front page of the first 1985 issue of *AA News* (January–February), the headline stated 'The Pressure's on for Boycott' and the tone of the article beneath was extremely optimistic as it accounted for the current state of the transnational anti-apartheid movement:

> On both sides of the Atlantic, anti-apartheid activists have been making life uncomfortable for some of the South African govern-ment's most powerful and influential allies in the western world ... . For all of us in the British Anti-Apartheid Movement – particularly as our own March Month of Boycott Action approaches – the hard work and achievements of our counterparts in the US, Scandinavia and elsewhere should be both an inspiration and a challenge.

In the Swedish media, attention was not only paid to events in South Africa during the first months of 1985; a large number of articles were related to a debate on anti-apartheid strategies going on in a number of sec-tors of the Swedish society. The law banning new investments was criticized for being ineffective and demands were made that the Social Democratic government impose further legal restrictions, not only on new investments but also on import of goods from South Africa. As it was revealed that major Swedish companies had ignored the 1979 law, there was an increasing media focus on the presence of Swedish companies in South Africa, includ-ing investigative articles on work conditions. In the context of the churches as well as the unions, demands for disinvestment were made. Following a debate on the 'Swedish South Africa law', as it was called, in parliament on 20 February, pressure rose on the government to make the law stricter. On 21 February, an editorial in DN connected the debate to the situation in South Africa, mentioning recent arrests of anti-apartheid leaders, and that hundreds of blacks had been killed during demonstrations and strikes during the last years. The editorial further turned against Moderaterna (the Conservative Party) and the Swedish industrialists – arguing that their arguments against the law were weak. One of the most important arguments put forth was, according to the editorial, a claim that it was only 'the extremist exile organization ANC' that advocated a ban on investment, while the black population, according to an often quoted opinion poll in South Africa, were of a different opinion. This must however be seen in relation to the fact that South African law prohibited public statements advocating sanctions. More weight should however, according to the editorial, be put to statements made by Desmund Tutu and the UDF, who in spite of great risk advocated sanctions.

As the UDF and Desmond Tutu, representing the churches, had appeared as strong anti-apartheid voices inside South Africa, the ANC had become less visible in the Swedish media than previously. However, on 17 March, four days before the Langa shootings, there was a full-page interview with Winnie Mandela in the largest labour daily, *Aftonbladet*. It directly related to the ongoing Swedish debate as the headline stated 'Take Your Bloody Money and Go!'. It was unsigned, but those who had read the latest issue of the AGIS' publication *Afrikabulletinen* (no. 2/85), probably noted that there was a similar interview with Winnie Mandela signed Herman Andersson – a pseudonym for anti-apartheid journalist and AGIS/ISAK activist Magnus Walan.

The 1985 British sanctions debate started in the beginning of January, as editorials commented the visit to South Africa by Senator Edward Kennedy. The comments displayed different positions on the sanctions issue that were to be repeated during the year. Just as important however, is that it also introduced the *frame of internal division* that was an important element in the established media's representation of the anti-apartheid movement during the year – a frame that stood in sharp contrast to the *AA News* reports on unity of the anti-apartheid movement internationally as well as in South Africa.

The editorials of the *Guardian* ('Where Teddy wasn't Ready') and the *Daily Telegraph* ('Insensitive Senator') on 15 January agreed that Kennedy's visit had turned out an embarrassment for Kennedy as well as for his host, Desmond Tutu. They also agreed that the purpose of Kennedy's visit was an attempt to win new support for himself and the Democrats in the United States after Reagan's election triumph in 1984, which according to the editorial in the *Guardian* immediately had been followed by 'sudden but sustained protest against apartheid'. According to the *Guardian*, the recent American protests

appears to have been provoked by television film night after night of the protracted and violent confrontation between the South African police and demonstrators opposed to the new constitution that excludes the black majority.

Both editorials further argued that Kennedy, eager to show support for the anti-apartheid movement through his journey to South Africa, had only showed his ignorance about the fact that South Africa, according to the *Guardian*, 'is a lot more complicated than it looks', or in the words of the *Daily Telegraph*, that it is 'a more complex society than the visiting politician can grasp'. 'Complexity' turned out to be another word for 'internally split' – not referring to splits between the ruling whites and the discriminated coloureds and blacks, but within the black community. According to the *Guardian*, Kennedy's tour 'threw into sharper relief than for some time the split which has been growing over the past decade within black opposition to apartheid'. Further, the tendency of 'black power', which according to the same article opposed a non-racial solution, 'now looks stronger than at any time'.

If the British press thus put an emphasis on internal division within the South African anti-apartheid movement in January, particularly the *Guardian* would during the following months also focus on an internal split in the context of British AAM. On 25 February, an article in the *Guardian* titled 'Apartheid Group Expels "Mavericks" ', written by Seumas Milne, reported that the national committee of AAM had decided to close its City of London group after two years of conflict between the group and the national leadership of AAM (see Chapter 3). It also reported that 12 Labour MPs, including Tony Benn, had signed a statement against the expulsion of City Apartheid.

The debate on sanctions during 1985 had two components. First, it was debated whether the British Government, following the Commonwealth, as well as the EEC, should impose sanctions against South Africa. Second, the strategy of 'disinvestment' was debated, focusing on the American anti-apartheid movement as a crucial actor and inspiration for activists in other parts of the world. For example, in an article in the *Daily Telegraph* on 18 March, titled 'Sanctions will Hit the Wrong Target', Stephen Glover argued against disinvestment. According to Glover, the transnational anti-apartheid movement was not in tune with the majority of those they claimed to be in solidarity with – on the contrary, they represented the voice of extremists:

Black trade unionists in South Africa are on the whole opposed to disinvestment. So are all but the most extreme black leaders there.

Thus, if the sanctions debate was fuelled by the shootings in Langa on Sharpeville day, it was already on its feet earlier during the year.

Langa in the press: 'an uncanny resemblance of Sharpeville'

Comparing the way that the shootings in Langa were reported on the front pages of *The Times*, the *Guardian*, DN and SvD on 22 March with the reports from Sharpeville 25 years earlier, there are obvious differences regarding the description of the event and the use of language, as any images of a rioting mob provoking the police to shoot were absent. For example *The Times'* front page stated '17 Blacks Killed by Police in South Africa' and in the introduction to the article, written by Michael Hornsley, comparisons to Sharpeville 1960 were made:

> South African police killed at least 17 people yesterday and injured 36 others'... Yesterday's shootings bore an uncanny resemblance of those at Sharpeville 25 years ago'.

Further, citing the comments of the Minister of Law and Order, Louis La Grange, Hornsley wrote that he *'claimed* (my italics) that the police had been forced to fire in self-defence'. The major tendency of the reports in the other three papers was similar; the police had shot into a peaceful demonstration. DN did however report that although the protest in Langa had been peaceful, 'from several places, there were reports about disturbances and riots'. The front page article in the *Guardian* reported that 'wildly conflicting accounts of the clash emerged last night', but the introduction to the article, as well as its headline ('South African Police Gun Down 17 Blacks') emphasized the version that the shootings were unprovoked.

The frame of battle between extremists was however put into play on the same day in an editorial in *The Times*, titled 'Sharpeville Jubilee'. On the one hand, it stated that 'only the South African police could commemorate the Sharpeville silver jubilee by shooting dead eighteen more blacks'. On the other hand, it ended by contrasting peaceful change with violence, as it used the events in Langa to remind the readers of

> that there are those in South Africa who do not necessarily agree – or might not have the patience to wait. Disasters like that two days ago can only lend strength to their cause.

SvD's editorial on 23 March is also worth paying attention to as it contained reflections on *how* the events had been reported on. The immediate reason for this reflection was a statement by Ronald Reagan that 'law and order' must be upheld also in South Africa and that the police in Langa had shot to defend themselves against a rioting mob. Here SvD expressed ambivalence. On the one hand, it argued that 'on first thought a counter attack from an attacked police force is easier to understand than naked and unprovoked violence'. But on the other hand, the editorial argued, 'ultimately, this distinction is not interesting', because 'in a society which sets the principle of equality of human value aside, there is no right. There is, by definition, no law and order that can be defended'.

In the wake of the Langa shootings, the temperature of the debate on sanctions and disinvestment rose. As the language of moral indignation got stronger, opponents to sanctions also seemed to be more on the offensive, the debate getting increasingly polarized. According to *AA News* (July–August), 25,000 people marched in London on Soweto day, demanding 'Sanctions Now!' in a demonstration organized by AAM. In Britain, established media's attention to the domestic anti-apartheid movement further increased. Two days after the Langa shootings, Seumas Milne published another article in the *Guardian* on the issue of the expulsion of the City group, titled 'Separate Developments in Common/Seumas Milne on a Split in Anti-Apartheid'. This time, Milne put a heavier focus on the *frame of internal split:*

> The news that the Anti-Apartheid Movement has closed down its dissident City of London local group has taken some students of political sectarianism by surprise. For the 25-year old solidarity movement has in the past avoided the factionalism that afflicts other radical groups.

Thus, Milne presented as news in itself that a movement that previously had 'managed to bring together activists from the ultra-left through to the Conservative Party', now was involved in 'unprecedented conflict'. In an editorial on 28 March, the *Daily Telegraph* attacked Bishop Trevor Huddleston in his capacity of the President of AAM, who 'would have us believe that revolution is around the corner' in South Africa. It related the Bishop's 'excessively apocalyptic cast of mind' to the sanctions issue, arguing that some believe that there is a chance 'to expedite matters by the introduction of sanctions':

> Here hope really does run wild, for while sanctions might no doubt harm South Africa – or at any rate, her blacks – they are unlikely, if history is anything to go by, to bring members of the Government to their knobbly Afrikaner knees.

While opponents to sanctions in the British press thus continued to portray their counterparts as idealistic, and emphasized a harsh economic view of the issue, protagonists mainly emphasized the moral argument. For example, an editorial in the *Guardian* on 15 April compared the sanctions campaign to the international campaign to end slavery, arguing that as 'with the slavery in the early days of the abolition campaign, the first question is not what others may or may not do, but what we are going to do ourselves against apartheid'.

In Sweden, national self-interest became clearly visible in the intensified debate during the end of summer when an 'unholy alliance' between conservatives and the Metal union emerged. In an article in conservative SvD on 23 August, titled 'Stock-Therapy Against Apartheid', Göran Albinsson Bruner argued against disinvestment, applauding Leif Blomberg, the chairman of the Metal Union, because he dares 'saying the simple truth' to his members: 'We do not overthrow apartheid by selling our shares'. In August, the Metal union held a congress, which got wide attention in the press. It decided against selling its shares in Sandvik, a Swedish company with subsidiaries in South Africa. Although the motivation of the decision emphasized the 'ineffectiveness of sanctions', economically as well as morally, there was no doubt that protection of jobs played a role. After a three week long campaign, only 70 out of 4500 workers at Sandvik had signed a petition brought out by a group that called themselves 'Metal Workers Against Apartheid', demanding that Swedish companies should withdraw from South Africa ('70 out of 4500 is Against Apartheid', *Arbetarbladet* 30 August).

As it became increasingly obvious that the 'reform policy' of the Botha regime was a failure, those who had defended it instead sharpened their criticism against the South African liberation movement, particularly the ANC, but also the UDF. This meant that the debate on possible alternatives to apartheid was further polarized, as the liberal side tended to show a more sympathetic approach to the ANC than a decade earlier. This cleavage between positions was clearly visible in the editorials commenting on the state of emergency in the *Guardian* and the *Daily Telegraph* on 22 July. In an editorial titled 'Burning the House Down', the *Daily Telegraph* claimed that the ANC, as SWAPO, 'have become a Soviet-linked terror organization which no South African Government could conceivably countenance in the foreseeable future'. The *Guardian's* editorial dismissed the argument that the ANC and the UDF organized the violence in the townships as a theory of conspiracy invented by the apartheid regime. On 24 August, the *Guardian* published another article on AAM, titled 'A White Hunter in Mandela Street', that was in sharp contrast to Milne's critical articles during spring. As the major part of the article consisted of long quotes from AAM's executive secretary Mike Terry, who, according to the article 'senses that a new dawn is nigh', it largely functioned as a mediation of the message of the movement to the readers.

'Which black opposition?'

As violence in South Africa increased, an important discursive strategy of the conservative press was the attempt to make anti-apartheid an issue of violence or non-violence. For those defending non-violence, reliable allies had always existed in the churches. An editorial in the *Daily Telegraph* on 24 July referred to a speech by Desmond Tutu in which he had threatened to leave the country if the necklacing of suspected 'collaborators' in the townships did not stop. The text ended thanking 'God that Bishop Tutu ... may be called upon eventually to help untangle the web' (of violence in South Africa). However, as 1985 was a year in which churches all over the world were radicalized on anti-apartheid issues, such allies became fewer. In October, a high-level delegation of the British Churches returned from a visit to South Africa, expressing doubts that non-violent change was still possible ('Churchmen See the "Final Phase" Begin, the *Guardian*, 4 October). On 7 December, in an article titled 'Tutu Says Evil of Apartheid Allows Christians to Use Force', *The Times* reported that Desmond Tutu in a speech at a meeting of the World Council of Churches (WCC) in Harare had said that 'advocates of non-violent change in South Africa were irrelevant and that individual Christians were justified in using force against apartheid'.

In an editorial comment to the Rubicon speech on 17 August, the *Daily Telegraph* wrote that 'the best interpretation' that could be made of Botha's speech was that 'he is willing to concede that the days when whites could decide the future of South Africa by themselves now are over, but that he cannot spell out what alternative he really has in mind'. This seems to have been true also for the British Conservatives, judging from the editorials in the *Daily Telegraph* and *The Times*. On 25 October, the *Daily Telegraph* ran an editorial titled 'Which Black Opposition?', addressing not just British Conservatives, but also anti-apartheid Liberals, in which it singled out Mangosuthu Buthelezi as the only leader sticking to non-violence, and thus providing the only possible anti-apartheid alternative:

> Chief Buthelezi is a strong black leader, beholden to no one, whose message that violence is both indecent and avoidable and should be attractive to both Liberals and Conservatives.

However, it remained unclear what kind of legitimacy his 'black leadership' should be based on in a future South Africa. While the *Guardian* in its editorial at this time stated that it fully supported the UDF's demands of a democracy based on 'one man one vote', conservative editorials in *The Times* and the *Daily Telegraph* were silent on this issue.

While the *Guardian* started to open up a space within the established press for the ANC to appear as an acceptable alternative force, *AA News* reported in its November issue that AAM on the 2 November had provided the President of the ANC, Oliver Tambo, a platform from which he could speak to 150,000 people, who marched against apartheid in London. A week earlier, on 24 October, *The Times* had reported that Oliver Tambo had been invited to give evidence to an all-party select committee of the House of the Commons (while Margaret Thatcher was away on a trip to the United States). If the ANC thus was beginning to regain a broader public recognition, the article also reported about loud protests from the Conservatives, who persisted in focusing on the issue of violence, as Geoffrey Howe was quoted stating that 'We do not engage in contact with organizations of this kind which are actually engaging in violence at the moment'.

In Sweden, the ANC once again appeared as the main South African movement organization when a rock concert in support of the ANC was held in November in Göteborg. The concert was broadcast by Swedish television and brought together the alternative left wing rock scene with a number of mainstream artists, and included a speech by Prime Minister Olof Palme.[11] Different from the Mandela concerts in Britain, the Swedish ANC concert was not organized by any of the leading anti-apartheid organizations. The local Africa Groups in Göteborg supported the organizing of the concert and were present with its information, but the concert was not even mentioned in AGIS' *Afrikabulletinen*.

In contrast to this emerging broader acceptance of the ANC was an article titled 'Mandela the Manipulated' by Roger Scrutton, editor of the *Salisbury Review*, published in *The Times* on 17 December. Commenting on the monument that the Greater London Council had raised to Nelson Mandela, Scrutton portrayed Mandela and the ANC as avant-garde Cold War terror warriors, threatening not just white South Africa, but the whole Western world:

> Now as then, the ANC is to be the spearhead of Soviet domination. Should it accomplish its purpose not only will the people of South Africa be deprived of their little freedom, but the West as a whole will receive a political, economical and strategic blow from which it will never recover.

Considering that influential members of the political and economical elite in the West shared this view, the end of the Cold War was certainly an important factor in the process that brought apartheid down. However, as the press material clearly indicates, the pressure of the transnational anti-apartheid movement on political leaders in South Africa as well as internationally, and on leading banks and corporations, had never been stronger than it was in the late 1980s. This was implicitly also the main message of the editorial of the *Guardian* on 30 December, as it began stating that 'South Africa has had a degree of sustained international attention in 1985 unmatched since the Anglo-Boer War'. However, its title nevertheless summarized a pessimistic conclusion: it had been 'South Africa's tragic year of missed chances'.

In Sweden intensified anti-apartheid mobilization in South Africa, as well as in Sweden, once again led to governmental action. On 17 December 1985 a decision was made in the Swedish parliament to impose a ban on South African agricultural products. Further, during the parliamentary debate demands were made of further restrictions on trade with South Africa, referring to a decision taken in Danish Parliament on 13 December.[12] In the process that followed, all parties except Moderaterna (the Conservatives) supported such a law, which was finally imposed in March 1987.

The release of Mandela

As the country internally appeared as ungovernable, and externally was under huge international pressure, the year of 1985 to many observers looked as the beginning of the end of white domination in South Africa.

However, the apartheid regime did not only manage to resist demands of serious change for another five years, but did also keep up its intensified repression. With the exception of a short period in 1986 the state of emergency remained until 1990.[13] When Nelson Mandela finally was released in February 1990, the fall of the apartheid regime once again to many observers seemed closer than ever. However, as Mandela himself declared in his speech on the day he was released, the anti-apartheid struggle was far from over. Rather, in Mandela's view, the struggle had to be intensified. And it was this message that dominated the front pages of the newspapers the day after Mandela's release, as images showed him and Winnie Mandela greeting the masses in Cape Town with clenched fists. The reports and comments in the liberal and conservative press were however based on different frames. In this respect, the major British and Swedish media presented similar patterns. In Sweden DN's front page headline made clear how Mandela's gesture should be interpreted – 'A Clenched Fist for Freedom'. SvD also showed the image of Nelson and Winnie with clenched fists. Another front page headline did however modify the image of celebration as it reported 'One Killed Six Hurt When Police Opened Fire'. Similarly, in Britain the front page headline of the *Guardian* emphasized celebration and reconciliation, while *The Times* put more emphasis on disruption and Mandela's militancy: 'Black Leader Strolls to Freedom While Police Open Fire on Looters/ Fight Goes On Says Mandela/No Option But to Continue the Struggle'.

The editorials further emphasized the tendencies of the front page reports. The *Guardian* and DN supported Mandela's message, arguing that his release did not change the fact that the apartheid regime was still in power. DN's editorial argued that De Klerk', 'who can be expected to resist full democracy, one man one vote', had a specific purpose with releasing Mandela at this moment. It was intended to impress on the foreign ministers of the EEC meeting in a week's time in Dublin, where Margaret Thatcher, according to a recent promise, would push for a lifting of sanctions. The editorial in the *Guardian* argued that it would be inappropriate to congratulate F.W. De Klerk for his 'realism'. Here, the killing of five demonstrators by police in Katlehon Township the evening before Mandela was released was mentioned as a reminder that the apartheid system was still in full force:

> It was a baleful descent to so much rejoicing. Not just the equipment but the mental outlook which produces torture, false evidence and deaths in captivity is in full place – a Frankenstein machine which could still undermine Mr. De Klerk.

Mandela's release was thus 'not the end but a punctuation mark in the obituary for apartheid'. The editorials in SvD and *The Times* did on the other hand emphasize the frame of internal division, arguing that the world must now reward De Klerk for his reform policy. The editorial in SvD, titled 'The Myth Mandela', painted a scenario of a South Africa plagued by factional violence. The ANC had based its particular status on the Mandela myth, the editorial argued, but when Mandela 'becomes real', it could lead to further internal tensions. Similarly, the editorial in *The Times* stated that Mandela now was changing the burden of imprisonment for the much heavier burden of his country's hope. As the Cold War was more or less over, even the communist flag seemed rather harmless compared to the threat of factionalism:

> Indeed, the ANC flag, which shares with the hammer and sickle of the South African Communist Party pride of place at most opposition rallies in the black townships, is today little more than a flag of convenience for mutually hostile factions both within the organization and outside.

Further, the editorial argued that Margaret Thatcher was responding correctly to De Klerk when she offered to lift sanctions against South Africa, and argued that the United States and EEC should follow rather than listen to the 'pusillanimous advice of Neil Kinnock, Sir Sonny Ramphal and all those who dread the end of the anti-apartheid industry'.

Thus, already on the day after Mandela' release, new positions in the debate were taken, although the arguments brought forth were basically repetitions of old ones, as supporters of De Klerk reopened the debate on almost every form of anti-apartheid action that the international anti-apartheid movement successfully had launched since 1959.

If the press in Britain and Sweden tended to focus its comments on the situation in South Africa immediately after Mandela's release, the focus shifted when Mandela visited the two countries in March and April. Now, the comments were directly related to the solidarity movements as well as to the anti-apartheid policies of the governments in the respective countries. In Britain, Mandela came for the second Wembley concert on 16 April, organized by AAM and visited by 77,000 people.

On 17 April, the front page of the *Guardian* carried the headline 'Diplomacy from Mandela Amid Wembley Uproar' above an image of the crowd at Wembley. The articles in the *Guardian* paid specific attention to the fact that anti-apartheid, in Britain, as well as globally, now was a highly mediatized, and even commercialized, phenomenon; the front page article began by painting a picture of the merchandise sold outside of Wembley, as it cited a heated argument between two black men regarding the fact that one of them, a merchandiser of Mandela t-shirts, did not know that Mandela's name was copyrighted.

The fact that the anti-apartheid movement, especially in Britain, now had become an established and highly mediated phenomenon also reintroduced *the frame of the anti-apartheid industry* (see Chapter 6). The expression was now frequently used when arguing that the call for further sanctions and boycotts did not serve the interests of the black South African population, but of a professionalized 'solidarity movement elite' who feared the end of apartheid because it would make them superfluous. The front page article in *The Times* on 17 April did however mainly focus on what it perceived to be an attack on Margaret Thatcher and the British Government – as a headline stated 'Mandela Chides Thatcher'.

In Sweden the renewed sanctions debate after Mandela's release debate peaked around 12 March, when Mandela arrived in Sweden and called for increasing pressure on the South African government in his public speeches in the Swedish Parliament, Uppsala Church and, finally, in front of 12,000 people in the Globe Arena. This was a significant moment in the debate that would guide Sweden's policy for the next four years, and not an easy one for those who opposed sanctions, as three decades of anti-apartheid mobilization, organized from below as well as from above, had created a climate in which it was difficult to question Mandela's authority.

The rally at the Globe Arena on 16 March clearly reflected the position and character of the Swedish anti-apartheid movement after 30 years of solidarity action. It was organized by AGIS and ISAK, who led the Committee for the Release of Nelson Mandela, including around 60 NGOs and all of the established Swedish political parties except the conservative Moderaterna and their youth Section. For the gala, AGIS and ISAK had been granted one million SEK by the Swedish government (through SIDA).[14] The day before, on 15 March, the Swedish Parliament had decided to extend the embargo to include trade in services. It is further significant of the strength of the Swedish anti-apartheid opinion that Moderaterna, who had always been harsh critics of the Swedish government's anti-apartheid policy, did not dare to initiate changes in this policy when it became the leading party in the non-socialist government that came into power in September 1991. The embargo was lifted only after Mandela had called for the lifting of sanctions in a speech to the UN General Assembly in September 1993; the Swedish government's support to the ANC stopped in January 1994.[15]

Mandela's visit to Sweden was thus an occasion for the celebration and confirmation of a victory for the Swedish anti-apartheid movement, the event, and the way it was reported in the media, further strengthening the position of its appeal for continued support to the South African liberation movement. In the Swedish media's sometimes euphoric self-celebration, this internationalist solidarity event was also an articulation of a kind of nationalism, as expressed for example in the tabloid *Expressen*, Sweden's largest daily, as its large headlines on 12 March proclaimed that 'A Whole World Followed Every Step' as Mandela had put his foot on Swedish soil.

Conclusion: the beginning of the end

Just as in the cases of Sharpeville and Soweto, extensive focus on South Africa following the Langa shootings appeared as a 'natural response' to an extraordinary violent event, with a potential of stirring up a moral outrage in the West. However, just as in the previous cases, the huge media attention to South Africa that followed on the shootings had been preceded by increasing mobilization in South Africa and in solidarity circles, something which was also reflected in media reports.

The fact that a new massacre occurred in South Africa on the day that marked the 25th anniversary of the shootings in Sharpeville gave rise not just to comparisons between the two massacres, but also to a discussion on whether South Africa had undergone any significant change during the period between the two events. One might also ask: had media reporting on the violence, and the editorial comments on the situation in South Africa and on the anti-apartheid movement, undergone any significant change during this period?

Comparing the shootings in Sharpeville, Soweto and Langa, historical accounts have established that the three occasions were similar in the sense that South African police started to shoot at, and actually killing, unarmed participants in a demonstration. The major tendency of media reporting in the newspapers in Britain and Sweden was however different in 1985 compared to 1960 and 1976. In 1985, the front-page headlines, as well as the articles, did not give the same impression of the shootings being a response to a violent and threatening crowd of Africans. Further, it is notable that an editorial in the Swedish conservative SvD actually brought up the issue of the news narration of the sequence of events in Langa as an important issue, worthy of a critical discussion. Considering the strength of the global anti-apartheid movement at the time, and that it had at this time established a number of contacts with the established press, it seems reasonable to assume that the anti-apartheid movement had contributed to the changing perspectives and self-reflexivity of the press, as well as to the actual change of the frames of reporting.

This change did not mean that the established press unambiguously presented a picture that was clearly in favour of the anti-apartheid movement. On the day after the shootings in Langa, *The Times* editorial used the *frame of battle between extremists*, connecting it to a *frame of internal division* with reference to the South African anti-apartheid movement. The frame of internal division is close to the frame of moderates versus extremists that was widely used in 1960, but has a different function. While the latter implicates support for one part of the anti-apartheid movement, the former rather discredits the movements as such, as it depicts it as incapable of performing unity, and thus questions its capacity of performing the role as 'realistic alternative'.

Although the frame of internal division was present both in the liberal and the conservative press during 1985, and especially so in Britain, it was however not a dominant perspective. The most dominant tendency of the debate in 1985 was *the increasing polarization regarding the representation of the anti-apartheid movement*. On the one hand, there were a significant number of articles explicitly discrediting anti-apartheid. For example, the ANC could be labelled as 'terrorists', while AAM could be described as 'sectarian' and ISAK as 'extremist'. On the other hand, there were also an increasing amount of articles presenting the ANC, AAM and ISAK as 'respectable' acting subjects – their views sometimes expressed in news articles through long quotes or by representatives in opinion articles.

If 1985 thus marked some general shifts in the apartheid/anti-apartheid debate, the release of Nelson Mandela in 1990 to a certain extent meant, perhaps a bit unexpectedly, a return to positions taken early in the debate. The fact that the end of apartheid seemed close added another twist to *the frame of the anti-apartheid industry*; it was implied that the resistance to the lifting of sanctions could be seen as an expression of the fear of professional anti-apartheid activists who felt that the end of apartheid, and thus of anti-apartheid, would make them unemployed.

In Sweden however, this frame was absent in 1990, something which must be understood in relation to a consensus culture defining a post-war epoch of non-governmental and governmental internationalism in Sweden, culminating four years after the murder of its engineer Olof Palme. This internationalism was, however, not without ambivalences and contradictions. On the one hand, the construction of the Swedish nation as a leading force in a global struggle for justice was a successful mobilizing element in the ideological repertoire of post-war Swedish Social Democracy, thus serving domestic and particularistic interests. Further, it was based on a rather Eurocentric perception of the world. On the other hand, this internationalism was part of a much broader wave of global solidarity that, as we have seen in this book, did not confine itself to empty declarations, but did involve frequent interaction with, and substantial material support to, the struggle for liberation in Southern Africa.

Conclusion: Anti-Apartheid and the Emergence of a Global Civil Society

Not an easy affair

In retrospect, support to the struggle against apartheid in South Africa might appear to have been something uncontroversial in most parts of the world. And sometimes it was. At certain moments, events in South Africa that were extensively reported by mass media and caused a moral outrage all over the world made it easier to get public attention for anti-apartheid organizations; as for example immediately after the Sharpeville shootings in 1960, the Soweto uprising in 1976 or the killing of Steven Biko in 1977. But to *sustain* support to the struggle in South Africa against apartheid through the decades from the 1950s until the 1990s, and especially to support the call for sanctions made by the South African liberation movement, was not always an easy affair. Even at those moments when the major media's attention to, and explicitly expressed indignation over, the apartheid regime peaked, it did not necessarily mean that it was in favour of the anti-apartheid movement.

Further, the anti-apartheid movement was not a homogenous phenomenon. The construction of its collective identity and its major action strategies was not a smooth process defined solely by consensus building. In this book I have tried to show that the dynamic of the anti-apartheid struggle must be analysed as a complex pattern of social interaction, involving conflicts and tensions not just in relation to the movement's adversaries, but also *within* the space of action that the movement created. To construct and sustain a sense of collective identity, while at the same time recognizing, and allowing space for, the discursive diversity characterizing a 'movement of movements', was a challenge to anti-apartheid activists – and more generally for other social movement activists during the last decades, as movements stretch across borders, uniting groups and individuals based in extremely wide ranges of cultural, social and political contexts.

It might be argued that in a 'movement of movements' such as anti-apartheid, which focus on a single issue, seeking as broad support as possible, collective identity is generally a weak element. This might indeed be true for more short-lived one-issue movements. In the case of anti-apartheid however, the transformation of a social order (the South African) was on the agenda, and the movement was engaged in sustained collective action that lasted for decades. This would not have been possible without a strong element of collective identification.

In terms of collective identity, sustained transnational anti-apartheid action across borders was made possible through the construction of *an imagined community of solidarity activists*. I think it is particularly useful to use Benedict Anderson's influential concept here, since it emphasizes the possibility of a shared sense of community among people dispersed over large geographical distances, not the least with the help of communication media. To borrow an expression from John B. Thompson, the transnational anti-apartheid movement was constituted by 'action at a distance'. According to Thompson, this is a form of action that, through the use of various forms of communication media, 'enables individuals to act for others who are dispersed in space and time, as well as enabling individuals to act in response to actions and events taking place in distant locales'.[1] However, not just media, but also mobility – or travel – played a crucial role in the organization, mobilization and articulation of anti-apartheid across borders. I would like to argue that the central aspects of the construction of a movement space for transnational anti-apartheid action, *which formed an important part of a wider process of the emergence of a global civil society during the post-war era*, can be analysed through the following interrelated themes, which will be discussed in this chapter: (1) transnational organization and mobilization (2) media and (3) mobility (travel).

Further, linking the inside and the outside of the movement, the inner tensions and differences of the anti-apartheid struggle should be seen as articulations of the conflicts that were an integral part of the *structural contexts* that conditioned its action space. First, there was a 'two-sidedness' of the anti-apartheid struggle, as *it simultaneously engaged in national and transnational/global politics*. This should be seen as a response to the contradictory processes of world politics during the period in which it was active; *on the one hand the continued process of nation building and on the other hand the intensified process of globalization, making borders of nation states and national identities increasingly porous.*

Second, if the world was becoming increasingly 'postcolonial' during the period of the anti-apartheid struggle, the post-war period might still be seen as a re-articulation of the political, economical and cultural links established during the colonial era. The legacy of colonialism was not just present in the inter-state alliances in the UN Security Council, opposing isolation of South Africa, but also in the movement itself, creating tensions and ambivalences. For example, it defined the relations between South African exile movements and Western solidarity movements. Solidarity organizations were dependent on good relations with the exile movements for its legitimacy in relation to its supporters and the general public. However, just as important, it was the other way around as well. For example, it was very difficult for the ANC or the PAC, being perceived as 'black' and 'foreign' organizations, to stage their own public meetings in Britain in the 1960s.[2] However, with AAM providing the platform through organizing the meeting, the ANC and the PAC leaders could give public voice to their issue. This interdependence between exile and solidarity organizations highlights some of the paradoxes characterizing the condition of postcoloniality, in which colonial dependencies can be reproduced, re-articulated as well as sometimes transcended. Finally, the globalization of politics during the post-war era was to a large extent a matter of *a division of any significant political field along the Cold War lines.*

Anti-apartheid politics further points to the 'Janus face' of the United Nations as a central institution of global politics, constituted during the Cold War era. On the one hand, as an international organization, the United Nations is subjected to the power hierarchy of the inter-state system. The dominant state powers in the Security Council can block or manipulate decisions in accordance with their national interests, as was the case with the issue of effective sanctions against South Africa. On the other hand, the United Nations might also be seen as a part of a global civil society, as relatively independent UN organizations such as the Special Committee Against Apartheid interact with NGOs from various countries, bypassing the state level, and giving space for transnational social movements opposing the interests of dominant state powers.[3]

In this context, anti-apartheid action at particular moments constructed what Homi Bhabha has called a *third space*, understood as 'an intervention into a situation that has become extremely polarized'.[4] As a position, 'third space' does not signify neutrality, rather it is a condition in which the conflicts, contradictions and ambivalences of a political order is felt most strongly. This was indeed the condition in which the means and strategies of anti-apartheid *collective action* were developed and sustained.

Organizing and mobilizing transnational anti-apartheid

Looking at the most important forms of activism, organization and mobilization of the anti-apartheid movement, a crucial aspect was, as in most social movements, the forming of movement organizations. Some of them were national, such as AAM, some of them were international, such as IDAF, and some of them consisted of networks of local groups, such as the Africa Groups in Sweden (before they were formed into a national organization, AGIS). These organizations were all part of a transnational solidarity network, which on the Southern Hemisphere had important nodes in Dar Es Salaam and Lusaka, and on the Northern Hemisphere in London and New York. London was vital in its capacity as a 'postcolonial capital', where the ANC had its main exile office and where South African exiles initiated AAM, and New York was instrumental as the site for the United Nations. The anti-apartheid struggle also involved alliances between states and actors in global civil society, as states in a few cases funded, and exchanged information with, movement organizations across national borders.

Transnational anti-apartheid mobilization occurred in three waves, or phases, involving three political generations of activists, who emphasized different forms of action strategies. *The first phase*, which is mainly associated with the name of 'Sharpeville', was initiated with the call from the South African Congress movement for an international boycott in 1958. Here, South African activists played a key role not just in South Africa, but also internationally, particularly in Britain. In solidarity circles activists from previously existing movements, such as the churches, the labour movement and the anti-colonial movement played a crucial role in defining the movement's initial action forms. While an important action form in this phase was the boycott, it was also a phase when major international organizations – such as IDAF and AAM, the latter's organization modelled on the labour movement – were set up. Younger activists were also involved.

The second transnational phase occurred when the young generation of the student protests entered the movement in the late 1960s. In both Britain and Sweden, sports events became the target of direct action. Although these actions in both cases were successful in the sense that the games were stopped, they nevertheless created some tension in relation to the previous generation of activists, who feared that the 'militancy' of the student activists would alienate a broader support base of the movement. Generational tension was also sometimes related to ideology, as the students picked up marxism in a re-radicalized form, criticizing the reformist approach of the worker's movement as well as of the churches and the liberals.

The third phase of transnational mobilization occurred in the 1980s in connection with the internal uprising led by the UDF and COSATU, and reached an important peak in 1985. While the whole action repertoire developed during the past decades was now put in use, the main focus was on the sanctions issue, as movement organizations put increasing pressure on their respective governments, as well as on international organizations such as the Commonwealth and the United Nations. The visibility of a third generation of activists, based on the second wave of new social movements emerging in the early 1980s (the peace, the women's and the green movement) was mainly manifested in an increasing emphasis on culture and symbolic action, sometimes highly media-oriented. In terms of influence, the movement was however dominated by the previous generations of activists, who were running organiza-tions that at the time had reached a certain degree of professionaliza-tion, and was engaging in political pressure on a relatively high level. When a younger generation was demanding, and engaging in, more radical forms of extra-parliamentary action, this created tension.

Mediated interaction and information politics

One of the important structural changes facilitating anti-apartheid activism across borders was obviously the increasing role of the media during the period of anti-apartheid struggle. However, the role of the media must not be over-emphasized, as is so often the case in studies of transnationalism and globalization. As we have seen, travel, or mobility, was also a crucial aspect of transnational activism. As the narratives of the activists show, the existence of a transnational network of 'political exiles' seemed to have played a particularly important role for the emergence of solidarity groups and movements in different parts of the world. Thus, face-to-face interaction with 'distant others', was an integral part of sustained global anti-apartheid activism.

John B. Thompson has argued that the development of the modern media, taking off in second half of the fifteenth century, has been an integral part of modernization and globalization, but nevertheless has been strongly under-emphasized in the social sciences. In his social theory of the media, Thompson makes a distinction between three forms of interaction: (1) face-to-face interaction, which takes place in a context of co-presence (2) mediated interaction, which involves communication across distance, through the use of a technical medium (letters, telephone, Internet), and (3) mediated quasi-interaction, which refers to modern mass media, and is characterized by the fact that it is 'produced for an indefinite range of potential recipients' and could be defined as 'monological'.[5]

According to the analysis of Thompson and many others, modernity and globalization means an increasing importance for mediated and quasi-mediated interaction – at the expense of face-to-face interaction. The role of the media might indeed have been under-emphasized in classical and post-war social science. However, in relation to studies and theories of transnationalism and globalization during the last decade, it might on the contrary be argued that the role of the media has been over-emphasized. Important for the processes of globalization of culture, politics and economy is also the increasing mobility across borders, including different forms of migration and temporary travel, particularly following the emergence of a global system of air traffic after the Second World War.[6] This development has created expanded possibilities for face-to-face interaction between people based at different locations in the world. The considerable changes in the patterns and possibilities of travel means an increasing importance for a form of face-to-face inter-action that I would define as *extended face-to-face interaction*, taking place in a context of increased possibilities of mobility, and characterized by its temporary character.

For any social movement involving action at a distance, which of course to a large extent is the case of transnational solidarity move-ments, media and information work become crucial. However, action at a distance in the context of the anti-apartheid movement was made pos-sible not just through the media, but also through travel. As was shown in Chapter 1, travel played an important role for the construction of transnational anti-apartheid networks, campaigns, strategies and identities. A substantial number of key activists, who might be called 'activist travellers', played an important role through travelling across the world, participating in meetings and conferences, making speeches, appearing in the media and, most important, exchanging information and sharing experiences with fellow activists.

I am arguing that the key to an analysis of the construction of trans-national anti-apartheid networks is to look at the combination of on the one hand mediated interaction, particularly the development of a number of media strategies, related to the emergence of new media and media technologies, and on the other hand face-to-face interaction, including exchange of information and experiences between individuals representing groups, communities and organizations with different locations in the world.[7]

Margaret E. Keck and Kathryn Sikkink define 'information politics' as 'the ability to quickly and credibly generate politically usable information and move it to where it will have the most impact'.[8] Looking at information politics in the context of anti-apartheid, it is obvious that generating information to a large extent also involved conflict and struggle. Generating and moving information in the context of the anti-apartheid movement can only be understood as a vital activity if it is seen as part of a wider struggle of information and interpretation, related to national as well as global articulations of the political meaning of issues of 'race', 'apartheid', 'anti-apartheid', 'democracy', 'national sovereignty' and 'human rights'.

In this respect, it is once again important to situate the anti-apartheid struggle in the context of the new social movements and the post-war phase of globalization that produces new structural conditions with different social implications in different parts of the world. This is a period in which we see the growth of a new form of capitalism that Manuel Castells has termed 'informational', and in which the struggle over the control of information, symbols and knowledge is becoming increasingly important for structural reasons.[9] Consequently, a defining aspect of the new social movements is an emphasis on information politics. This is something that has been theorized in the context of social movement studies, however, as argued in the Introduction, often with a Eurocentric bias.[10] Social movement's increasing media orientation and turn to information politics has not just taken place in the context of advanced capitalist nation states, but is a global phenomenon. As the case of anti-apartheid shows, not just the solidarity movements of the North, but also the liberation movements of the South, developed a sophisticated politics of information, including carefully thought-out media strategies aimed at different contexts.

If information politics in the context of globalization has become increasingly important for social movements all over the world, it is nevertheless important to emphasize the specific characteristics of each movement and political struggle. In the context of the anti-apartheid movement, information politics had a special meaning because of the nature of its struggle. As a movement whose actions to a large extent aimed at influencing governments, as well as ordinary people, to boycott

South African goods (and cultural workers) and to impose sanctions on South Africa, it involved numerous forms of production, dissemination, as well as struggles for information.

There is no doubt that the transnational anti-apartheid movement was always dependent on, and influenced, processes in South Africa. The moves of the apartheid government in order to resist international pressure were not alone in making an impact on its actions. All of the three major protest waves of the transnational movement were initiated by the South African liberation movement. However, there was no simple causal logic at play. Rather, how national events influenced the international process were largely dependent on how the information about these events were mediated. This is one of the reasons for the crucial role of the media, and this is why alternative information channels were vital at times when the large media were restricted and influenced by South African media strategies.

Mobility – travel and exile

The action at a distance that constituted anti-apartheid as a trans-national movement was not only facilitated by the media but also by mobility; temporary travel, student visits facilitated by scholarships and 'exile journeys'. This facilitated face-to-face interaction between individual activists who were based in different parts of the world or were coming from different places of origin. Of course, far from all of the people who participated in the movement travelled, but among those who did were key activists, who could be understood as 'spiders' in the webs of global anti-apartheid activism. They were people such as Michel Lapsley, who through individual moves and movements were connecting places, organizations and networks.

Travel, or mobility, had different functions within the movement. *First*, as we have seen, *conferences played an important role* as a space for networking, discussions and co-ordination of national as well as transnational campaigns. *Second, the exiled South Africans played an important role as organizers and mobilizers*, travelling extensively around the world, making speeches at solidarity meetings and thus giving 'the other' a public face.

Third, according to accounts of solidarity activists *travel was related to an emotional aspect of solidarity activism*, crucial for the individual's motivation to engage in, as well as to sustain, solidarity action through the years. For some activists journeys to South Africa meant making direct experiences of the apartheid system that became a starting point for a commitment to the struggle. *More important, travel facilitated personal encounters between South African activists and solidarity activists,* sometimes developing into friendships. Some activists mention temporary visits by South Africans, for example by the UDF in the 1980s, as an important source of inspiration for the everyday routines of solidarity activism. It seems however, that it was the presence of exiled South Africans that was the most important aspect in the process of giving 'the other' a face on the level of personal relations in the context of the solidarity movement. *Hence, through making identification with 'distant others' something concrete for grassroots activists, travel seemed to have been a crucial element in making anti-apartheid solidarity possible.*

Considering the important role ascribed to the presence of South African exiles by solidarity activists, it is reasonable to conclude that this is an important factor in explaining the fact that solidarity with the South African liberation movement had a stronger and wider support base in Europe and the United States than did the liberation movements of other countries in Southern Africa; the latter did not have as strong an exile presence in the Western countries as did the South African organizations.

An imagined community of solidarity activists

This book has largely focused on the activities of organizations and activists that were crucial nodes in the networks of national and transnational anti-apartheid activism. However, it is important to underline the significance of the everyday activism that was performed in the context of a movement culture that largely existed beyond media reporting and public attention, and which constituted a fundamental aspect of the transnational anti-apartheid solidarity movement. Swedish activist Per Herngren accounts as follows the anti-apartheid activities of a local group of an organization affiliated to ISAK:

> In the local group that I belonged to, activism was mainly about the boycott, and about music and dance at local festivals organized for fundraising purposes. We noticed the presence of the anti-apartheid movement in the media in brief news items or articles a couple of times every year, but we were never engaged in any media work. It was the chairman of ISAK and a few others who took care of that. However, when an anti-apartheid activist made a statement in the press you often knew who it was, and therefore the central work never felt far away.[11]

If this statement argues that central and local parts of a social movement organization, through a kind of division of labour, complemented each other, other activists that I have interviewed have emphasized differences regarding influence between activists in the centre and the periphery of the movement, particularly in connection with participation in international meetings and conferences. One example is the account of local AAM activist Margaret Ling, who however also gives an example of the fact that an important form of transnational interaction occurred directly between local groups in Sweden and Britain, thus bypassing the central organizations:

> Anne-Marie Kihlberg of the Africa Groups in Göteborg and I had been in touch for quite a few years; we'd corresponded and talked on the phone, but we had never met until apartheid was over. And when we did meet we sat down and talked about how we hadn't had the chance to go to these various conferences abroad, that it was always the top executives who did that. Travel was not necessary for the lower ranks, for one to feel that there was an international anti-apartheid movement and that we were part of it.[12]

In the context of the movement culture, some activists were of course more active than others were. Some activists lived a large part of their everyday life within the movement culture, thus engaging in *politics as a form of life*. For others, participating in a movement culture might have been limited to occasional visits to collective events, such as going to demonstrations, wearing a 'political T-shirt', and boycotting South African goods when shopping in the local supermarket, thus largely performing anti-apartheid activism as individual action, engaging in what might be termed *lifestyle politics*. But whatever the degree of the involvement in the movement culture, these everyday actions can be conceptualized as *life politics*, something which, as defined by Anthony Giddens, is part of the process of increasing individualization in the context of late modernity.[13] The emergence of contemporary life politics should also be understood in relation to wider economic, political and cultural changes, including an increasing globalization of the economy and the media. An important part of life politics is that it politicizes consumption through the notion that the individual can perform a political action not just as a citizen, but also as a consumer, as in the boycott.[14]

Although I agree with Giddens that the phenomenon of life politics can be conceived as an individualization of politics, I would however rather define it as *expressing a new relation between individual and collective political action*, emerging in contemporary society, and largely depending on communication through the media. Participating in a boycott, through not buying South African goods, is certainly an individulized form of political action, but it presupposes a collective organization of the boycott and a collective articulation of its political meaning, which in the case of anti-apartheid was done by organizations such as AAM, the ANC or ISAK, using established and alternative media as channels of communication.

Already a few days after the Sharpeville massacre in 1960, both *The Times* and the *Guardian* paid attention to *the style and symbols of the anti-apartheid protesters* in London, as for example manifested in the Ying and Yang shaped AA-symbol worn as a badge. Cultural links with the anti-nuclear movement in terms of a shared – new form of – political culture were also pointed out in the press reports. These articles did not only highlight the emergence of a 'movement politics of style' as part of an emerging new social movement culture, but also shows us that the symbolic dimension of movement activism was part of what attracted attention from the media. In fact, this shows that the Sharpeville shootings took place at the moment of the emergence of a new and young political culture in Europe (much later named 'new social movements'), standing close to, and later deeply intertwined with, the explosion of a much broader youth culture in which rock music would play a central role.

The British AAM was initiated under the name of the Boycott Movement, and *I would conclude that the boycott continued to be the most important form of activism and mobilization* in the context of the anti-apartheid movement. While an aim of the economic, cultural and sports boycotts was putting direct pressure on the South African government, the boycott also functioned as a form of mobilization and 'consciousness raising'. Through the launching of boycott campaigns, the organizations offered people an opportunity for 'everyday' participation in solidarity action.

Connecting individual, local and symbolic action to transnational collective action, it could also be argued that participating in a boycott, or wearing an anti-apartheid T-shirt, could be seen as a form of expressive action that was a fundamental aspect of the construction of the collective identity of the movement. It was an act through which the individual subject could feel that s/he became part of an imagined global community of solidarity activists. In this sense, the boycott was a form of 'identification at a distance' through local action. From this point of view the boycott also *emotionally* connected grass-roots activists in different parts of the world.[15]

The emergence of a global civil society

Since late eighteenth century, up until its 'rediscovery' during the 1980s, the various definitions of the concept of 'civil society' has been associated with the political space of the modern nation state. The recently emerging discourse on a 'global', 'international' or 'transnational' civil society thus implies the notion of the emergence of *a global political space*.[16]

However, scepticism toward the notion of a global civil society has also been frequently expressed. One common objection is that 'civil society' implies a certain level of social and cultural integration, articulated politically in the form of a national identity.[17] However, I would argue that the notion of cultural homogeneity as a defining aspect of modern national civil society, taken for granted by many social scientists, universalizes the particular conditions of certain Western nation states (and it might even be argued that not even in Western Europe was there ever the kind of homogenous national identities that has been taken for granted in dominant scientific as well as in political discourses). However, in spite of this, it still might make sense to be sceptical about the possibilities of constructing, on a global level, public spheres and political identities corresponding to those that historically have emerged in the context of the nation state, and which have been fundamental for democratic politics. It is quite obvious that the concept of civil society needs to be reformulated when transferred from theories of the nation state to theories of a global society.

This discussion is particularly relevant for analysis and research on transnationalism in the context of social movement studies, which until quite recently largely has emphasized national movements and contexts. Even scholars of transnationalism such as Margaret E. Keck and Kathryn Sikkink have been sceptical about the emergence of a global civil society, as they have argued that 'there is a lack of convincing studies of the sustained and specific processes through which individuals and organizations create ... something resembling a global civil society'.[18] Contrary to this, I would like to argue that it makes sense to define certain developments during the twentieth century, including the history of the transnational anti-apartheid movement, in terms of the emergence of a global civil society. In this sense the interactions of the anti-apartheid movement was part of the construction of a global political culture during the Cold War.

The rise of a global civil society was part of a process of intensified political globalization during the post-war era – and was of course related to processes of economic and cultural globalization. Here, it is also relevant to make an analytical distinction between *globalization from above* and *globalization from below*.[19] The increasing number and importance of inter-governmental organizations (IGO's) constitute political globalization from above, a highly significant process of the twentieth century. In 1907, there were 37 IGO's, while at the time of the end of apartheid, there were 260. The process intensified during the decades after the Second World War; treaties embracing IGO's increased from 6351 in 1945 to 14,061 in 1975.[20] The process of political globalization from below during the twentieth century, of which the emergency of a global civil society was part, was constituted by the increasing number of NGO's, transnational networks and social movements organizing across borders. In 1909, there were 176 NGOs working internationally, while at the time when apartheid ended, there were 28 900.[21]

Another objection to the use of the concept of civil society in relation to a global context is that in previous theories, it was always in one way or another defined by its relations to the state – and it is hardly possible to argue that there exists a global state. Rather, just as global civil society is characterized by diversity, its actors relate to diverse counterparts; transnational corporations, supra-national institutions as well as nation states. Here, it might be useful to introduce James Rosenau's notion of 'the two worlds of world politics'. On the one hand, there is the state-centred world, characterized by centralized political organization and consisting of just over 200 actors. On the other hand, there is the multi-centred world, in which hundreds of thousands of actors operate across borders.[22] It is a world characterized by a de-centred power structure and complex interdependencies. In order to influence and change social structures, actors in the multi-centred world need to have access to large networks, and contemporary alliances are frequently formed for specific purposes. In this sense, the multi-centred world is similar to Manuel Castells' 'network society'.[23]

The two worlds of world politics both overlap and interact with each other, sometimes in contradictory ways. Conflicts between the two worlds can occur, as alliances formed in the context of the multi-centred world put pressure on a nation state, questioning its sovereignty on a particular issue, or as in the case of the apartheid regime, its legitimacy.

During the last decades social movements have increasingly operated simultaneously in the two worlds of world politics, thus mobilizing public opinion both in the context of different national civil societies and in the context of global civil society. Adding to the complexity of political globalization, it must also be emphasized that not just social movements, NGO's and corporations, but also states, can be actors in the multi-centred world. However, while states in the context of the state-centric world are defined by territorial sovereignty, they perform different functions as they enter the multi-centred world. Ulrich Beck has coined the term 'transnation states' in order to define the new role that states play as they act in relation to various issues in the context of the multi-centric arena.[24] In this context, states are no longer political spaces defined by their territorial sovereignty, but one of many political actors, which enter into alliances with other actors, such as corporations or even social movements. Beck mentions the campaigns against Shell's dumping of an oil platform in the North Sea, and against France's nuclear testing in the Pacific Ocean, both taking place in 1995, as examples of coalitions between states and social movements, expressing a new kind of politics emerging with contemporary globalization. However, two decades before that, the anti-apartheid movement formed alliances with states such as India, Nigeria, Tanzania and Sweden.

To sum up, in a global context 'civil society' must be thought of as a political space of a different character in relation to *national* civil society. I define global civil society as *a political space in which a diversity of political cultures interact and intersect*. Contrary to national civil society, global civil society does not have a single political counterpart. Rather, actors in global civil society often act simultaneously in different political arenas, in opposition to, and sometimes in alliance with, supra-national organizations as well as nation states and local Councils.[25]

As the number and activity of NGO's has continued to increase after the end of the Cold War, direct relations between NGO's/INGO's and the UN has continued to become more and more direct. Enhanced co-operation with NGOs has also been a central issue in the attempts to reform the UN made by UN General Secretary Kofi Annan, who in 1999 wrote:

> In the United Nations a few decades ago, the Governments of Member States were virtually the sole players in the international process; non-governmental organizations were seen as mere supporters and mobilizers of public opinion in favour of the goals and values of the UN Charter. Today, the cultural gap between NGO's and the UN is rapidly and happily disappearing ... NGOs are often on the ground before the international community gives the UN a mandate to act.[26]

In this context the large UN/NGO conferences, and their counterpart conferences defined in terms 'non-official' alternatives, have played an extremely important role in facilitating and reproducing transnational movement networks. As has been argued in this book, the interaction between the UN and the transnational anti-apartheid movement played a significant role for the emergence of these forms of co-operation.

To conclude, I argue that the history of the anti-apartheid struggle provides an important historical case for the analysis of present-day global politics, as it is evident that the present mobilization of a global civil society in relation to economic globalization and supra-national political institutions such as WTO, IMF and the World Bank, has historical links to the post-war, transnational political culture that the anti-apartheid movement formed an important part of. Movement organizations, action forms and networks that were formed and developed in the anti-apartheid struggle are present in this contemporary context, making the transnational anti-apartheid movement an important historical resource for contemporary global civil society, as a number of key anti-apartheid activists in contemporary mobilization act as movement mediators.

If the system of nation states, the postcolonial condition and the Cold War were the most crucial historical and structural contexts for the growth of a global civil society after the Second World War, it might be argued that, considering the changes that have taken place since the early 1990s, the structural conditions of social movement action in contemporary global civil society are qualitatively different. The most important global change that has taken place is of course the end of the Cold War. However, if the fall of the Berlin wall seemed to widen the space for political action across borders, a bipolar division of global politics was once again introduced after 11 September 2001 and the declaration of the global 'war against terrorism'. Further, the alliance of states that subsequently went to war in Afghanistan and Iraq also confirmed that nation states can still be powerful, and that the hierarchy of the system of nations that was constituted during the colonial era still matters.

In this context social movement activism once again could be conceived as 'an intervention into a situation that has become extremely polarized', thus constructing an action space in which the conflicts, contradictions and ambivalences of 'the new world order' order is felt most strongly.

Further, an important similarity between the transnational anti-apartheid movement and the wave of global mobilization emerging at the turn of the millennium, is the co-existence of 'old' and new movements, as an important role in the global World Social Forums is played by churches and particularly labour unions, showing a renewed internationalist orientation in response to the latest phase of economic globalization.[27]

To conclude, there are many continuities and similarities between the transnational anti-apartheid movement and the contemporary 'global justice movement'. There is however a certain displacement; while both movements simultaneously mobilize nationally and transnationally, the anti-apartheid movement put a stronger emphasis on pressuring national governments to impose sanctions, while the present global justice movement puts more weight on addressing supra-national institutions and organizations such as the WTO, IMF, the World Bank or G8; a change reflecting the increasing globalization of politics and economy. However, for this new global solidarity movement to achieve its goal, that is, decreasing social cleavages globally, it must nevertheless engage in the same kind of 'unholy alliances' between movements, states and supra-national organizations that were formed during the struggle against apartheid.

The meaning(s) of solidarity

In the *transnational* anti-apartheid movement, 'solidarity' was the central identity concept. The activists that I have interviewed, whether political exiles, church activists, communists, union activists, women's activists, liberals or activists of anti-apartheid organizations, shared an identification with the concept of solidarity. Solidarity was the general concept that defined the movement's collective identity, its ideas and its practices.[28] Whatever one was doing, whatever one was participating in, an organization, a demonstration, a boycott, it was defined as an act of solidarity. Solidarity was thus constructed as a fundamental value in the transnational anti-apartheid movement.

But beyond any idealistic or romantic understanding of 'solidarity', what did it actually mean in the context of the transnational anti-apartheid movement's discourses/practices? In the sociological understanding of the concept, as defined by French sociologist Émile Durkheim, 'solidarity' refers to social integration; it signifies the social bonding that keeps society together. However, in a sociological context 'society' has often implicitly referred to local or 'national society'. In the context of the global anti-apartheid movement 'solidarity' defined interaction between localities at a distance, across national borders. As AGIS activist Mai Palmberg defines it, it was 'the unconditional support to a group of people who struggle for their rights in a distant place'.[29] Hence, it implied a notion of a world society. However, within this very general frame of meaning, it could be defined in various ways in movement discourse, and it could refer to many different, and sometimes conflicting, practices.

In a sense, in global solidarity, there are no 'Others', as it implies universalism. However, global anti-apartheid solidarity, as any other practice constructing a collective identity, involved drawing a number of borders between 'us' and 'them'. The fundamental Other of the transnational anti-apartheid movement was of course the apartheid regime. In the case of the solidarity movements in Britain and Sweden, other important Others were the state, national corporations with subsidiaries in South Africa and their political allies. However, constructing collective identity does not just involve drawing borders in relation to 'enemies'. As I argued in Chapter 3, 'solidarity' often implicitly referred to national identity, as it was defined as solidarity of one (national) people with another. Solidarity activism thus implied a 'we' helping 'them' – the 'objects' of solidarity. Further, it involved the internal struggle between particular interests, national or organizational, creating tensions and conflicts.

Doing my interviews, I have asked my informants what they actually did when they were acting as solidarity activists. However, I have also asked them, as a general reflection over the meaning of their actions, to define solidarity. Here, the main tensions were defined in terms of theory/practice and universalism/particularism. With a few exceptions, activists immediately responded to my question by making a distinction between solidarity and charity, which they associated with a relation of inequality, and with a religious (Christian) rather than a political understanding of social relations. In contrast, 'solidarity' was defined as implying a value of social equality and a political analysis of the conditions which created a need for solidarity.

When attempting to define the interaction that solidarity involved, that between the subject and the object of solidarity, the tension between universalism and particularism was a recurring theme in my informant's reflections.[30] As AGIS activist Bertil Högberg stated, there was in the anti-apartheid movement an attempt to define and to practice a solidarity that was based on 'an empathy with, and an engagement in, other people's situation, a subject–subject relation'. However, the practice of the solidarity movement was most often constructed in terms of 'subject–object, where the people in South Africa, their organizations, became the object of our solidarity'.[31]

It is possible to discern number of ways to negotiate the tension between universalism and particularism inherent in the concept of solidarity as generally defined in this context. According to one view solidarity is based on social justice as a value in combination with an analysis establishing that social structures are constituted by webs of interdependency. From this point of view, solidarity can be defined as the mutual recognition of self-interest between peoples. This view invokes an imagined future. For example Ingvar Flink, veteran AGIS activist, illustrated this view by referring to PAIGC leader Amilcar Cabral as he during a visit to Sweden in the 1960s stated that 'When we have become liberated, I hope that we might come here and help you some time if you get into trouble'.[32]

Another view is a value- or norm-oriented approach, based on an ethical stand. Solidarity is according this view an act of identification, recognizing that identification with others is what constitutes the identity of the individual. It is also a definition that puts a strong emphasis on an emotional aspect, particularly in the form of the identification with the Other's suffering. Being close to, or even rooted in, a certain form of Christian ethics, this was a definition that many of the church activists put forth, as for example Brian Brown of the British Council of Churches:

> I would say it is standing alongside, an entering into the existential experience of someone else, in as far as one is able. Total solidarity is nonsense; I can never stand in your shoes, only you can. But in as far as empathy, and sensitivity and love and knowledge and identification allow I can get alongside you to be in solidarity, which is walking with, and empathizing, feeling with, and struggling with. It is something that I think is part of our Christian calling ... it is a whole depth of theological dimension that we haven't ever properly articulated within the church of Christ.[33]

This ethical view could however also be articulated in a secularist discourse, bearing humanist, or existentialist connotations, as in the definition by Per Wästberg:

> You experience yourself in the encounter with another human being. I encounter a person who appears to be different from me, he can be black, but he has also an apparent ability to laugh and cry for the same reasons as I, and he has also a lot of other similarities with me, but he does not have my chances, my resources, he might be in a disadvantageous position. And then an emotion arises in me that he or she just as well could be me and therefore I have to act in solidarity with that person in order not to isolate myself.[34]

A way to escape, or dissolve, the duality of the relation between the subject and the object of solidarity action, is to invoke a third element, a cause, which the action is in solidarity with. For example AAM executive secretary Mike Terry states that 'I think you have to be in solidarity with something, you have to be in solidarity with the struggle, and that struggle has to be one with which you have some general affinity with its goals and strategies'.[35] AAM activist Margaret Ling referred to a quote by the FRELIMO leader Samora Machel:

> He said that 'solidarity is not charity but it's about two people who share the same vision, working together to achieve that, and I think that is what it is, you share a common vision of the world'. I think also that Samora Machel said, anyway this came from Mozambique, that the liberation struggle is like a train, going along, as it goes along some people might drop off the train, but the train goes on, and I feel that that very much described what happened.[36]

Bo Forsberg, a former chairman of ISAK, stretched the notion of the third even further, as he defined solidarity in terms of the ethical and political consequence of a recognition of the global interdependency of contemporary world society. He further stated that while the concept had been out of fashion for a while, it would very soon return. It would take less than three months before he was proved right. I was doing the interview with Forsberg and another former anti-apartheid activist in Stockholm in September 1999, while they were busy interacting with NGO's in various parts of the world, preparing a protest against the WTO meeting in Seattle in December. 'It' s going to be big', they told me. Their organization Diakonia, previously a member of the Swedish anti-apartheid coalition ISAK, was one of the 1448 organizations that signed the 'Appeal from the international civil society' that was published on the Internet during the protests in Seattle in December 1999. With reference to the anti-apartheid struggle as well as to the contemporary context, Forsberg argued that solidarity is

> an insight regarding mutual dependency and mutual responsibility related to the fact that we live in a world in which we, to an increasing extent, are dependent on each other, and therefore have to take a common responsibility. I think that solidarity, which today is a word that is an object of ridicule, will return pretty soon, in connection with the issue of the transfer of resources from North to South, and with the fact that we are facing common international challenges of a kind that we have never been confronted with before.[37]

What we can perhaps learn from these reflection's on global solidarity made by individual's who have devoted a large part of their lives attempting to practice it, is that if the construction of a common ground is necessary for collective action in support of justice, there will always be different interpretations of what is just, and on what the appropriate means to achieve justice are. As any discourse aspiring to unite people all over the world makes universalist claims, while at the same time interpreting the meaning of global solidarity from a particular point of view, there will always be a tension between universalism and particularism in the imagined communities of an increasingly globalized world. Thus, the meaning of solidarity across borders will be multiple, and those interpretations that reach a relative hegemony will be challenged by the alternative interpretations of its others.

Epilogue: The Legacy of Anti-Apartheid

On 10 May 1994, in the wake of South Africa's first democratic elections, the presidential installation of Nelson Mandela was celebrated. It took place in front of the Union Buildings in Pretoria, the administrative centre of the apartheid State from 1948, the same year that the UN Declaration of Human Rights was announced. In front of a dancing and singing crowd, Nelson Mandela presided over a powerful manifestation of the new Rainbow Nation, broadcast live by television all over the world. More than 6000 international guests, including government representatives from 150 countries, underlined the fact that this was an event of global concern.

When the tenth anniversary of this event was commemorated, far from all comments on the achievements of a decade of ANC rule was celebratory. To some commentators South Africa represented a political failure, arguing that the ANC had betrayed the people they once represented. Criticism of the ANC government has been directed at its lack of firm response to HIV/AIDS and at the lack of resistance to demands of liberalization and privatization from influential transnational corporations, IMF and the World Bank. Those who are defending this policy have argued that such 'reforms' have been necessary in order to create wealth through economic growth. Nevertheless, these 'reforms' have failed to create new jobs and have left large groups of South Africans still living in poverty.

In these debates, South Africa's problems are often put into a national framework. Poverty, increasing social cleavages and the AIDS disaster are presented as problems that have to be solved through national politics. South Africa's present problems are however related to global processes over which national politics has little control. Thus, just as apartheid was never just a national concern – in spite of the Apartheid regime's constant references to national sovereignty – South Africa's present situation demands political action stretching beyond its national borders.

Further, when South Africa's present state is debated, the legacy of apartheid is often, rightly, put high on the agenda. But what about the legacy of global anti-apartheid, and particularly of the solidarity movement, when South Africa is facing the consequences of an intensified economic globalization?

In Britain AAM was transformed into Action for South Africa (ACTSA) in 1994, the latter engaged in solidarity work in Southern Africa, keeping a large part of the former's organizational support base. Just like many other previous anti-apartheid activists, groups and organizations, it was involved in the Jubilee 2000 campaign for cancellation of the debts of poor countries in the South. The approach of IDAF was continued in Canon Collins Educational Trust for Southern Africa (CCETSA – initially funded by the British Defence and Aid Fund in 1981) assisting South African students and different education projects in South Africa.[1] In Sweden, a network for solidarity with Southern Africa emerged out of ISAK. AGIS has continued solidarity work in relation to Southern Africa, slowly increasing its membership base. There are however other ways of acting upon the legacy of anti-apartheid solidarity – and the 'symbolical capital' it might have generated. For example, a former chairman of ISAK was an important facilitator when the Swedish government, in competition with several other countries, sold Swedish fighter planes (JAS) to South Africa for a substantial sum of money.

In June 2000, I interviewed former anti-apartheid media activist Danny Schechter, today working with Globalvision, an alternative media organization, and Mediawatch – The Global Media and Democracy Supersite, a project that aims at supporting media critique and media activism, and to which more than 400 groups and organizations from all over the world were connected at the time of the interview. As an example of the fact that different individuals can carry the learning processes of the anti-apartheid movement into very different contexts, he showed me Ben Cashdan's documentary 'The two Trevor's go to Washington'. It follows two South Africans, Trevor Manuel and Trevor Ngwame, both of them former anti-apartheid activists, on their journey to the IMF/World Bank meeting in Washington in 2000. Trevor Manuel visits the meeting as South Africa's minister of finance and as the chairman of the Boards of Governors of the International Monetary Fund and the World Bank. Trevor Ngwame is a grassroots activist from Soweto who goes to Washington to protest against the global policies of the IMF and the World Bank – following on the protests against the WTO meetings in

Seattle in December 1999.[2] In the film, there is also a short interview with an activist participating in a demonstration in Washington, Dennis Brutus, who started SAN-ROC (The South African Non-Racial Olympic Committee), which led the international campaign for a sports boycott on South Africa.

These examples do not only show that there are many different ways to deal with the legacy of anti-apartheid; they also highlight the continuities between the transnational anti-apartheid movement and present global mobilization as manifested in the global justice movement.

Notes

Prologue

1. Quoted from Krog 1999, p. 118f.
2. The TRC held was made possible through legislation created shortly after the first democratic elections were held in South Africa. The hearings were held between 1996 and 1998.
3. Michael Lapsley, centrally placed in the TRC, argues that it was impossible not to know (interview with Michael Lapsley).
4. For analyses of apartheid discourse, see for example, Beinart and Dubow 1995 (eds), Dubow 1995, Norval 1996 and Marks and Trapido (eds) 1987.

Introduction

1. Quoted from Sampson 1999, p. 415.
2. Mandela 1994.
3. Beinart 1994, Adler and Webster 2000, Seekings 2000.
4. Friedman and Atkinson 1994.
5. Worden 1994, Odén and Ohlson 1994.
6. Massie 1997, Crawford and Klotz (eds) 1999. Of course, most research make arguments for a combination of 'internal' and external' factors, although giving some more weight than others. For an example of such an analysis, with a high level of sophistication, see Price (1991), where two internal factors, economic decline and political violence, interacts with international pressure.
7. In 1990 he was targeted by a letter bomb, losing both hands and an eye. He finally returned to South Africa in 1992 and got involved in work with the Truth and Reconciliation Commission (TRC).
8. Interview with Michael Lapsley. For a biography on Lapsley, see Worsnip 1996.
9. Melucci 1996, Waterman 2001, Wignaraja (ed.) 1993, Cohen and Rai (eds) 2000, Della Porta and Tarrow (eds) 2005.
10. On global civil society, c.f. Kaldor 2003, Anheier et al. (eds) 2001 and 2004/05, Keane 2003, on the World Social Forums and the global justice movement, see Della Porta and Tarrow (eds) 2005, Sen et al. 2003, Waterman and Wills (eds) 2001, Patomäki and Teiviainen 2004, Bond 2001.
11. E. S. Reddy, e-mail 13 April 2005.
12. AAM Archive, MSS AAM 13 and M.
13. E.g. Keck and Sikkink 1998, Della Porta and Kriesi 1999, Cohen and Rai (eds) 2000, Della Porta and Tarrow (eds) 2005.
14. E.g. Jennett 1989, Voorhes 1999, Seekings 2000, Fieldhouse 2005.
15. This approach implies looking at norms, defined as 'shared understandings of standards for behaviour and interests', Klotz 1995, p. 14, as interacting

with self-interest in the context of international politics and institutions. Relations between norms and interest are thus depending on the context.

16. See for example Cohen and Rai (eds) 2000, Della Porta and Tarrow (eds) 2005, Tarrow 1998a, Keck and Sikkink 1998, Smith, J. *et al.* 1997.
17. Keck and Sikkink 1998, p. 1.
18. Herbstein 2004. On the role of the Christian element in the emergence of the anti-apartheid movement in Britain, see Skinner 2004, 2005. On the role of IDAF internationally, see also Shepherd 1977.
19. Fieldhouse 2005, p. 5.
20. Trevor Huddleston (1913–99) was born in England and became an Anglican priest. In 1943, he was sent by his church community to Sophiatown in South Africa, an experience about which he wrote the book *Naught for Your Comfort*, which was published in 1955, the same year in which Huddleston returned to England. Huddleston hade made close friends with ANC leaders and spent most of his life in commitment to the struggle against apartheid. He was Vice President of AAM between from 1961 until 1981, when he became its president, a position he held until its dissolution in 1995. It is however unclear whether Trevor Huddleston actually appeared at the meeting in 1959 – a letter was recently found in the AAM archives in which Huddleston apologizes that he has another appointment (correspondance with C. Gurney, 14 April 2005).
21. AAM Archive, MSS AAM 1. See also Gurney 2000a.
22. A/RES/1598 (XV), 13 April 1961, quoted from UN 1994, p. 249f.
23. AAM Annual Report 1965, AAM Archive.
24. AAM Archive, MSS AAM 1306. *AA News*, 4(1) 1968.
25. Hall 2000, p. 52.
26. Jennett 1989.
27. On 'new social movements', Melucci 1989, 1996, who coined the term. For overviews Della Porta and Diani 1999, Cohen and Rai (eds) 2000 and Kriesi *et al.* 1995, Gilroy (1987) provides an important link between NSM theory and cultural studies.
28. E. g. Wignaraja (ed.) 1993.
29. Laclau 1985, p. 30.
30. Jennett 1989, pp. 136, 147, Jennett and Stewart 1989, p. 21.
31. Beck 1999.
32. For a criticism of a Eurocentric bias in globalization theories, see for example Paolini 1997, Castells 1996a, p. 14f, and in relation to NSM theory, Vahabzadeh 2001, p. 624.
33. See for example Young 2001, 2004, Spivak 1999, Bhabha 1994.
34. Herbstein 2004.
35. Interview with Dorothy Robinson, who was active in the Africa Bureau in the late 1950s and AAM in the early 1960s.
36. This is an understanding of social movements influenced mainly by the works of Melucci 1989 and 1996 and Eyerman and Jamison 1991. See also Thörn 1997.
37. Tilly 1978, McAdam 1996, Tarrow 1998, Della Porta and Diani 1999. For a discussion on the 'identity paradigm' versus Resource Mobilization Theory (RMT), see Cohen and Arato 1992.
38. For an updated and systematic discussion on the relation between social movement mobilization, national and international POS, see Sikkink 2005.

However Sikkink still argues that when both national and international POS are open, activists 'will, I believe, privilege domestic political change', p. 165.

39. I define globalization as the historical emergence of a world society, including economic, political and cultural processes, which establish relatively stable and complex relations of power and interdependency across vast distances (see Thörn 2002, Follér and Thörn (eds) 2005 and Abiri and Thörn (eds) 2005). This is a definiton being close to the ones presented in Giddens 1990 and Held *et al.* 1999. In the debate on globalization, some scholars make a distinction between internationalization and globalization (i.e. Hirst and Thompson 1996), while others, including this author, view globalization as a process involving a complex interplay between international processes, denoting interaction between national organizations (such as a state or a labour union) and transnational processes, referring to interaction across national borders. Further, in Chapter 2, I will make a distinction between political globalization from above and from below (Falk 1999). The former is constituted by the increasing number and importance of inter-governmental organizations (IGOs); the latter by the increasing number of NGOs, social movements and activist networks organizing across borders.

40. It might be argued that the Cold War was a rearticulation of the colonial world order, and thus constituted a form of postcoloniality, but I will try to show that it is fruitful to make an analytical distinction between the two. For enlightening discussions on concepts of 'postcolonialism' and 'postcoloniality', see for example Young 2004, 2001, Spivak 1999 and Hall 1996.

41. For a similar approach to the struggle against apartheid from an international relations perspective, see Klotz 1995.

42. My approach is close to theories on political culture developed in the context of cultural theory and cultural sociology, including neo-marxist approaches influenced by Antonio Gramsci. In this tradition the dynamics of political culture is conceived in terms of antagonism and conflict, rather than consensus. See for example Laclau and Mouffe 1986, Mouffe 1988 and Morley and Chen (eds) 1996. An important historical work on social movements and political culture is Wuthnow 1989. For an overview of different conceptions of 'political culture' see Somers 1995.

43. I will sometimes use the term 'liberation movements/SMOs' and 'solidarity movements/SMOs' to distinguish between collective action that ultimately aimed at gaining state power in South Africa, and those movements that acted in support of the former. However, the concept of 'the transnational anti-apartheid movement' included both of these types of movements/SMOs.

44. Eyerman and Jamison 1991, Peterson and Thörn 1994.

45. E. g. Hartley 1992, Kellner 1990, Dahlgren 1995. On the concept of 'mediatization', see Fornäs 1995.

46. Meyrowitz 1985, Thompson 1995, Tomlinson 1999.

47. Keane 1991, p. 143.

48. Habermas 1989, Calhoun (ed.) 1992, Cohen and Arato 1992, Beck 1996.

49. Gitlin 1980, Zoonen 1992, Peterson and Thörn 1999, Couldry and Curran (eds) 2003, Opel and Pompper (eds) 2003, Jong *et al.* (eds) 2005.

50. Hallin 1986.

51. E. g. Dayan and Katz 1992. For a critical di_.ussion on the assumption that 'icons of outrage', as mediated in news does have political or social effects, see also Perlmutter 1998.
52. Karis, Carter and Gerhart vol. 3 (1972–77), p. 295.
53. On the BBC coverage of South Africa before Sharpeville, see Smith 1993.
54. E. g. Wallerstein 1991, Mignolo 2000, Beck 1999.
55. Mignolo 2000.
56. Anzaldúa 1999, Bhabha 1994.
57. The direct support to the ANC from the Swedish state started in 1972/73 with the modest sum of 35,000 Swedish kronor (SEK). In the following year it increased to 215,000 SEK. By 1994, the ANC had received a total sum of 896 million SEK, Sellström 2002, pp. 34, 397 and 900.
58. Sellström 2002, interviews with Magnus Walan, Bertil Högberg and Sören Lindh.
59. ISAK Annual Report 1989/90, p. 1, Labour Movement Archive. The AGIS Annual Reports in the 1970s does not account for the number of members. Its monthly publication, *Afrikabulletinen* had 1100 subscribers 1977/78. In 1990, it had 2150 subscribers, AGIS Annual Report 1977/78 and 1989/90, Labour Movement Archive.
60. Hall 1993, Laclau (ed.) 1994, Morley and Chen 1996.
61. Gamson 1988, p. 225.
62. Gitlin 1980, p. 7. See also Hall 1993.
63. Gitlin 1980, p. 22.
64. Gamson 1992.
65. Gamson 1989.
66. For the British newspapers, I have used the collection of press cuttings assembled at the Royal Institute of Commonwealth Affairs in London. The section on relations between Great Britain and South Africa provided cuttings from nine daily newspapers in 1960 (*The Times, Daily Telegraph, Guardian, Daily Express, Daily Herald, Daily Worker, Financial Times, Observer, Sunday Times*), ten in 1969–70 and 1976 (adding *Sunday Telegraph* to the previous), four in 1985 (*Financial Times, Daily Telegraph, Guardian, The Times*) and five in 1990 (adding *Independent*). For the Swedish press, I have used the section on relations between Sweden and South Africa at the Press archive at Uppsala University, which includes cuttings from all daily Swedish newspapers.
67. This means a particular focus on *AA News* in Britain, published by AAM, and *Afrikabulletinen* and *Södra Afrika Nyheter* in Sweden, published by AGIS. In 1960, when these publications did not yet exist, I used *Boycott News* in Britain. Because the labour movement was the main movement context for anti-apartheid at this time, I also included the TUC magazine *Labour* and *T & G WU Record* in Britain, and *Metallarbetaren*, published by the Metal Union in Sweden.
68. Foucault 1981.
69. Here I use the term 'ideology' as reinterpreted in the context of discourse analysis by Ernesto Laclau 1990, p. 92.

1 Narratives of Transnational Anti-Apartheid Activism

1. Keck and Sikkink 1998, p. 216.
2. Eyerman and Jamison 1991, p. 3.

3. Eyerman and Jamison 1991, p. 94ff.
4. Reddy was promoted to Director of the Centre Against Apartheid in 1976 (set up to demonstrate greater commitment of the UN to action against apartheid), and became Assistant Secretary-General of the UN in 1983 – until he retired in 1985. Where no other references are made, the following is based on my interview with E. S. Reddy. See also Reddy 1986 and 1987. For a collection of his articles, see www.anc.org.za/un/reddy. See also Korey 1998 and Shepherd 1977.
5. Interview with Jennifer Davis. Among the people that have stated that Reddy and the Special Committe played an extremely important role in facilitating the transnational mobilization of the anti-apartheid movement are other key activists in Britain and the United States like Mike Terry (AAM), George Houser (ACOA) as well as journalist and author Denis Herbstein.
6. As for example at the Beijing Women's Conference in 1995, where 4000 NGOs gathered for the alternative meeting, Dickenson 1997.
7. Interview with Denis Herbstein. See also Herbstein 2004.
8. UN 1994, p. 26.
9. Shepherd 1977, p. 51.
10. The other was the Swedish author and journalist Per Wästberg, see Sellström 1999 and Kasmal and Kasmal 1974.
11. Where no other references are made, the following is based on my interview with Gunnar Helander. See also Sellström's interview with Helander in Sellström (ed.) 1999.
12. Sellström 1999, p. 112.
13. Interview with Gunnar Helander.
14. Sellström (ed.) 1999, p. 285.
15. Helander was also appointed to the Consultative Committee on Humanitarian Assistance (CCHA) (see Chapter 3).
16. Interview with Gunnar Helander.
17. Sellström 2002, p. 433.
18. Sellström 1999.
19. *The Economist* 29/6 1974, quoted from Sellström 2002, p. 437.
20. However, since news about the meeting was being leaked to the press, Tambo withdrew. Interview with Gunnar Helander, see also Sellström, (ed.) 1999, p. 288.
21. Where no other references are made, the following is based on my interview with Sobizana Mngqikana.
22. By this time, there were six established ANC missions in the world: Lusaka, Dar Es Salaam, Algiers, Cairo, New Delhi and London, Sellström 2002, p. 398.
23. *Dagens Nyheter*, 7/9 1977 and 17/9 1977.
24. Mngqikana was received at the Ministry of Foreign Affairs in March 1974 (Sellström 2002, p. 398) and also had frequent contacts with the international secretary of the Social Democratic party, Bernt Carlsson, interview with Sobizana Mngqikana.
25. Quote from Sellström 2002, p. 441.
26. The interview was made in *Dagens eko*, and was also referred to in *Dagens Nyheter* 23/12 1974 ('Sydafrikaresan blir ett propagandajippo').
27. In the early 1960s in London, Mngqikana had met representatives from the locally constituted Swedish South Africa committees, one of the earliest transnational contacts of AAM.

28. Sellström 2002, p. 429. In Stockholm, there was a 'Support Group for South Africa's People' that supported the ANC before the Africa Groups did.
29. Afrikagrupperna 1972, pp. 6 and 84ff.
30. Where no other references are made, the following is based on my interview with Margaret Ling.
31. Interview with Margaret Ling.
32. MSS AAM 333.
33. The notion of 'life politics' is borrowed from Giddens 1991. For a critical discussion, see the concluding chapter.
34. Interview with Tariq Mellet (previously Patrick de Goede).
35. AGIS Congress Report 1977, p. 22.
36. AGIS 1978, Palmberg (ed.) 1983. For an account of the process of writing the book, see Palmberg 2004. Where no other references are made, the following is based on my interview with Palmberg.
37. Ruth First was assassinated by a letter bomb in Maputo in 1982. Joe Slovo was appointed as the Minister of Housing in Nelson Mandela's government in 1994, but died from cancer in 1995.
38. AGIS 1983, p. ii.
39. Ibid., p. 75.

2   The Globalization of the Anti-Apartheid Movement

1. Tarrow 1998a, p. 240. See also Della Porta and Kriesi 1999. More recently, Della Porta and Tarrow (2005) have started to put more emphasis on global developments, arguing that such developments have transformed social movements' environments since the 1960s (p. 1) and formulating a theory of 'complex internationalism' (p. 227ff.).
2. Tarrow 1998b.
3. On the history of the ANC, see e. g. Lodge 1983, Lodge and Nasson 1991, Karis, Carter and Gerhart (1972–77), Dubow 2000. Where no other references are made, the following account of the history of the ANC and the PAC are built on Lodge 1983, Chapters 3, 10 and 12 and Lodge and Nasson 1991, part III.
4. Quoted from Lodge 1983, p. 85.
5. See for example Sibeko 1976.
6. Initially an attempt was made to establish co-operation between the two organizations in the South African United Front (SAUF), gaining support from independent African states and European Social Democrats and being active in Accra, Cairo, Dar Es Salaam and London. Internal division did however lead to a break up of SAUF after just 18 months.
7. Interview with E. S. Reddy.
8. For a comprehensive analysis of the history of the UDF, see Seekings 2000.
9. Massie, 1997, p. 565f.
10. Quotes from Barber 1999, p. 247f.
11. Barber 1999, p. 312.
12. Lodge and Nasson 1991, p. 24 and p. 173.
13. Sellström 2002, p. 485. Olof Palme (1927–86) served as chairman of the Swedish Social Democratic Party from 1969 and as Swedish prime minister from 1969 to 1976 and from 1982 to 1986. He was assassinated on 28 February

1986 in Stockholm, by a yet unknown assailant. The assasination occurred one week after the conference 'Swedish People's Parliament Against Apartheid', where Palme appeared together with Oliver Tambo and a number of other prominent anti-apartheid profiles from all over the world. In 1996, Eugene de Kock, former South African death squad commander, stated in the Pretoria Supreme Court that the apartheid regime had been behind the assassination. Swedish police investigating the murder visited South Africa to interview Kock and other former members of South Africa's security forces, but came back without evidence that would hold in court.

14. Interview with Mike Terry.
15. The importance of these early contacts is clearly established by Sellström 1999 and 1999 (ed.) as well as in my interviews with David Wirmark and Anna-Greta Leijon.
16. Interview with George Houser.
17. On the US divestment movement, see Voorhes 1999.
18. Voorhes 1999, p. 140.
19. *AA News*, March issue 1970.
20. On AAM's cultural boycott, see Fieldhouse 2005, p. 103ff.
21. AAM: 'Memorandum to the ANC: "Cultural and Academic Boycotts" ', Mayibuye Archives.
22. Interview with Ronald Segal.
23. Fieldhouse 2005, p. 49f. The papers from the conference were published by Penguin in a book titled *Sanctions Against South Africa* (Segal 1964).
24. Fieldhouse 2005, p. 76.
25. Massie 1997, p. 355 and 408f.
26. Interview with Christabel Gurney.
27. Massie 1997, p. 252ff.
28. Quoted from Fieldhouse, p. 265.
29. The following account on Lars-Gunnar Eriksson and the 'IUEF affair' is based on Sellström 2002, Wästberg 1995 and Herbstein 2004.
30. Sellström 1999, p. 557.
31. Quoted from Sellström 1999, p. 562.
32. Keck and Sikkink 1998.
33. When the issue was brought up in the Security Council it was articulated as 'a threat against world peace and security'.
34. *The United Nations and Apartheid 1948–1994*, p. 30.
35. As defined by Klotz 1995, p. 27.
36. Fieldhouse 2005, p. 250, e-mail conversation with Christabel Gurney 2005–05–23.
37. Ibid., 1995.
38. UN (1994).
39. Klotz 1995, Chapter 5.
40. Ibid., Chapter 7.
41. Interview with Patsy Robertson, Commonwealth Secretariat, Ethel de Keyser, AAM, Mike Terry, AAM.
42. For a theoretical discussion on the interaction between social movements and the UN, see also Passy 1999.
43. Interview with Jennifer Davis.

44. Neither the Scandinavian countries, who otherwise strongly supported the South African liberation struggle, joined the committee.
45. Della Porta and Kriesi 1999.

3   National Politics in a Global Context

1. Gurney 2000, p. 137f.
2. Fieldhouse 2005, p. 156f.
3. It also excluded a secret deal known as 'the Simonstown agreement', Fieldhouse 2005, p. 79.
4. Fieldhouse 2005, Klotz 1995, Chapter 7.
5. Hochschild 1998, Shepherd 1977.
6. Interview with Brian Brown. Brown also represented the BCC in the Southern Africa Coalition, in which British churches, unions and AAM co-operated against apartheid.
7. Between 1947 and 1990 the Swedish state publicly criticized South Africa 138 times publicly, Bjereld 1992, p. 65.
8. Bjereld 1992.
9. Quotes from Sellström 1999, p. 67. For the notion of 'parallellity of interest', see Sellström 1999, who, following the theory on national foreign policy of Marie Demker (1996), argues that Sweden's support to the liberation struggle in Southern Africa was based on the objectives of national security, ideological affinity, economic opportunity and public legitimacy (p. 513f).
10. A volunteer Scandinavian Corps and Ambulance Unit that travelled from Scandinavia to participate on the Boer side consisted of 113 men and 4 women, Sellström 1999, p. 119. For a report from the participation of Swedish volunteers in the war, see for example *Göteborgs-Posten* 23 March 1900.
11. In a formal sense, Sweden's most lasting and famous colonial conquest was the Caribbean island of St Barthélemy, which was purchased from France in 1784 and was sold back to the French in 1877. In the late Seventeenth century there was a Swedish colony named New Sweden in Delaware, North America, and the Swedish Afrikakompaniet had a colony named *Cabo Corso* on the coast of present Guinea.
12. Winqwist 1978, Sellström 1997.
13. Rosenblad 1992.
14. Rosenblad 1992, p. 107.
15. On the speech and the British reactions, as reported in the Swedish press, see also 'Palme vid "anständighetens gräns" ', by Thomas Bergström in *Expressen* 30 September 1971.
16. Interviews with Vella Pillay, Mike Terry, Sören Lindh and Magnus Walan.
17. Interview with Mike Terry.
18. Interviews with Anne Page (previoiusly Anne Darnborough), Ethel de Keyser, Vella Pillay, Dorothy Robinson and Ronald Segal.
19. Interview with Ethel de Keyser.
20. AAM 1963, p. 3.
21. Darnborough 1967, p. 22.
22. AAM Annual Report 1967/1968, p. 18.
23. AAM 1986, p. 1.

24. AAM 1986, p. 3.
25. Most activists of the 1960s that I have interviewed agree on this view. See also Sanders 2000, Chapter 4.
26. Sanders 2000, p. 115.
27. Fieldhouse 2005, p. 191.
28. Interview with Ethel de Keyser, Mike Terry and Vella Pillay. See also Fieldhouse 2005, p. 472. According to Denis Herbstein, neither the IDAF received any state funding (although it received funding from other governments, including the Swedish). Interview with Denis Herbstein.
29. Interview with Mike Terry.
30. Sellström 1999, p. 70ff.
31. While this perception might not have been held about ISAK in general, it was known that AGIS activists played a key role in the activist core of ISAK. Carl Tham, Director General of SIDA and chairman of CCHA, states that '... the Africa Groups was probably not perceived as sufficiently strong, you should remember that there were very strict rules of secrecy'.
32. Interview with Sören Lindh and Magnus Walan and telephone conversation with Maj-Lis Lööw. See also Nordenmark 1991, p. 114.
33. As highlighted by Sanders (2000) in his chapter on AAM.
34. Interview with Ethel de Keyser.
35. Interview with Victoria Brittain.
36. Interview with Ethel de Keyser.
37. According to Roger Fieldhouse, fundraising events were an extremely important source of income for AAM – in 1970–71 accounting for half of the income, and during the 1980s, when a fundraising committee was set up, it 'had become crucial to the financial viability of the Movement' (p. 306).
38. For a comparison of new social movements in Europe, including the case of Sweden, see Brand 1985 and Thörn 2002.
39. Interview with Bertil Högberg.
40. Interview with Mai Palmberg.
41. Solomon 1996.
42. However, for practical reasons a 'secret', or informal, chairman was elected after much compromising, interview with Bertil Högberg.
43. AAM Annual Report 1990, p. 33, AGIS Annual Report 1988/89, p. 8, and ISAK Annual Report 1990/91, p. 8 (Labour Movement Archive).
44. Quoted from Rhodes 2000.
45. Interview with Ethel de Keyser and Barbara Rogers. See also Sanders 2000, p. 94. The tension was fuelled by Peter Hain's book *Don't Play with Apartheid: The Background to the Stop the Seventy Tour* Campaign, which came out in 1971.
46. Interview with E.S. Reddy.
47. Interview with Ingvar Flink.
48. Interview with Sören Lindh.
49. Draft Reply to PAC/CPC Memo, ANC London papers.
50. Interview with Hans Tollin.
51. According to Per Wästberg, personal friend of Olof Palme, it was easy for an ANC representative to be received by the Swedish Prime Minister.
52. Interview with Sören Lindh and Lindiwe Mabusa.

53. Interview with Magnus Walan.
54. *Afrikabulletinen* 43/1978, p. 3.
55. In fact the only important union joining ISAK was the Public Servants Union (Statstjänstemannaförbundet), which was part of the white collar TCO.
56. Gurney 2000b, p. 2.
57. Interview with Mike Terry.
58. Fieldhouse 2005, p. 377, and AAM Annual Report 1990, p. 44.
59. Interview with Mike Walsh.
60. Fieldhouse 2005, p. 392.
61. For an account of the conflict related to CLAAG, see Fieldhouse 2005, p. 218ff.
62. Gurney 2000b, p. 18, interview with Jack Jones.
63. Quoted from Fieldhouse 2005, p. 348.
64. Quoted from Fieldhouse, p. 349.
65. Fieldhouse 2005, p. 345.
66. In its Annual Report 1989/90, ISAK stated that it dissociated itself from 'sabotage actions carried out by groups outside of ISAK', p. 10.
67. Fieldhouse 2005, p. 319. There were also professional groups, specialists groups, youth and students groups and regional committees within AAM.
68. Interview with Hans Tollin. Conversations with Anne-Mari Kihlberg, Africa Groups in Göteborg and Per Herngren, local activist in an organization affiliated to ISAK.
69. Interview with Margaret Ling.
70. McAdam 1996.
71. Della Porta and Kriesi 1999, p. 17, See also Sikkink 2005.
72. McAdam, McCarthy & Zald 1996.

4   The Struggle Over Information and Interpretation

1. Interview with Anne and Bruce Page. However, as is shown by James Sanders (2000), AAM put less emphasis on, and had a more difficult time with, the established media in the 1970s. This was again changed in the 1980s, when AAM developed new media skills (interview with Victoria Britain and Mike Terry).
2. ANC 1987.
3. Interview with Nceba Faku and Ben Mahase.
4. Interview with Lucky Malgas. The PAC had however (just like the ANC) access to UN radio transmissions to South Africa.
5. Interview with Anthony Sampson.
6. Quoted from Sanders 2000, p. 63.
7. Sanders 2000, p. 3.
8. Ibid., p. 65.
9. See Sanders 2000, p. 70ff.
10. Interview with Michael Lapsley.
11. Merrett 1994.
12. Gray 1985.
13. Gray 1985.
14. Interview with Denis Herbstein. For an analysis of the world of foreign correspondents, see Hannerz 2004.
15. Sanders 2000, p. 38ff.

16. Interview with Magnus Walan.
17. On apartheid media strategies, see Laurence 1979.
18. Merrett 1994, p. 119.
19. Interview with Dorothy Robinson.
20. Interview with Anne Page.
21. Interview with Bruce Page.
22. During the 1970s AAM did however not have contacts in South Africa, something which was a huge problem for the journal. E-mail conversation with Christabel Gurney, 10–05–2005.
23. Interview with Anne Page.
24. Interview with Tariq Mellet (Patrick de Goede).
25. Interview with Barry Feinberg.
26. Shepherd 1977, p. 51.
27. Interview with Barry Feinberg.
28. Interview with Mike Terry.
29. Peterson and Thörn 1994, 1999.
30. E. g. Ewald and Thörn 1994.
31. For example such conferences were organized by the Commonwealth Secretariat (co-sponsored by the Association of British Editors, Harvard University and the African-American Institute) in London in 1988 ('South Africa – Controlling the News'). There was also one in East Berlin in 1981 and one in Lima in 1988 (interview with E. S. Reddy).
32. For discussions on alternative media and 'radical journalism', e. g. Atton 2001.
33. Interview with Anne Page (previously Anne Darnborough).
34. Schechter 1997. Where no other references are made, the following is based on my interview with Danny Schechter.
35. Interview with Denis Herbstein.
36. Interview with Denis Herbstein.
37. Interview with Victoria Brittain.
38. Interview with Per Wästberg.
39. Interview with Anthony Sampson.
40. On the 'dramaturgical approach' see Peterson and Thörn 1994 and 1999, on 'protest simulacra', see Della Porta and Kriesi 1999.
41. Interview with Ethel de Keyser.
42. AAM Annual Report 1969/1970, p. 23f, AAM Archive.
43. Sanders 2000, p. 93f.
44. Sanders 2000, p. 93.
45. Sanders 2000, p. 93.
46. Interview with Barry Feinberg.
47. Interview with Barry Feinberg.
48. Interview with Tariq Mellet.
49. Interview with Tariq Mellet.
50. Interview with Tariq Mellet.
51. Eyerman and Jamison 1991.

5   Beginnings: Sharpeville and the Boycott Debates

1. Massie 1997, p. 63f.
2. Quoted in Massie 1997, p. 64.

3. Worden 1994, p. 107.
4. *Metallarbetaren*, no. 1/2, 1960, p. 16.
5. This is for example confirmed by Howard Smith (1993) in his study of the coverage of South Africa by the BBC before Sharpeville.
6. The Uppsala University Press Archive has collected 56 articles in Swedish newspapers debating the boycott during March–May 1960.
7. See for example Sanders 2000.
8. See for example Eyerman and Jamison 1991, Chapter 1.

6   Sports as Politics: The Battle of Båstad and 'Stop the 70s Tour'

1. For analyses on the anti-apartheid sports campaigns, see Black 1999, Guelke 1993 and Nixon 1994.
2. Lindblom 1968, p. 10 and interviews with Ingvar Flink, Ann Schlyter and Hans Tollin. For a discussion of the Båstad events in the context of the protest year of 1968, see Bjereld and Demker 2005.
3. Lindblom 1968, p. 10.
4. Lindblom 1968, p. 12.
5. Lindblom 1968, p. 44.
6. Quoted from Lindblom 1968, p. 33.
7. The course of events are well documented in Lindblom 1968.
8. Interviews with Ingvar Flink and Ann Schlyter.
9. For an account of this process, see Hain 1996, p. 49ff.
10. AAM Annual Report 19697/0, p. 19.
11. Hain 1996, p. 52.
12. Hain 1996, p. 54.
13. Verbatim Press Service 167/70, 21 of May 1970.
14. Sanders 2000, p. 88.
15. Interview with Bruce Page.

7   'A New Black Militancy' – Before and After the Soweto Uprising

1. For historical accounts of the Soweto uprising, see Lodge 1983, Worden 1994, Barber 1999, Massie 1997.
2. Quoted from Sanders 2000, p. 163. Sanders adds: 'It is now accepted that the Soweto uprising represented a crucial juncture in contemporary South African history'. See also Worden 1994, p. 10.
3. Sanders 2000, p. 171.
4. Sanders 2000, p. 109. On the Durban strikes, c.f. Beinart 1994, p. 222ff, Worden 1994, p. 118ff.
5. Barber 1999, p. 213.
6. Interview with Nceba Faku.
7. C.f. Massie 1997, p. 394.
8. Massie 1997, p. 390.
9. Massie 1997, p. 390ff. In spite of demands that Kissinger should cancel the talks when the news about the shootings in Soweto came out, the talks in

Bavaria were held between 20 and 24 June. Further talks were held in September, in both Zürich and Pretoria.

10. In his chapter on the international media's coverage of Soweto, James Sanders is arguing that:'Although the signs that unrest was intensifying in the schools of Soweto had been apparent for some time, most of the stringers and correspondents were caught unprepared by the events of 16 June 1976' (p. 164). Sanders gives one example of this, quoting Caminada's article in *The Times* on 14 June, but also names three 'exceptions', one of them Tutu's article in the *Guardian* cited earlier. In this chapter, I have showed that if there were stringers and correspondents in South Africa that were unprepared for Soweto, enough coverage was published during the first half of 1976, at least in Britain, to make observant newspaper editors, as well as readers, aware of the emerging wave of anti-apartheid mobilization in South Africa. It was rather Caminada's article that was the exception. As even *The Times* editorial on 17 June admitted, 'an explosion' had long been predicted.
11. Quoted from Sanders 2000, p. 169.
12. Nordenmark 1991, p. 89.
13. Nordenmark 1991, p. 100.
14. Sanders 2000, p. 170. See also O' Meara 1996, p. 180 and Barber 1999, p. 213.
15. The *Daily Telegraph* 'Has Vorster got a policy?', 24 August 1976.
16. Beinart 1994, p. 221.
17. Barber 1999, p. 215f.
18. Massie 1997 and interview with George Houser.

8   Sharpeville Revisited and the Release of Nelson Mandela

1. Barber 1999, Beinart 1994, p. 245ff. and Worden 1994, p. 123.
2. Barber 1999, p. 230f.
3. Beinart 1994, p. 237.
4. Barber 1999, p. 237.
5. Massie 1997.
6. On the roots of the UDF in the Soweto uprising, see Seekings 2000. On the economic and demographic context, see Beinart 1994, p. 240ff.
7. Quoted from Barber 1999, p. 244.
8. Worden 1994, p. 139.
9. Quoted from Massie 1997, p. 586f.
10. Massie 1997, p. 618ff.
11 On the concert, see Sellström 1999, p. 300.
12 Nordenmark 1991, p. 114f.
13 Worden 1994, p. 130.
14. Sellström 1999, p. 823.
15. Sellström 1999, p. 832ff.

Conclusion

1. Thompson 1995, p. 82
2. Interview with Reg September.

3. For a theoretical discussion on the interaction between social movements and the UN, see also Passy 1999.
4. On the notion of 'third space', see Bhabha 1994. The particular definition of the concept above was used in a lecture by Homi Bhabha in Göteborg on 19 September 2002.
5. Thompson 1995, p. 82ff.
6. On the globalization of culture, see for example, Pieterse 2004, Tomlinson 1999, Clifford 1997, Hannerz 1996.
7. For an important analysis of the dynamics of media and migration in contemporary cultural globalization, see Appadurai 1996. For a theoretical discussion of travel and mobility, see Urry 2000.
8. Keck and Sikkink 1998, p. 16.
9. Lash and Urry 1994, Castells 1996 and 2001.
10. However, this is now beginning to change, as analyses of the new wave of globalization, occurring around the turn of the Millennium, are being published. See for example Jong *et al.* (eds) 2005, Olesen 2005, Opel and Pompper (eds) 2003, Couldry and Curran (eds) 2003.
11. E-mail conversation with Per Herngren, 11 May 2005.
12. Interview with Margaret Ling.
13. Giddens 1991, Chapter 7.
14. Recently this form of action has been conceptualized as 'political consumerism', see Micheletti 2003 and Micheletti, Follesdal and Stolle (eds) 2003. On the emergence of new forms of political action in connection with individualization, see also Beck 1996.
15. For an elaboration on the role of emotions in the context of social movement theory, see Wettergren 2005.
16. For a historical and conceptual discussion of 'global civil society', see Kaldor 2003 or Keane 2003.
17. E. g. Hirst and Thompson 1996.
18. Keck and Sikkink 1998, p. 33. For a more recent discussion on transnational activism, see Sikkink 2005.
19. Falk 1999.
20. Held *et al.* 1999, p. 53.
21. McGrew (ed.) 1997. However, it must be recognized that far from all of these organizations can be considered as taking part in the process of political globalization. In the context of the debate on a global civil society, scepticism toward the concept of 'NGO' has also, quite rightly, been expressed. The concept of NGO is an extremely broad term used to signify various types of non-governmental organizations. In theories and research on civil society, NGOs are often assumed to be voluntary organizations, characterized by a democratic orientation. This often refers both to internal democracy and to 'making democracy work' in the context of the society in which the NGOs are active. However organizations classified as NGOs can be involved in a quite wide range of activities, and do not per definition promote democracy. In some cases, particularly in the context of international aid, NGOs are simply the extensions of states and their interests. In other cases, they are highly professionalized and rather business like, more or less functioning as enterprises. For a critical discussion on NGOs, see Ottaway and Carothers (eds) 2000 and Hanlon 1991.
22. Rosenau 1990 and 1997.

23. Castells 1996b.
24. Beck 1999.
25. For the notion of 'multi-level political game', see Della Porta and Kriesi 1999.
26. Annan 1999, p. xiv.
27. On the global justice movement, the World Social Forums, and the presence of old and new movements, see Sen *et al.* (eds) 2003, Waterman and Willis (eds) 2001, Della Porta 2005.
28. Most of the activists that I have interviewed in this project (including activists based in churches, unions, solidarity organizations and exiled liberation movements), state that the concept of solidarity was a defining concept of the theory and practice of the struggle in which they participated. The concept of solidarity can also be found in various anti-apartheid documents and statements produced by actors with different ideological commitments.
29. Interview with Mai Palmberg.
30. For an insightful reflection on the theme of particularism/universalism, see Laclau 1996, and on the concept of solidarity, see Liedman 1999.
31. Interview with Bertil Högberg.
32. Interview with Ingvar Flink.
33. Interview with Brian Brown.
34. Interview with Per Wästberg.
35. Interview with Mike Terry.
36. Interview with Margaret Ling.
37. Interview with Mike Terry.

Epilogue

1. On ACTSA and CCETSA, see Fieldhouse 2005, p. 491ff.
2. On South Africa, the IMF, the World Bank and the global justice movement, see Bond 2001.

References

AAM (1986) *A Tiny Little Bit: An Assessment of Britain's Record of Action Against South Africa*, London: AAM.

Abiri, E. and Thörn, H. (eds) (2005) *Horizons: Perspectives on a Global Africa*, Lund and Göteborg: Studentlitteratur/Museum of World Culture/Göteborg University.

Adler, G. and Webster, E. (eds) (2000) *Trade Unions and Democratization in South Africa, 1985–1997*, Witwatersrand: Witwatersrand UP.

Afrikagrupperna (1972) *Afrika. Imperialism och befrielsekamp*, Lund: Afrikagrupperna i Sverige.

AGIS (1978) *Befrielsekampen i Afrika*, Stockholm: AGIS.

Ainslie, R. and Robinson, D. (1963) *The Collaborators*, London: AAM.

Allison, L. (ed) *The Changing Politics of Sport*, Manchester: Manchester UP.

ANC (1987) 'The Pretoria Regime's Media Policy and its Impact Abroad', Arusha Conference: The World United Against Apartheid for a Democratic South Africa, Reference: AC/BP-09/87. Mayibuye Archives/133.

Anderson, B. (1991) *Imagined Communities: Reflections on the Origin and Spread of Nationalism*, London and New York: Verso.

Anheier, H., Glasius, M. and Kaldor, M. (2001) *Global Civil Society 2001*, Oxford: Oxford UP.

Anheier, H., Glasius, M. and Kaldor, M. (2004/5) *Global Civil Society*, London: Sage.

Annan, K. (1999) 'Foreward', in Foster, J. W. and Anand, A. (eds) (1999) *Whose World is it Anyway? Civil Society, the United Nations and the Multilateral Future*, Ottawa: United Nations in Canada.

Anzaldúa, G. (1999) *Borderlands/La Frontera: The New Mestiza.* Second edition, San Fransisco: Aunt Lute Books.

Appadurai, A. (1997) *Modernity at Large: Cultural Dimensions of Globalization*, Minneapolis, MN: University of Minnesota Press.

Asmal, K. and Asmal, L. (1974) 'Anti-Apartheid Movements in Western Europe', *Notes and Documents*, no. 4.

Atton, C. (2000) 'News Cultures and New Social Movements: Radical Journalism and the Mainstream Media', in *Journalism Studies*, 3 (4), pp. 491–505.

Atton, C. (2001) *Alternative Media*, London: Sage.

Barber, J. (1999) *South Africa in the Twentieth Century*, Oxford: Blackwell.

Beck, U. (1996) *The Reinvention of Politics: Rethinking Modernity in the Global Social Order*, Cambridge: Polity Press.

Beck, U. (1999) *What is Globalization?*, Cambridge: Polity Press.

Beinart, W. (1994) *Twentieth Century South Africa*, Oxford: Oxford UP.

Beinart, W. and Dubow, S. (eds) (1995) *Segregation and Apartheid in Twentieth-Century South Africa*, London and New York: Routledge.

Bhabha, H. K. (1994) *The Location of Culture*, London & New York: Routledge.

Bjereld, U. (1992) *Kritiker eller medlare? Sveriges utrikespolitiska roller 1945–1990*, Stockholm: Nerenius & Santérus.

Bjereld, U. and Demker, M. (2005) *I vattumannens tid: en bok on 1968 års uppror och dess betydelse idag*, Stockholm: Hjalmarsson & Högberg.

Black, D. R. (1999) ' "Not Cricket": The Effects and Effectiveness of the Sport Boycott', in Crawford, N. C. and Klotz A. (eds) *How Sanctions Work: Lessons from South Africa*, London: Macmillan.

Bond, P. (2001) *Against Global Apartheid: South Africa Meets the World Bank, IMF and International Finance*, Cape Town: UCT Press.

Brand, K.-W. (1985) *Neue soziale Bewegungen in Westeuropa and den USA: ein internationaler Vergleich*, Frankfurt: Campus.

Calhoun, C. (ed.) (1992) *Habermas and the Public Sphere*, Cambridge, MA: MIT Press.

Castells, M. (1996a) 'The Net and the Self: Working Notes for a Critical Theory of the Informational Society', *Critique of Anthropology* 1(16), pp. 9–38.

Castells, M. (1996b) *The Information Age: Economy, Society and Culture, Vol. 1: The Rise of the Network Society*, Oxford: Blackwell.

Castells, M. (2001) *The Internet Galaxy: Reflections on the Internet, Business and Society*, Oxford: Oxford UP.

Clifford, J. (1997) *Routes: Travel and Translation in the Late Twentieth Century*, Cambridge, MA: Harvard UP.

Cohen, J. L. and Arato, A. (1992) *Civil Society and Political Theory*, Cambridge, MA: MIT Press.

Cohen, R. and Rai, S. (eds.) (2000) *Global Social Movements*, London: Athlone Press.

Couldry, N. and Curran, J. (eds) (2003) *Contesting Media Power: Alternative Media in a Networked World*, Lanham, MD: Rowman and Littlefield.

Crawford, N. C. and Klotz, A. (eds) (1999) *How Sanctions Work: Lessons From South Africa*, London: Macmillan.

Dahlgren, P. (1995) *Television and the Public Sphere: Citizenship, Democracy and the Media*, London: Sage.

Darnborough, A. (1967) *Labour's Record on Southern Africa*, London: AAM.

Dayan, D. and Katz E. (1992) *Media Events: The Live Broadcasting of History*, Cambridge, MA: Harvard UP.

Della Porta, D. and Diani, M. (1999) *Social Movements: An Introduction*, Oxford: Blackwell.

Della Porta, D. and Kriesi, H. (1999) 'Introduction', in Della Porta, D., Kriesi, H. and Rucht (eds) *Social Movements in a Globalizing World*, London: Macmillan.

Della Porta, D., Kriesi, H. and Rucht (eds) (1999) *Social Movements in a Globalizing World*, London: Macmillan.

Della Porta, D. and Tarrow, S. (eds) (2005) *Transnational Protest and Global Activism: People, Passions and Power*, Oxford: Rowman & Littlefield.

Demker, M. (1996) *Sverige och Algeriets frigörelse 1954–1962: Kriget som förändrade svensk utrikespolitik*, Stockholm: Nerenius & Santérus.

Dickenson, D. (1997) 'Counting Women in: Globalization, Democratization and the Women's Movement', in McGrew, A., ed., *The Transformation of Democracy? Globalization and Territorial Democracy*, Cambridge: Polity Press.

Downing, J. D. H. (2001) *Radical Media: Rebellious Communication and Social Movements*, London: Sage.

Dubow, S. (1995) *Scientific Racism in Modern South Africa*, Cambridge: Cambridge UP.

Dubow, S. (2000) *The African National Congress*, Johannesburg: Jonathan Ball Publishers.

Ewald, J. and Thörn, H. (1994) *Peace Monitoring in South Africa: An Evaluation of a Cooperation Between Swedish and South African Organisations*, Stockholm: The Swedish UN-Association.

Eyerman, R. and Jamison, A. (1991) *Social Movements: A Cognitive Approach*, Pennsylvania: Penn State UP.

Falk, R. (1999) *Predatory Globalization: A Critique*, Cambridge: Polity Press.

Fieldhouse, R. (2005) *Anti-Apartheid: A History of the Movement in Britain. A Study in Pressure Group Politics*, London: Merlin Press.

First, R., Steele, J. and Gurney, C. (1972) *The South African Connection: Western Involvement in Apartheid*, London: Temple Smith.

Follér, M. and H. Thörn (eds) (2005) *No Name Fever: AIDS in the Age of Globalization*, Lund and Göteborg: Studentlitteratur/Museum of World Culture/Göteborg University.

Fornäs, J. (1995) *Cultural Theory and Late Modernity*, London: Sage.

Foucault, M. (1981) 'The Order of Discourse' in Young, R. J. C. (ed) *Untying the Text: A Post-Structuralist Reader*, London and Boston: Routledge & Kegan Paul.

Friedman, S. and Atkinson, D. (1994) *The Small Miracle: South Africa's Negotiated Settlement*, Johannesburg: Ravan Press.

Gamson, W. A. (1988) 'Politcal Discourse and Collective Action,' *International Social Movement Research*, 1, pp. 219–44.

Gamson, W. A. and Modigliani, A. (1989) 'Media Discourse and Public Opinion on Nuclear Power: A Constructionist Approach', *American Journal of Sociology* (95) 1, pp. 1–37.

Giddens, A. (1990) *The Consequences of Modernity*, Cambridge: Polity Press.

Giddens, A. (1991) *Modernity and Self-Identity: Self and Society in the Late Modern Age*, Cambridge: Polity Press.

Gilroy, P. (1987) *'There Ain't no Black in the Union Jack': The Cultural Politics of Race and Nation*, London: Hutchinson.

Gitlin, T. (1980) *The Whole World is Watching: Mass Media in the Making and Unmaking of the New Left*, Berkeley, CA: UCLA Press.

Gray, M. (1985) 'Press Under Pressure: Militarization and Propaganda in South Africa 1977–1985', unpublished paper, ANC London papers, Cape Town: Mayibuye Archives.

Guelke, A. (1993) 'Sport and the End of Apartheid', in Allison, L. (ed.) *The Changing Politics of Sport*, Manchester: Manchester UP.

Gurney, C. (2000a) ' "A Great Cause": The Origins of the Anti-Apartheid Movement, June 1959–March 1960', *Journal of Southern African Studies* (26) 1, pp. 123–44.

Gurney, C. (2000b) 'Solidarity or Sell-Out?: the British Labour Movement and Apartheid in the 1960s and 1970s', paper presented at the University of Sussex, March 2000.

Habermas, J. (1989) *The Structural Transformation of the Public Sphere: An Inquiry into a Category of Bourgeois Society*, Cambridge, MA: MIT Press.

Hain, P. (1971) *Don't Play with Apartheid: The Background to the Stop the Seventy Tour Campaign*, London: Allen & Unwin.

Hain, P. (1996) *Sing the Beloved Country: the Struggle for the New South Africa*, London and Chicago: Pluto Press.

Hall, S. (1993) 'Encoding, Decoding' in During, S., (ed), *The Cultural Studies Reader*, London and New York: Routledge.

Hall, S. (1996) 'When was the "Post-Colonial": Thinking at the Limit', in Chambers, I. and Curtis, L. (eds), *The Post-Colonial Question: Common Skies, Divided Horizons*, London and New York: Routledge.

Hall, S. (2000) 'The AAM and the Race-ing of Britain', in *The Anti-Apartheid Movement: A 40-year Perspective. Symposium Report*, London: Anti-Apartheid Movement Archives Committee.

Hallin, D. C. (1986), *The 'Uncensored War': The Media and Vietnam*, New York: Oxford UP.

Hanagan, M., Moch, L. P., Brake, W. (eds) (1998) *Challenging Authority: The Historical Study of Contentious Politics*, Minneapolis: University of Minnesota Press.

Hanlon, J. (1991) *Mozambique: Who Calls the Shots?*, Oxford: James Currey.

Hannerz, U (1996) *Transnational Connections: Culture, People, Places*, London and New York: Routledge.

Hannerz, U. (2004) *Foreign News: Exploring the World of Foreign Correspondents*, Chicago: Chicago Press.

Hartley, J. (1992) *The Politics of Pictures: The Creation of the Public in the Age of Popular Media*, London and New York: Routledge.

Held, D., McGrew, A., Goldblatt, D. and Perraton, J. (1999) *Global Transformations: Politics, Economics and Culture*, Cambridge: Polity Press.

Herbstein, D. (2004) *White Lies: Canon Collins and the Secret War against Apartheid*, Cape Town: HSRC Press.

Hirst, P. and Thompson, G. (1999) *Globalization in Question: The International Economy and the Possibilities of Governance*, Malden, MA: Polity Press.

Hochschild, A. (2000) *King Leopold's Ghost: A Story of Greed, Terror and Heroism in the Colonial Africa*, London: Macmillan.

Huddleston, T. (1956) *Naught for Your Comfort*, London: Collins.

Jennett C. (1989) 'Signals to South Africa: The Australian Anti-Apartheid Movement', in Jennett C. and Stewart, R. G. (eds), *Politics of the Future: the Role of Social Movements*, Melbourne: Macmillan.

Jennett C. and Stewart, R. G. (eds) (1989) *Politics of the Future: the Role of Social Movements*, Melbourne: Macmillan.

Jong, de W. D. Shaw, M. and Stammers, N. (eds) (2005) *Global Activism, Global Media*, London and Ann Arbor: Pluto Press.

Kaldor, M. (2003) *Global Civil Society: An Answer to War*, Oxford: Blackwell.

Karis, T. and Carter, G. and Gerhart, K. M. (eds) (1972–77) *From Protest to Challenge: A Documentary History of African Politics in South Africa 1882–1964*, Stanford, CA: Hoover. Vol 1 (1972): *Protest and Hope: 1882–1934, Vol. 2* (1973): *Hope and Challenge 1935–1952, Vol. 3* (1977): *Challenge and Violence: 1953–1964*, Vol. 4: *Political Profiles 1882–1964*.

Keane, J. (1991) *The Media and Democracy*, Cambridge: Polity Press.

Keane, J. (2003) *Global Civil Society?* Cambridge: Cambridge UP.

Keck, M. E. and Sikkink, K. (1998) *Activists Beyond Borders: Advocacy Networks in International Politics*, Ithaca and London: Cornell UP.

Kellner, D (1990) *Television and the Crisis of Democracy*, Boulder, CA: Westview Press.

Kellner, D. (1995) *Media Culture: Cultural Studies, Identity and Politics Betweeen the Modern and the Postmodern*, London and New York: Routledge.

Klotz, A. (1995) *Norms in International Relations: The Struggle Against Apartheid*, Ithaca and London: Cornell University Press.

Korey, W. (1998) *NGOs and the Universal Declaration of Human Rights: 'A Curious Grapevine'*, New York: St Martin's Press.

Kriesi, H., Koopmans, R., Duyvendak, J. W. and Giugni, M. G. (1995) *New Social Movements in Western Europe: A Comparative Analysis*, Minneapolis, MN: University of Minnesota Press.

Krog, A. (1999) *Country of My Skull*, London: Vintage.

Laclau, E. (1985) 'New Social Movements and the Plurality of the Social', in Slater, D. (ed), *New Social Movements and the State in Latin America*, Amsterdam: CEDLA.

Laclau, E. (1990) *New Reflections on the Revolution of Our Time*, London and New York: Verso.

Laclau, E. (ed.) (1994) *The Making of Political Identities*, London and New York: Verso.

Laclau, E. (1996) *Emancipation(s)*, London and New York: Verso.

Laclau, E. and Mouffe, C. (1986) *Hegemony and Socialist Strategy: Towards a Radical Democractic Politics*, London and New York: Verso.

Lash, S. and Urry, J. (1994) *Economies of Signs and Space*, London and New York: Routledge.

Laurence, J. (1979) *Race, Propaganda and South Africa*, London: Victor Gollancz.

Liedman, S.-E. (2000) *Att se sig själv i andra: Om solidaritet*, Stockholm: Bonnier.

Lindblom, B. (1968) *Fallet Båstad: en studie i svensk opionionsbildning*, Stockholm: Wahlström & Widstrand.

Lodge, T. (1983) *Black Politics in South Africa Since 1945*, London and New York: Longman.

Lodge, T. and Nasson, B. (eds) (1991) *All, Here, and Now: Black Politics in South Africa in the 1980s*, Cape Town: David Philip.

Mandela, N. (1994) *Long Walk to Freedom. The Autobiography of Nelson Mandela*, Boston, MA: Little, Brown and Co.

Marks, S. and Trapido, S. (eds) (1987) *The Politics of Race, Class and Nationalism in Twentieth Century South Africa*, London: Longman.

Massie, R. K. (1997) *Loosing the Bonds: The United States and South Africa in the Apartheid Years*, New York: Doubleday.

McAdam, D. (1996) 'Conceptual Origins, Current Problems, Future Decisions', in McCarthy, J. D. and Zald M. N., (eds), *Comparative Perspectives on Social Movements: Political Opportunities, Mobilizing Structures and Cultural Framings*, Cambridge: Cambridge UP.

McAdam, D., McCarthy, J. D. and Zald, M. N. (eds) (1996) *Comparative Perspectives on Social Movements: Opportunities, Mobilizing Structures and Framing*, Cambridge: University Press.

McGrew (ed.) (1997) *The Transformation of Democracy? Globalization and Territorial Democracy*, Cambridge: Polity Press.

Melucci, A. (1989) *Nomads of the Present: Social Movements and Individual Needs in Contemporary Society*, London: Hutchinson.

Melucci, A. (1996) *Challenging Codes: Collective Action in the Information Age*, Cambridge: Cambridge UP.

Merret, C. (1994) *A Culture of Censorship: Secrecy and Intellectual Repression in South Africa*, Cape Town: David Philip.

Meyrowtiz, J. (1985) *No Sense of Place: The Impact of Electronic Media on Social Behaviour*, New York and Oxford: Oxford University Press.

Micheletti, M. (2003) *Political Virtue and Shopping: Individuals, Consumerism and Collective Action*, London and New York: Palgrave Macmillan.

Micheletti, M., Follesdal, A. and Dietlind, S. (eds) (2003) *Politics, Products and Markets: Exploring Political Consumerism Past and Present*, New Brunswick, NJ: Transaction Publishers.

Mignolo, W. D. (2000) *Local Histories/Global Designs: Coloniality, Subaltern Knowledges and Border Thinking*. Princeton, NJ: Princeton UP.

Morley, D. and Chen, K.-H. (eds) (1996) *Stuart Hall: Critical Dialogues in Cultural Studies*, London and New York: Routledge.

Mouffe, C. (1988) 'Hegemony and New Political Subjects: Towards a New Concept of Democracy', in Grossberg, L. and Nelson, C. (eds) *Marxism and the Interpretation of Cultures*, London: Macmillan.

Nixon, R. (1994) *Homelands, Harlem and Hollywood: South African Culture and the World Beyond*, London and New York: Routledge.

Nordenmark, O. (1991) *Aktiv utrikespolitik: Sverige – Södra Afrika 1969–1987*, Stockholm: Almqvist & Wiksell.

Norval, A. (1996) *Deconstructing Apartheid Discourse*, London: Verso.

Odén, B. and Ohlson, T. (1994) 'South Africa – A Conflict Study', in Odén, B. *et al.* (eds), *The South African Tripod: Studies of Economics, Politics and Conflict*, Uppsala: Nordiska Afrikainstitutet.

Odén, B. et. al. (eds) (1994) *The South African Tripod: Studies of Economics, Politics and Conflict*, Uppsala: Nordiska Afrikainstitutet.

Olesen, T. (2005) *International Zapatismo: Globalization and the Construction of Solidarity*, London: Zed.

O' Meara, D. (1996) *Forty Lost Years: The Apartheid State and the Politics of the National Party 1948–1994*, Johannesburg: Ravan Press.

Opel, A. and Pompper, D. (eds) (2003) *Representing Resistance: Media, Civil Disobedience and the Global Justice Movement*, Westport, Conn.: Praeger.

Ottaway, M. and Carothers, T. (eds) (2000) *Funding Virtue: Civil Society Aid and Democracy Promotion*, Washington: Carnegie Endowment for Int. Peace.

Palmberg, M. (ed.) (1983) *The Struggle for Africa*, London: Zed.

Palmberg, M. (2004) 'The Struggle for Africa Revisited', unpublished paper, Nordiska Afrikainstitutet.

Paolini, A. (1997) 'Globalization', in Darby, P. (ed), *At the Edge of International Relations: Post-Colonialism, Gender and Dependency*, London and New York: Pinter.

Passy, F. (1999) 'Supranational Political Opportunities as a Channel of Globalization of Political Conflicts: The Case of the Rights of Indigenous Peoples', in Della Porta, D., Kriesi, H. and Rucht (eds), *Social Movements in a Globalizing World*, London: Macmillan.

Patomäki, H. and Teivainen, T. (2004) 'The World Social Forum: An Open Space or a Movements of Movements?', *Theory, Culture and Society*, 21, (6), pp. 145–54.

Perlmutter, D. D. (1998) *Photojournalism and Foreign Policy: Icons of Outrage in International Crises*, New York: Praeger.

Peterson, A. and Thörn, H. (1994) 'Social Movements as Communicative Praxis – A Case Study of the Plowshares movement', *YOUNG: Nordic Journal for Youth Research*, 2 (2), pp. 17–36.

Peterson, A. and Thörn, H. (1999) 'Movimientos sociales y modernidad de los medios de communicación. Industrias de los medios de communicación: amigos o enemigos?', *in Comunicación y Sociedad*, 35, pp. 11–44.

Pieterse, J. N. (2004) *Globalization and Culture: Global Mélange*, Oxford: Rowman & Littlefield.

Price, R. (1991) *The Apartheid State in Crisis: Political Transformation of South Africa, 1975–1990*, Oxford: Oxford UP.

Reddy, E. S. (1986) *Apartheid, the United Nations and the International Community: A Collection of Speeches and Papers*, New Delhi: Vikas.

Reddy, E. S. (1987) *Struggle for Freedom in Southern Africa: its International Significance*, New Delhi: Mainstream.

Rhodes, D. (2000) 'The Anti-Apartheid Movement in Britain', unpublished MPhil. Thesis, Faculty of Social Sciences, University of Oxford.

Rosenau, J. N. (1990) *Turbulence in World Politics: A Theory of Change and Continuity*, Princeton, NJ: Princeton UP.

Rosenau, J. N. (1997) *Along the Domestic-Foreign Frontier: Exploring Governance in a Turbulent World*, Cambridge: Cambridge UP.

Rosenblad, J.-G. (1992) *Nation, nationalism och identitet: Sydafrika i svensk sekelskiftesdebatt*, Nora: Nya Doxa.

Salomon, K. (1996) *Rebeller i takt med tiden: FNL-rörelsen och 60-talets politiska ritualer*, Stockholm: Rabén & Prisma.

Sampson, A. (1999) *Mandela: The Authorized Biography*, London: HarperCollins.

Sanders, J. (2000) *South Africa and the International Media 1972–1979: A Struggle for Representation*, London: Frank Kass.

Schechter, D. (1997) *The More You Watch the Less You Know: News Wars (sub)Merged Hopes, Media Adventures*, New York; Seven Stories Press.

Seekings, J. (2000) *The UDF: A History of the United Democratic Front in South Africa 1983–1991*, Cape Town: David Philip.

Segal, R. (1964) *Sanctions Against South Africa*, Harmondsworth: Penguin.

Sellström, T. (1999) *Sweden and National Liberation in Southern Africa, vol 1: Formation of a Popular Opinion 1950–1970*, Uppsala: Nordiska Afrikainstitutet.

Sellström, T. (ed) (1999) *Liberation in Southern Africa: Regional and Swedish Voices*, Uppsala: Nordiska Afrikainstitutet.

Sellström, T. (2002) *Sweden and National Liberation in Southern Africa, vol 2: Solidarity and Assistance 1970–1994*, Uppsala: Nordiska Afrikainstitutet.

Sen, J. *et al.* (2003) *World Social Forum: Challenging Empires: Reading the World Social Forum*, New Delhi: Viveka Foundation.

Shepherd, G. W. (1977) *Anti-Apartheid: Transnational Conflict and Western Policy in the Liberation of South Africa*, Westport, Conn.: Greenwood Press.

Sibeko, D. M. (1976) 'The Sharpeville Massacre: Its Historical Significance in the Struggle Against Apartheid', *Notes and Documents*, no. 8.

Sikkink, K. (2005) 'Patterns of Dynamic Multi-Level Governance and the Insider-Outsider Coalition', in Della Porta, D. and Tarrow, S. (eds), *Transnational Protest and Global Activism: People, Passions and Power*, Oxford: Rowman & Littlefield.

Skinner, R. (2004) 'The Wartime Roots of Anti-Apartheid: Pastoral Mission, Local Activism and International Politics', in *South African Historical Journal*, 50, pp. 12–26.

Skinner, R. (2005) 'Christian Reconstruction, Secular Politics: Michael Scott and the Campaign for Right and Justice, 1943–45', in Dubow, S. and Jeeves, A. (eds), *Worlds of Possibilities: South Africa's 1940s*, Cape Town: Double Storey.

Smith, H. (1993) 'Apartheid, Sharpeville and "Impartiality": the Reporting of South Africa on BBC Television 1948–1961', *Historical Journal of Film, Radio and Television*, 13 (3), pp. 251–98.

Smith, J., Chatfield, C. and Pagnucco, R. (1997) *Transnational Social Movements and Global Politics: Solidarity Beyond the State*, Syracuse: Syracuse UP.

Somers, M. (1995) 'What's Political or Cultural about Political Culture and the Public Sphere? Toward an Historical Sociology of Concept Formation', in *Sociological Theory*, 13 (2), pp. 113–44.

Spivak, G. S. (1999) *A Critique of Postcolonial Reason: Toward a History of the Vanishing Present*, Cambridge, MA: Harvard UP.

Tarrow, S. (1998a) 'Fishnets, Internets and Catnets: Globalization and Transnational Collective Action', in Hanagan, M., Moch, L. P. and Brake, W. (eds), *Challenging Authority: The Historical Study of Contentious Politics*, Minneapolis, MN: University of Minnesota Press.

Tarrow, S. (1998b) *Power in Movement: Social Movements and Contentious Politics*, Cambridge: Cambridge UP.

Thompson, John B. (1995) *The Media and Modernity: A Social Theory of the Media*, Cambridge: Polity Press.

Thörn, H. (1997) *Modernitet, sociologi och sociala rörelser*, Göteborg: Sociologiska institutionen, Göteborgs universitet.

Thörn, H. (2002) *Globaliseringens dimensioner: nationalstat, världssamhälle, demokrati och sociala rörelser*, Stockholm: Atlas.

Tilly, C. (1978) *From Mobilization to Revolution*, Reading, MA: Addison-Wesley.

Tomlinson, J. (1999) *Globalization and Culture*, Cambridge: Polity Press.

UN (1994) *The United Nations and Apartheid 1948–1994*, New York: United Nations.

Vahabzadeh, P. (2001) 'A Critique of Ultimate Referentiality in the New Social Movement Theory of Alberto Melucci', *Canadian Journal of Sociology* 26: 611–33.

Voorhes, M. (1999) 'The US Divestment Movement', in Crawford, N. C. and Klotz, A. (eds), *How Sanctions Work: Lessons from South Africa*, London: Macmillan.

Wallerstein, I. (1991) *Geopolitics and Geoculture: Essays on the Changing World System.* Cambridge: Cambridge UP.

Waterman, P. and Willis, J. (eds) (2001) *Place, Space and the New Labour Internationalisms: Beyond the Fragments?* Oxford: Blackwell.

Waterman, P. (2001) *Globalization, Social Movements and the New Internationalisms*, London and New York: Continuum.

Wettergren, Å. (2005) *Moving and Jamming: Implications for Social Movement Theory*, Karlstad: Karlstad University Studies.

Wignaraja, P. (ed.) (1993) *New Social Movements in the South: Empowering People*, London: Zed.

Winquist, A. (1978) *Scandinavians and South Africa: Their Impact on the Cultural, Social and Economic Development of pre-1902 South Africa*, Cape Town and Rotterdam: A.A. Balkema.

Worden, N. (1994) *The Making of Modern South Africa: Conquest, Segregation and Apartheid*, Oxford: Blackwell.

Worsnip, M. (1996) *Priest and Partisan: A South African Journey.* Melbourne: Ocean Press.

Wuthnow, R. (1989) *Communities of Discourse: Ideology and Social Structure in the Reformation, the Enlightenment, and European Socialism*, Cambridge, MA: Harvard UP.

Wästberg, P. (1995) *I Sydafrika: Resan mot friheten*, Stockholm: Wahlström & Widstrand.

Young, R. J. C, (ed) (1981) *Untying the Text: A Post-Structuralist Reader.* London and Boston: Routledge & Kegan Paul.

Young, R. J. C. (2001) *Postcolonialism: An Historical Introduction.* Oxford and Malden, Mass.: Blackwell.

Young, R. J. C. (2004) *White Mythologies: Writing History and the West.* Second edition, London and New York: Routledge.

Zoonen, E. A. van (1992) 'The Women's Movement and the Media: Constructing a Public Identity', *European Journal of Communication*, 7 (4), pp. 453–76.

Archives

ANC Historical Documents Archive, www.anc.org.za

Bodleian Library, Oxford
Archive of the Anti-Apartheid Movement, 1959–95 (AAM Archive):
M: Overseas anti-apartheid organisations, 1963–95.
M2: Correspondence and Papers, 1963–95.
MSS AAM 1: Committee of African Organisations' papers concerning establishment of Boycott Movement, 1959–60.
MSS AAM 13: AAM annual reports, 1962–90, and political reports, 1992–93.
MSS AAM 333: Women's Committee minutes 1980–94
MSS AAM 1306: Circular letters to overseas anti-apartheid organisations and contact lists, 1964–95.

British Library, London
Press Cuttings of the Royal Institute of Commonwealth Affairs, 1960, 1968–70 and 1976

The Labour Movement Archive, Stockholm
AGIS Annual Reports
ISAK Annual Reports

Mayibuye Centre, University of Western Cape, Cape Town
ANC London papers

The Nordic Africa Institute Library, Uppsala
ISAK Annual Reports

The Press Archive, Uppsala University
Press Cuttings from 1960, 1968, 1976, 1985 and 1990

The Press Library, Royal Institute of Commonwealth Affairs, London
Press Cuttings, 1985 and 1990

TUC Library Collections, London, Metropolitan University
Labour
T & GWU Record

British newspapers and magazines

AA News
Daily Express
Daily Herald
Daily Telegraph
Guardian
Independent

Labour
Observer
Sunday Telegraph
Sunday Times
T & GWU Record
The Times

Swedish newspapers and magazines

Afrikabulletinen
Aftonbladet (AB)
Arbetarbladet
Arbetet
Dagens Nyheter (DN)
Eskilstunakuriren
Expressen
Göteborgs-Posten
Kvällsposten
Metallarbetaren
Nordvästra Skånes Tidningar (NST)
Nyheterna
Stockholmstidningen
Svenska Dagbladet (SvD)
Södra Afrika Nyheter

Interviews*

Name	Organization/ activity	Place/date
Björn Andréasson	LO	Stockholm 01–10–1999
Kerstin Bjurman	AGIS	Stockholm 01–10–1999
Paul Blomfield**	AAM	Sheffield 25–03–2000
Victoria Brittain	Journalist	Göteborg 05–02–2000
Brian Brown	CI/BCC	London 03–03–2000
Jennifer Davis	UM/ACOA	New York 20–06–2000
Nceba Faku	BCM/ANC	Göteborg 05–08–2000
Barry Feinberg	ANC/AAM/IDAF	Cape Town 13–02–2001
Ingvar Flink	AGIS	Stockholm 28–09–1999
Bo Forsberg	Diakonia/ISAK	Stockholm 30–09–1999
Christabel Gurney	AAM	London 25–10–2000
Gunnar Helander	Author/SSAK/IDAF/ CCHA	Västerås 16–11–1999
Denis Herbstein	Author/Journalist	London 29–02–2000
Lars Herneklint	Journalist	Stockholm 24–03–2000
George Houser	ACOA	New York 20–06–2000
Bob Hughes (Lord of Woodside)	AAM/LP	London 24–10–2000
Lars Hult	AGIS/ISAK	Stockholm 30–09–1999
Bertil Högberg	AGIS/ISAK	Uppsala 29–09–1999
Anders Johansson	JSAK/journalist	Eskilstuna 17–11–1999
Lena Johansson	AGIS/SIDA	Stockholm 27–09–1999
Jack Jones*	T&GWU	London 17–02–2000
Suresh Kamath	AAM/ACTSA	London 07–03–2000
Louise Kasmal	Irish AAM	Cape Town 13–02–2001
Ethel de Keyser	AAM/IDAF/CCETSA	London 03–03–2000
Michael Lapsley	ANC/TRC	Göteborg 15–06–2000
Anna-Greta Leijon	SSU/SAP	Stockholm 18–02–2000
Sören Lindh	AGIS/ISAK	Stockholm 02–10–1999
Margaret Ling	AAM/IDAF	London 29–02–2000
Lindiwe Mabuza	ANC	Cape Town 16–02–2001
Ben Mahase	ANC/UDF/AGIS	Stockholm 01–10–1999
Lucky Malgas	PAC	Göteborg 16–08–2000
Tariq Mellet	ANC/SACP/SACTU/ IDAF	Cape Town 22–02–2001
Sobizana Mngqikana	ANC	Stockholm 16–02–2000
Lawson Naidoo	ANC	Cape Town 21–02–2001

* All interviews made by the author, except * by Christabel Gurney and ** by David Rhodes. The interviews made by the author were semi-structured, lasting between one and three hours.

Johan Nordenfelt	UN	Stockholm 31–05–2000
Anne Page	AAM	London 01–11–2000
Bruce Page	Journalist	London 01–11–2000
Mai Palmberg	AGIS	Uppsala 27–09–1999
Vella Pillay	BM/AAM	London 07–03–2000
Enuga S. Reddy	UN	New York 19–06–2000 and 21–06–2000
Barbara Rogers	Journalist	London 30–10–2000
Patsy Robertson	Commonwealth Secretariat	London 001027
Dorothy Robinson	AAM/IDAF	London 02–03–2000
Anthony Sampson	Author/journalist	London 03–08–2000
Ronald Segal	Author/journalist/ AAM	London 28–10–2000
Danny Schechter	Author/journalist/ film producer	New York 20–06–2000
Ann Schlyter	AGIS	Uppsala 28–09–1999
Reg September	ANC	Cape Town 21–02–2001
Michael Terry	AAM	London 28–02–2000 and 07–03–2000
Carl Tham	SIDA/SAP/FPU	Göteborg 20–09–2000
Hans Tollin	AGIS	Göteborg 14–09–1999
Magnus Walan	AGIS/ISAK	Stockholm 30–09–1999
Mike Walsh*	TUC	London 04–02–2000
David Wirmark	WAY/Folkpartiet	Stockholm 16–02–2000
Per Wästberg	Author/journalist/ IDAF/CCHA	Stockholm 29–09–1999

Conversation/correspondence

Christabel Gurney, AAM, conversations and e-mail correspondence 2000–05
Per Herngren, Christian Student Movement/ISAK, e-mail correspondence May 2005
Anne-Mari Kihlberg, AGIS/ISAK, conversations 2000–02
Maj-Lis Lööw, SDP, Sweden, telephone conversation 10–05–2005
Enuga S. Reddy, UN, e-mail correspondence 2000–05
Tor Sellström, Senior Researcher, Nordic Africa Institute, conversation 28–09–1999
Raymond Suttner, ANC, South African Ambassador to Sweden, conversation, Stockholm, 20–09–2000

Index

242

.